D1881225

BENGAL DISTRICT GAZETTEER HOWRAH

BENGAL DISTRICT GAZETTEER
HOWRAH

BY

L. S. S. OMALLEY

GYAN

© **Author**

All rights reserved. No part of this work may be reproduced, stored, adapted, or transmitted in any form or by any means, electronic, mechanical, photocopying, micro-filming, recording or otherwise, or translated in any language, without the prior written permission of the copyright owner and the publisher. The book is sold subject to the condition that it shall not, by way of trade or otherwise, be lent, resold, hired out, or otherwise circulated without the prior publisher's written consent in any form of binding or cover other than that in which it is published.

The views and opinions expressed in this book are author(s) own and the facts reported by them have been verified to the extent possible, and the publishers are not in any way liable for the same.

ISBN : 978-81-212-1818-4 (HB)

First Published, 1909

Published, 2018

Published by

Gyan Publishing House
5, Ansari Road
Daryaganj, New Delhi-110002
Phone: 011-47034999, 9811692060
www.gyanbooks.com
E-mail: books@gyanbooks.com

Printed at: G. Print Process, Delhi.

PLAN OF CONTENTS.

TABLE OF CONTENTS.

CHAPTER I.

PHYSICAL ASPECTS.

CHAPTER II.

HISTORY.

CHAPTER III.

THE PEOPLE.

CHAPTER IV.

PUBLIC HEALTH.

CHAPTER V.

AGRICULTURE.

CHAPTER VI.

CANALS, DRAINAGE AND EMBANKMENTS.

CHAPTER VII.

NATURAL CALAMITIES.

CHAPTER VIII.

RENTS, WAGES AND PRICES.

CHAPTER IX.

OCCUPATIONS, MANUFACTURES AND TRADE.

CHAPTER X.

FACTORY INDUSTRIES.

CHAPTER XI.

MEANS OF COMMUNICATION.

CHAPTER XII.

GENERAL ADMINISTRATION.

CHAPTER XIII.

LOCAL SELF-GOVERNMENT.

CHAPTER XIV.

EDUCATION.

CHAPTER XV.

GAZETTEER.

GAZETTEER

OF THE

HOWRAH DISTRICT.

CHAPTER I.

PHYSICAL ASPECTS.

THE district of Howrah is situated in the south-east of the Burdwān Division between 22° 13′ and 22° 47′ north latitude and between 87° 51′ and 88° 22′ east longitude. With an area of 510 square miles and a population of 850,514 persons, it is the smallest district in Bengal and has a less numerous population than any district in the Province except Angul, Palāmau, Singhbhūm and Darjeeling. Its area is less than that of an average Bengal subdivision, but the district is slightly bigger than Bedfordshire and contains 58,000 more inhabitants than the county of Middlesex. GENERAL DESCRIPTION.

The district is bounded on the north by the Arāmbāgh and Serampore subdivisions of the Hooghly district; on the east by the Barrackpore, Alipore and Diamond Harbour subdivisions of the 24-Parganas; on the south by the Tamluk subdivision of Midnapore; and on the west partly by the Tamluk and Ghātāl subdivisions of the latter district and partly by the Arāmbāgh subdivision of the Hooghly district. The boundaries are partly natural and partly artificial. On the west and south-west the river Rūpnārāyan, and on the east and south-east the river Hooghly constitute natural boundaries, while on the north the boundary is formed by the Bally (Bāli) *Khāl* and an artificial line marking the southern limit of the Hooghly district. Boundaries.

In general shape, the district of Howrah is an irregular triangle bounded on two sides by great rivers, the apex of which lies at their confluence near Fort Mornington. Its extreme natural from east to west is about 28 miles, and its extreme Configuration.

length from north to south is nearly 40 miles. Hemmed in between the Hooghly on the east and the Rūpnārāyan on the west, and intersected by the Dāmodar, the Howrah district consists of a flat alluvial plain, with a gradual, almost imperceptible, rise towards the north and north-west, the general flow of drainage being consequently to the south and south-east. The product of these rivers and their branches, it comprises two main divisions, viz., the raised river banks and the large marshes or lowlands that separate them. In this way three distinct tracts are formed, each with a depression in the centre bounded by the high banks of the rivers, viz., an eastern tract stretching away from the Hooghly and its branch the Saraswatī, a central tract traversed by the Dāmodar and its branch the Kānā Dāmodar or Kausikī, and a western tract consisting of the country between the Dāmodar and the Rūpnārāyan. The upper courses of the Dāmodar and the Rūpnārāyan are somewhat higher than the Hooghly ; and in the intervening country are numerous watercourses or creeks, called *khāls*, which run dry or are very shallow in the hot weather.

In the interior the country is broken up into extensive swamps (*jhils*), or depressions, which form a vast sheet of water in the rains. There is little high land except on the banks of the rivers, whose windings the villages follow. These villages have a quiet beauty of their own, being surrounded by a dark belt of mangoes, feathery palms and clustering bamboos, while rich rice fields stretch to the verge of the reed-bordered marshes. Between Mākardah and Bargachhiā (Bargechhe), however, the country is so low that for miles not a single house or tree is visible, the monotonous sameness of this flat fen being broken only by the banks of the Rājāpur channel. South of the Bengal-Nāgpur line, from Kolāghāt to Uluberiā, the scenery changes. The rivers become broader, the currents stronger, and the land more fluvial in nature. The villages are situated at greater distances, while the country has to be protected from inundation by long embankments. Roads are few in number. and boats, or the paths along the embankments, are the chief means of communication. In the rains the floods often burst through the embankments or pour in through the creeks, spreading far and wide over the country. This tract then resembles an inland sea, from which the scattered villages stand out like islands ; while the rivers sweep on with increasing velocity, cutting away their banks and carrying an enormous volume of silt to the sea.

RIVER The chief rivers are (1) the Hooghly and its branch the (2) the cutting with two branches, the Kānā Dāmo-

The district is also intersected by numerous tributaries or effluents of the main rivers, which are generally called *khāls* or creeks. In the case of the Hooghly, these are the Bally (Bāli), Rājganj, Sānkrāil, Sijberiā and Champā *Khāls*, which are mostly tidal offshoots navigable by boats of 4 to 5 tons burden for short distances inland. The Sānkrāil and Sijberiā *Khāls* are the lower reaches of the Saraswatī and Kānā Dāmodar respectively. Into the Dāmodar fall a dozen channels, and into the Rūpnārāyan about half that number, the more important being the Madāriā, Bānspāti and Gāighātā (or Giāghātā) *Khāls* among the former, and the Bakshi *Khāl* among the latter. The Bakshi and Gāighātā *Khāls* join one another forming a tortuous passage between the two rivers, which is much used by country boats. The following is an account of the principal rivers of the district.

The Hooghly is the main westerly channel by which the waters of the Ganges enter the Bay of Bengal, its easterly channel being the Padmā. It is formed by the confluence of the Bhāgīrathī, Jalangī and Mātābhāngā; but among Hindus the name Bhāgīrathī is commonly given to the whole branch from Murshidābād southwards. It is so-called after king Bhagīrath, who, according to Hindu mythology, induced Gangā to come down from heaven. The legend runs that king Sagar being childless went to the Himālayas and underwent severe penances in order to obtain a son. The gods granted him 60,000 sons, and he commenced to perform the traditional horse sacrifice called *Asvamedha jajna*. A horse was turned loose to roam at will, and the whole Indian world was challenged to arrest its progress. If at the end of a year the horse returned safely and its retinue unconquered, the supremacy of the challenger would be patent, and as acknowledged suzerain over the whole country, he would solemnly sacrifice the horse to the gods. This crowning sacrifice could not be performed by king Sagar, for the god Indra in jealousy stole away the horse and hid it in the *Pātāla*, *i.e.*, the Indian hell, where the holy sage Kapila, an incarnation of Vishnu, was absorbed in meditation. The army of 60,000 princes, which escorted the horse, traced it up hill and down dale, till at last they found it grazing near Kapila. Suspecting him to be the thief, they rushed upon him, but fire darted from the angry eyes of the outraged sage, and they were burnt to ashes. After many long years, a descendant of Sagar named Bhagīrath, by his austere penances, induced Siva to permit the holy goddess Gangā (*i.e.*, the Ganges) to come down from the heavenly heights and bring salvation to his ancestors. Bhagīrath led the way till near the sea and then declared that he

Hooghly.

knew not the rest of the road. Thereupon Gangā, in order to make sure of reaching the ashes of the dead, divided herself into a hundred streams, one of which, by washing the ashes, completed their atonement for sin and redeemed their souls. Thus was the delta of the Ganges formed.

The name Bhāgīrathī, which commemorates this legend, literally means the Ganges, but in Bengal the name and sanctity of the river attach only to the westerly and most southerly branch now known as the Hooghly, for the worship of which the Dasaharā day is specially set aside. The portion below Sānkrāil is not considered sacred, however, perhaps because it was little used by boats in early times. Boatmen avoided this part of the main channel because of the difficulties of navigation and the danger of piratical raids, and went south-east by the branch flowing opposite Bator, which still survives as a small creek near Kālīghāt. It is called the Adi Gangā or the original Ganges, and has all the sanctity of that river. The river is also held sacred among Buddhists, and we find that Warren Hastings gave the Tāshi Lāmā of Tibet some land at Ghusuri in answer to his request that he might have "some land on the banks of the Ganges to which he might send his people to pray."* The monastery erected on this land may still be seen at Bhot-bāgān.

The river first touches the district at Bally, and, after flowing past Ghusuri and between the cities of Calcutta and Howrah, turns due west at Shālimār Point for a short distance along Garden Reach as far as Hangman Point. It then pursues a south-easterly course as far as Uluberiā, after which it describes another wide arc and then flows almost due south, receiving the Dāmodar opposite Faltā Point and the Rūpnārāyan opposite Hooghly Point. These great tributaries deflect the stream to th east for no less than 8 miles and have set up in it, just above the mouth of the Rūpnārāyan, the dreaded moving shoals known as the James and Mary Sands.

The reaches.

The deep channel alternates from left to right and *vice versa* according to the windings of the river, except where deflected by the large tributaries which debouch into it at the southern limit of this district. Proceeding from Howrah Bridge, the deep channel runs on the Calcutta side in the Calcutta Reach past the Fort and Kidderpore to Garden Reach. At Rājganj, opposite Hangman Point, it crosses over to the Howrah side, and follows the Sānkrāil Reach as far as Melancholy (Mānikhāli) Point. It then zigzags from left to right at each bend,

* Proceedings, Asiatic Society of Bengal, 1890, pages 140-148.

viz., to Jarmaker's Reach (left) to Coffrey Reach (right) and to Budge-Budge Reach (left). Thence a long bend brings the channel to the right through the Uluberiā and Māyāpur Reaches, the latter of which has a dangerous bar. The subsequent changes are to Rayāpur Reach (left), to Hog River Reach (right), and thence to the Fisherman's Anchorage or Reach (left). The influx of the Dāmodar now causes it to shoal up on the right bank, forming the Faltā Sands in the centre, so that there is only a narrow channel, the Faltā Reach, on the left bank. The next reaches are Naināu and Nurpur, both on the left, and after them come the notorious James and Mary Sands, with a narrow channel on each side called the Eastern Gut and the Western Gut. An account of these sands will be found in Chapter XV. The distances from Fort William are:—to Rājganj 6⅓ miles, to Uluberiā 19⅓ miles, to Faltā Point 35⅝ miles, and to Hooghly Point opposite the mouth of the Rūpnārāyan 42½ miles.*

Navigation. The chief perils to navigation are the James and Mary Sands and the Māyāpur Bar. Direct efforts to manipulate the channels across these shoals have not yielded favourable results. In 1868 experiments were conducted on the Māyāpur Bar, and spurs were run some distance below high water line from both banks of the river; but they were found inadequate to guide the flood and ebb tide into one channel, and no improvement resulted. In 1896 an engineering expert was brought out to consider the feasibility of improving the river, and he suggested that training walls should be built to regulate the channels across the James and Mary Sands and the Māyāpur Bar; but his recommendations were not considered practicable. A great deal has, however, been done of late years by the Port Commissioners to reduce the dangers of navigation.

All the available evidence tends to show that the Hooghly is not deteriorating as a waterway, but rather that it is improving. The rules for the Pilot establishment laid down in 1826 show that the draft of water at which pilots were authorized to take charge of ships in the river was from March to September 16½ feet from Calcutta to Diamond Harbour and 18 feet from Diamond Harbour to Saugor; while from October to February the depths were 17 feet and 18½ feet respectively. Four years later a revised rule was issued, by which vessels drawing 20 feet were allowed to navigate the river "with the aid of competent steamers at all times of the year up and down." Pilots were "strictly forbidden on pain of dismissal from the service from moving a vessel in the river

---

* S. R. Elson, *The River Hooghly, Calcutta to Saugor Island*, 1884.

on any account at a greater draft;" and vessels of greater draft were to be moored at Saugor or Diamond Harbour, as the case might be, until lightened to the proper draft. Since that time the draft of vessels moving up and down the Hooghly has greatly increased. The draft of the ten most deeply-laden vessels up to March 1906 was 27 feet 6 inches, but vessels of over 28 feet draft have navigated the river; and in June 1909 alone three steamers drawing 27 feet to 27 feet 11 inches left the Port of Calcutta.

Tides. The Hooghly is regularly affected by the tides, which rise at Kidderpore 15½ feet above the lowest tide-level in spring and 10½ feet in neap tides. During floods the mean springs rise as high as 19½ feet and the mean neaps 14½ feet. The tide travels to Calcutta from the Sāgar Roads in 4 hours and 9 minutes, and from Diamond Harbour in a little more than two hours, running at the rate of 17 miles an hour at Diamond Harbour, 22 miles at Māyāpur and 18 miles an hour at Fort William. In addition to tides, the Hooghly waters are affected by several other factors, such as the seasonable low readings of the barometer between March and September, the forcing of water into the river by strong southerly winds from March to August and out of it by northerly winds from November to February, and, lastly, by the floods which bring down a large body of fresh water from July to October. The difference due to these causes is about four feet, the highest level being in August and September, and the lowest in February and March.

The bore. Bores of more or less violence occur at perigee springs, especially in February, March and April. The bore is not felt much until it enters the more tortuous and contracted reaches above Hooghly Point, where it not only capsizes and swamps boats that have not been hauled off into deep water in time, but also affects vessels at anchor, forcing them to run upstream of their anchors with straightened cables, more especially if there is a strong southerly breeze. The following graphic description of the bore is given by a writer in the *Calcutta Review* of 1859:—"Upon the approach of this wave a distant murmur is heard, which turns into the cry *bān*! *bān*! *bān*! from the mouths of thousands of people, boatmen, sailors and others, who are always on the look out for this much dreaded wave. This cry is the signal for all sorts of craft to push out into the centre of the river, the only spot where the wave does not curl over and break. Should any boat or larger craft be caught in that portion of wave that breaks, instant destruction is inevitable. Numerous boats from the upcountry provinces are lost every year from the crews being ignorant either of the existence of the bore, or from not knowing the correct position to take up so as to meet it. Ships at anchor in Calcutta, though not exposed to the breaking portion of the wave, frequently part their cables when struck with the wave. Standing on the shore during the rapid rushing passage of the bore, it is a curious sight to see the lower portion of the river, or that nearest to the sea, six or eight feet higher than the upper portion of the river, the tide rising that number of feet in an instant. The height of the bore in the Hooghly varies from five to twelve feet; it is exceedingly dangerous in some parts of the river, but more moderate in others; it never breaks on both sides of the river at the same time. Deep water destroys its force, but shallow water, or a sand bank, brings out all its power and fury."

Accretions (*chars*) have been formed at various places on the Howrah side of the river, *e.g.*, at Ghusuri, Rāmkristapur, Sibpur (near the Engineering College), Sārengā and Uluberiā. These *chars* are very valuable, especially those at Rāmkristapur, which have been the source of a considerable income to the Port Commissioners. Elsewhere the bank is sloping and is largely utilized, outside municipal limits, for brick-making. A retired line of embankments runs along it up to the mouth of the Dāmodar, but, being under the charge of a number of co-sharing zamīndārs, is more or less in decay with many unrepaired breaches caused by floods. In 1906-07 a part of the line near Uluberiā had to be repaired by Government, at the cost of the landlords, to prevent floods causing serious damage to crops in the interior. The embankment between the mouths of the Dāmodar and the Rūpnārāyan is kept up by the Public Works Department.

Saraswatī. The Saraswatī, known locally as the Sarsati or Sarsuti, branches out from the Hooghly at Tribenī a few miles above Hooghly town, and enters the Howrah district near Bāluhāti (Baluti) as a small shallow stream. It then meanders on to the south in a tortuous course, and, keeping the Rājāpur *jhil* on the west, flows past Dumjor and Andul, falling into the Hooghly just above Sānkrāil. It is navigable up to Andul, but only by boats of 5 tons burden. Its high banks, and the remains of large boats occasionally dug out from its bed, show that once it must have been a broader and deeper stream. This inference is confirmed by the numerous large pools, called *dahas*, found in its bed, from which many river-side villages take their name, *e.g.*, Mākardah, Jhāpardah, Bhāndārdah, etc. The silting up of the river began some centuries ago, and its causes will be dealt with later in the section on changes in river courses.

Dāmodar. The Dāmodar is the only large river passing through the district. After forming the north-western boundary for seven miles, it enters the district near the village of Aknā and then flows south to Amtā, below which it receives the Gāighātā creek on its right bank. Leaving Amtā, it follows a winding southerly course to Bāgnān, and then flows to the south-east falling into the Hooghly opposite Faltā Point. Its total length within or touching the district is 45 miles. The Dāmodar is influenced by the tide as far as Rāspur two miles north of Amtā. At Amtā the spring tide rises 2 to 2½ feet in summer; ten miles lower down at Mahishrekhā the rise is 5 feet at neap and 8 feet at spring tides. During the summer, *i.e.*, from March to May, bores are felt as far up as Amtā, especially when strong southerly breezes are blowing. The height of the bore-wave varies according to weather and tides, but does not usually exceed 4 feet. The river has in summer 6 to 8 feet of water at Mahishrekhā and is not usually fordable below the junction of the Gāighātā *Khāl*. Above this point the river narrows rapidly, and at Amtā shrinks in the hot weather to a width of only 10 to 12 feet and a depth of a foot or so. Cargo boats do not ply as far up as Amtā after October, except during spring tides.

No important change in the course of the Dāmodar has taken place for many years past, but, on account of a large breach at Beguā in the Burdwān district, the volume of water passing down it has been much diminished, a large quantity being diverted from its present channel. No islands have been formed in the channel, except near Bānsberiā, but several large *churs* have sprung up along the banks, all more or less covered with grass, while a few are under cultivation. The banks are well-defined and vary from 6 to 15 feet in height. The river has been embanked on both sides, but the embankments on the upper part of the western side have not been maintained. It has been found that inundations on that side cause less damage, while the existence of embankments on both sides, by walling in the river and raising its bed, tends to cause heavy loss when breaches occur. The eastern embankment is now kept up by Government throughout, and also that portion of the western embankment which extends from the junction of the Gāighātā *Khāl* up to the Hooghly river. The flooded tracts produce excellent cold weather crops, especially pulses and tobacco. The Dāmodar is crossed at Mahishrekhā by the Orissa Trunk Road, a little lower down near Bāgnān by the Bengal-Nāgpur Railway, and about half a mile further down-stream by the High Level Canal.

Kānā Dāmodar. Of the several branches of the Dāmodar, two only call for special mention, viz., the Kānā Dāmodar or Kausikī and a branch on the west also called the Dāmodar. The Kānā Dāmodar enters this district on the east of Ichhānagar village, and flows south, winding its way to the west of the Rājāpur *jhil.* Finally, turning south-east, it falls into the Hooghly a mile north of Uluberiā town, after a course of nearly 20 miles in the district. A small stream now, it must have been more important in old days, as several large villages inhabited by the *bhadralok*, or respectable Hindu castes, lie along its course.

The western branch issues from the main channel of the Dāmodar in the extreme north of the district, and after a winding course of some 14 miles rejoins the Dāmodar 3 miles north-west of Amtā.

The Rūpnārāyan first touches this district on the south-west near Bhātorā village. It then flows south-east, receiving an accession of water from the Bakshi *Khāl*, and follows a generally south-easterly course to Tamluk. Here it bends to the east and finally falls into the Hooghly opposite Hooghly Point. The river nowhere intersects the district, but has a tortuous course along the boundary for some 35 miles. The stream widens considerably towards the mouth, and has at places a breadth of nearly 3 miles. The Rūpnārāyan is influenced by the tide throughout this portion of its course, and a heavy bore ascends it in the hot weather as far as the mouth of the Bakshi *Khāl.* It is nowhere fordable and is navigable by boats and small steamers all through the year. Several islands are found in the river channel, while accretions in the shape of grass-covered *chars* are not infrequent, especially on the right side. From the confluence of the Bakshi *Khāl* down to its mouth, the river is embanked along the left bank. The embankment, however, is what is known as a retired line; and in April and May the lands between it and the bed are inundated by spring tides and rendered unfit for cultivation by saline impregnations, except where minor embankments have been thrown up round the fields to keep out the brackish water. The river is crossed by the Bengal-Nāgpur Railway line at Kolāghāt (in the Midnapore district), and within a short distance of that place by the Orissa Trunk Road and the High Level Canal. Rūpnārāyan.

The Gāighātā (or Giāghātā) Bakshi *Khāl* is an improved natural waterway, 7½ miles in length, forming a connecting link between the Dāmodar and Rūpnārāyan rivers. The channel was taken over by the Public Works Department from the District Board of Howrah in 1894, and tolls are levied on it. Gāighātā Bakshi *Khāl.*

Within historic times great changes have taken place in the courses of the principal rivers. The changes have been greatest in the case of the Dāmodar. Formerly it discharged its waters CHANGES IN THE RIVER COURSES.

into the Hooghly near Nayāsarāi, 3 miles above Tribenī and about 39 miles north of Howrah. This channel appears gradually to have silted up, and in Rennell's map (1779-81) it is shown as the "Old Dummodah," from which it may be inferred that the volume of the main stream had been diverted from it. This diversion appears to have been the chief cause of the silting up of the Saraswatī at its head and of the decay of the port of Sātgāon. The channel must, therefore, have deteriorated by the middle of the 16th century, for in the *Ain-i-Akbarī* Hooghly is mentioned as a port superior to Sātgāon, though it does not appear in early maps, such as those of Gastaldi (1561) and De Barros (1553-1613), which show only Sātgāon.

Dāmodar.

The main volume of the Dāmodar water appears next to have flowed south along the channel now called the Kānā Dāmodar, De Barros, followed by Blaev (1650), shows the Dāmodar as debouching by two mouths above Pisolta, which has been identified with the modern village of Pichhaldaha close to Fort Mornington Point.* One of these mouths is the present mouth of the Dāmodar opposite Faltā Point, and the other is the Sijberiā *Khāl* above Uluberiā, by which the Kānā Dāmodar falls into the Hooghly. In the maps and accounts of the 17th century and the beginning of the 18th century the latter river was called the Jan Perdo, "a river for great ships" according to the chart of 1701. In Bowrey's map of the river Hooghly (1687) it is shown with small islands at its mouth, and these are also mentioned in 1676 by Streynsham Master. In Rennell's map, however, it is shown as a small stream without connection with the Dāmodar and without islands at its mouth; and at present it is a shallow silted-up stream, serving only to carry off local drainage. But it seems clear that it formed the main southerly channel of the Dāmodar up to the beginning of the 18th century, and its size and importance are still attested by the long marshes on either side, as well as by the populous villages crowded along its banks.

The present channel of the Dāmodar can be traced to the second half of the 16th century in De Barros' map, while in Bowrey's chart it appears as the Raspas, and in the pilot chart of 1703 as the Mondelghat, after the Mandalghāt *pargana* through which it flows. Gradually, as the eastern branches silted up at their mouths, it became the main channel. The Madāriā *Khāl* between the present channel and the Kānā Dāmodar is another old branch of the Dāmodar. This channel is shown in Rennell's Atlas of 1779 as branching off above Rājbalhāt and rejoining the

---

* C. R. Wilson, J. A. S. B., 1892. p. 112.

Dāmodar near Bāgnān, whereas it now falls into the parent stream above Amtā. Traces of the old course still survive in the Bānspāti *Khāl* and a number of pools (*dahas*), each about half a mile long and a quarter of a mile broad, at Dudkhāli, Chota Mairā, Bara Mairā, Jagannāthpur, Mansmāri, Dhāpa and Milki. It is said to have been navigable by ships, and it is reported that on its bank, at the village of Gobardhanpur 1½ miles from Bāgnān, there was formerly a place called Jāhājghātā, *i.e.*, the anchorage for ships. There was formerly also a branch to the west from Rājbalhāt to Amtā, but this also has silted up.

The changes in the lower portion of the Rūpnārāyan are also considerable. This river was known to Europeans up to the 18th century by a number of different names. It was called Ganga in the maps of Gastaldi and De Barros, Guenga in Blaev's map, Tamalee in Bowrey's chart, Tomberlie in the pilot chart of 1703, Patraghatta by Valentijn (1670), and finally the Rūpnārāyan by Rennell, who referred to it as "falsely called the Old Ganges." Similarly, in the older accounts, such as the *Da Asia* of De Barros, it went under the name Ganga, and in the later accounts of the 17th century it was designated Tumbolee (Hedges), Tumberleen (Master), and Tombolee (Bowrey). From Valentijn's map it appears that a large branch of the Dāmodar fell south into the Rūpnārāyan above Mandalghāt and Tamluk, while another branch running east fell into the Hooghly near Kālnā. The main channel of the Dāmodar is still connected with the Rūpnārāyan by the Kānā Dwārakeswar, and it is not unlikely that a large stream joined the Rūpnārāyan somewhere near Ghātāl. By these two branches boats could have come from the Bhāgīrathī to the Rūpnārāyan without difficulty, and this probably led to the idea of its being a branch of the Ganges. The next prominent fact is that the Rūpnārāyan is shown in older maps (Gastaldi, De Barros and Blaev) as discharging itself by two channels enclosing a large island at its mouth. The westerly channel disappears in Valentijn's map, Bowrey's chart and the pilot map of 1703 A.D.; and it appears, therefore, that it must have silted up and that the island became more or less joined to the mainland in Midnapore. The combined result of its discharging all its silt-laden water through the eastern channel alone and the close proximity of the main stream of the Dāmodar was the formation of the James and Mary Sands in the Hooghly. **Rūpnārāyan.**

It remains to note the deterioration of the Saraswatī, which seems to have been due to the diversion of the Dāmodar water from the upper reaches of the Hooghly. By Rennell's time (1779-81) it had so far silted up, that it was quite a small **Saraswatī.**

stream; and now it is merely a shallow narrow creek, except for a few miles above its outfall. It is shown as a large river in old maps as late as Valentijn's (based on information gathered in 1660-70) and was formerly used by country boats and small sloops for inland traffic, but there appear to be no good grounds for the common belief that it was once the main channel of the Hooghly or Ganges.

GEOLOGY. The district is composed of alluvium and presents no features of special geological interest. Judging from the results of the boring made in Calcutta in 1835-40, the depth of the deposit is very great. The boring reached a depth of 481 feet without signs of either a rocky bottom or marine beds. At a depth of 30 feet below the surface, *i.e.*, about 10 feet below sea-level, beds of peat with wood were found, which indicate the existence of ancient land surfaces. The wood in the upper peat beds was examined and found to be of two kinds, one of which was recognized as belonging to the *sundrī* tree (*Heritiera littoralis*), which grows in abundance on the muddy flats of the Ganges delta, while the other was probably the root of a climbling plant resembling *Briedelia*. At considerable depths, bones of terrestrial mammals and fluviatile reptiles were found, but the only fragments of shells noticed, at 380 feet, are said to have been of fresh-water species. At a depth of 175 to 185 feet, and of 300 to 325 feet, and again throughout the lower 85 feet of the bore-hole, pebbles were found in considerable quantities. The inference drawn is that the present site of Calcutta was near the margin of the alluvial plain, and that the land has undergone depression and has subsequently been covered by an accumulation of alluvial material. The geological formation of Howrah may be presumed to be the same.

The present conformation of the district is due to the action of its silt-laden rivers. "When the whole country is covered with water, moving rapidly towards the sea in the river channels, and stationary throughout the intervening marshes, the dead water of the marshes prevents the floods of the rivers from breaking out of the channels, and, by stopping the course of the silt-charged water along the edges of the creeks and streams, forces it to deposit the sediment it has in suspension. Hence gradually arises a system of river channels, traversing the country in many directions, between banks which are higher than the intervening flats, and these flats form persistent marshes, known in the Ganges delta as *jhils* or *bils*."*

* R. D. Oldham, *Manual of the Geology of India* (Calcutta, 1893), pages 432-34, 440-41.

Outside the Royal Botanic Garden at Sibpur, of which a description will be found in Chapter XV, there is little of especial interest to a botanist. The vegetation is composed almost exclusively of the aquatic and marsh plants to be met with in the alluvial rice fields of Bengal, such as *Hydrilla*, *Utricularia*, *Caesulia*, or of those semi-spontaneous plants that form the village shrubberies of Central Bengal, such as *Glycosmis*, *Trema*, *Urena*, *Solanum*, *Datura*, *Leonotis* and the like. Waste places are generally covered by a weedy vegetation, and one of the striking features of the district is the extent to which the weeds which occur in these places are exotic so far as Bengal is concerned. Many of them, indeed, such as *Scoparia*, *Ageratum*, *Evolvulus nummularius* and *Peperomia pellucida*, though now remarkably abundant, were originally natives of America. BOTANY.

The district being fringed with factories and under cultivation elsewhere, wild animals are scarce. The larger species are practically unrepresented, for there is no jungle which could furnish cover for big game. One or two leopards have, however, been reported in the district within recent years. One was killed by a local *shikāri* at Bāltikri 3 or 4 years ago, and another was reported to have been seen on some *hoglā* jungle in the grounds of the Civil Engineering College at Sibpur 2 years ago; but they were probably only stray visitors from the adjoining districts. Wild pig abound in parts of the Uluberiā subdivision, and a few are said to be found in the Jagatballabhpur thāna. Crocodiles are sometimes to be seen on the banks of the Hooghly and Dāmodar rivers during the winter months; and during the rains they frequently find their way into tanks and flooded lowlands near the river. In the cold weather snipe of two or three varieties are fairly numerous in the paddy fields within the Dumjor, Sānkrāil and Jagatballabhpur thānas in the headquarters subdivision, and also in the Uluberiā subdivision. The common, whistling and cotton teal are found in fair numbers in the flooded area between Māju and Amtā, and sometimes two or three of the commoner varieties of duck. FAUNA.

The principal varieties of river fish netted in the Hooghly river are *hilsā*, *bhetki*, *tengrā*, and, during the season, *tapsi* or mango-fish (*Polynemus paradiseus*). The Hooghly from Uluberiā to Diamond Harbour is, in fact, noted for the delicious fish last named, which is described by Walter Hamilton (1820), "as the best and highest flavoured fish not only in Bengal, but in the whole world." It is caught with or without roe in large numbers from April to June; and Uluberiā is a centre for its export. Members of the carp family are found in almost every tank, and *rui*, *mirgel* and *kātlā* spawn are reared extensivly. The impregnated eggs float in small lumps near the shallow edges of rivers and are collected in pieces of cloth by certain low caste people and also by fishermen. They are bought by the rearers at the rate of Rs. 5 to Rs. 8 for a handful, and put in shallow ponds, where they hatch in a few days. In about a month's time, it becomes possible to distinguish the various kinds. The fry are then caught with fine nets, sorted and put in different tanks; some also are disposed of to hawkers, who carry them about for sale to stockers of tanks. Amtā is a centre of this business.

CLIMATE. The climate of Howrah is very similar to that of Calcutta For practical purposes the year may be regarded as consisting of two seasons, the dry season from November to May and the wet season from June to October; but the dry season may be further subdivided into the cold weather and the hot weather, and the wet season into the advancing south-west monsoon (June to September) and the retreating monsoon (September-October).

In the cold weather there is but little cloud or rain, the fall varying from 0·13 inches in December to 0·99 inches in February. Humidity gradually diminishes from 70 per cent. of saturation in November to 60 per cent. in February. Heavy dews fall in November and the first half of December; but gradually they too become less frequent and less heavy, the pressure of aqueous vapour diminishing from 0·600 in November to 0·400 in February. At this season cold winds blow from the land side, veering from north-north-east to north-west, while the mean barometric pressure rises to 30·05 in December and January. The temperature falls very perceptibly, the coldest month being January, when the range of the thermometer is from 85° to 50° in the shade, the mean diurnal variation being considerable, viz., 20° to 25°. The beginning of November is affected by the retreating monsoon, and is often stormy, while a few cold-weather land-storms occur later; but Howrah does not lie in the usual track of storms and cyclones.

The hot weather begins in March and continues till the first week of June. Clouds now begin to appear more frequently, and the rainfall increases to about 5 inches in May. Humidity does not rise much, being only 70 to 80 per cent. in May; but the aqueous vapour pressure rises to about 0·850 in that month. The temperature rises steadily, until in May it goes up to 105°, with a mean diurnal variation of 15° to 20°. The heat in the evening is fortunately lowered by a steady sea-breeze from the south and occasionally the south-west, and also by "nor'westers" with sudden showers. Hail-storms in March and April sometimes occur; but other storms are comparatively few, breaking mostly in May. Just before the monsoon bursts, the winds frequently fail altogether and the weather becomes humid and sultry.

The south-west monsoon usually bursts in the second week of June, with heavy rain. The wind blows steadily from the south and occasionally from the south-south-east, while the barometric pressure falls from 29·60 to 29·45, but rises slightly to 29·75 in September. The temperature slowly falls having a maximum of 105° in early June and of 95° in September, the minimum in the latter month being 70°. Humidity and the aqueous vapour pressure are now at their highest, rising to 90 per cent. and 0·950 respectively. The heaviest rainfall occurs in July and August, when it is over 11 inches, with 15 to 20 rainy days in each month. Storms, chiefly originating in the north-west corner of the Bay of Bengal are frequent in these months; while a few land storms come up in July and August, but cyclones are comparatively rare. Owing to heavy rainfall and high humidity, the weather becomes oppressive in September, which is undoubtedly the most trying and unhealthy month in the year.

The second period of the wet season marks the retreat and final disappearance of the monsoon. The wind now changes gradually to north and the barometric pressure becomes variable, but rises to 29·90. The mean temperature slowly falls to 70° early in November and the nights become cooler, the mean diurnal variation being 15°. Rainfall diminishes to 4 inches in October, and there are only 5 to 10 rainy days in the month; humidity falls to 80 per cent. and the aqueous vapour pressure is from 0·800 to 0·850. Rain gives place to dews at night; but the chief peculiarity of this period is that in the wake of the retreating monsoon follow numerous storms.

Generally speaking, the healthiest season is from the middle of January to the middle of March, when it is mildly cold and fairly bracing. In the hot weather from the middle of March to the middle of May, the heat, though great in the day-time, is alleviated in the afternoon by a southerly sea-breeze. This season is consequently not unpleasant, and is fairly healthy. The most unhealthy season is from September to the middle of January, when dews fall and the air and earth are charged with moisture, malarial fevers and bowel complaints being common.

The district receives an abundant rainfall, but the quantity often varies greatly, rising, for instance, to 78·6 inches in 1900-01 and falling to 35·7 inches in 1895-96. The bulk falls in the season of the south-west monsoon, *i.e*, from June to September; and the smallest fall is in the cold weather, *i.e.*, from November Rainfall.

to February. The following table gives the average rainfall at the three recording stations for the cold, hot and rainy weathers.

Station.	Years recorded.	November to February.	March to May.	June to October.	Annual average.
Howrah ..	32—33	2·23	8·21	49·03	59·47
Mahishrekhā ...	25—26	2·31	8·09	47·75	58·15
Uluberiā ...	9—10	1·21	7·49	44·54	53·24

CHAPTER II.

HISTORY.

EARLY HISTORY.

THE history of Howrah, prior to the advent of European merchant adventurers, is practically unknown, and any attempt to trace it must necessarily lead along a wide and somewhat insecure track of conjecture. It may, however, be assumed that it was inhabited long before the Christian era, for adjoining it to the south lay Tāmralipti (Tamluk), a famous sea-port of Eastern India, often mentioned in the *Mahābhārata*, in the old scriptures of the Jainas and Buddhists, and in Ptolemy's Geography. It may also be inferred from the nature of the country, a low-lying fen land bounded by great waterways, that its earliest inhabitants belonged for the most part to fishing and boating tribes. Even now Kaibarttas, the great Bengali caste of fishermen and boatmen, form nearly a third of the total population of the district. At the dawn of history, it probably formed part of the territory of either the Suhmas or Tāmraliptas, and eventually became attached to Tāmralipti, which is mentioned as a separate kingdom up to the time of Yuan Chwang (Hiuen Tsiang), *i.e.*, until the close of the first half of the seventh century A.D. On the decline of Tamluk it probably passed under the rule of the more powerful Suhmas, or, as they were called later, the Rādhas.

In the beginning of the 12th century A.D. the area now included in the district may have acknowledged the suzerainty of Chodaganga, the first Ganga king of Orissa, who is credited in inscriptions with having conquered Mandar and pursued its king to the bank of the Ganges.* Mandar is evidently the earlier form of Mandāran, which is called distinctly in a late Sanskrit work *Mandārāvani*.† Presumably, therefore, the Gangas conquered and annexed Mandāran, and with it at least a part of this district. Moreover, in the palm-leaf chronicles of the Jagannāth temple, King Anangabhīmadeva (*circa* 1300 A.D.) is quoted as boasting that he extended the northern frontier of his kingdom from the

* M. M. Chakravarti, J.A.S.B., 1903, p. 110.

† *Bhavishyat Purāna*, Ind. Ant., XX, 420.

river Kānsbāns (near Bhadrakh in the Balasore district) to the river Danei-budhā. The latter is apparently the old Dāmodar, which as late as the 17th century was called Jan Perdo, *d* and *j* being interchangeable in the Oriyā language. If credence may be given to these records, the Ganga kingdom extended up to the old Dāmodar and included the Uluberiā subdivision, leaving the Howrah subdivision still in Rādha.

MUHAMMADAN RULE.

Towards the end of the 13th century the Muhammadans took possession of Sātgāon, and in all probability extended their conquest southwards as far as the mouth of the Dāmodar. But no early Muhammadan remains have been yet found in the district, and the distance from their capital, Lakhnautī or Panduā, must have precluded their exercising any effective rule over this outlying part of their dominions. The real rule of the Muhammadans probably began in the time of Husain Shāh (*circa* 1494-1520), who consolidated his power over Bengal and Bihār, and whose generals invaded Assam, Orissa and Chittagong. A generation later the district appears to have been overrun by the Oriyās, for their last Hindu king, Makundadeva Hari Chandan, was apparently in possession of the country as far north as Tribenī, where a broad flight of steps leading down to the Ganges is said to have been constructed under his orders. His hold over the country was soon lost, for in 1568 the army of the Bengal Sultān, Sulaimān Kararāni, drove him out, and finally conquered the whole country as far as the Chilkā lake. During the reign of this latter king a part of Howrah district, with the adjoining *mahāls*, was grouped into a new *sarkār* called after him Sulaimānābād.

On the defeat and death of his son Dāūd Kararāni in 1576 A.D., Bengal formally became a part of Akbar's empire. In 1582 Todar Mal drew up his famous rent-roll, which so far as the *sūbah* of Bengal was concerned merely accepted the state of things as it existed during Afghān rule from the reign of Sher Shāh to that of Sulaimān Kararāni. From this rent-roll the district appears to have been distributed between three *sarkārs*, Sātgāon, Sulaimānābād and Mandāran, and the following *mahāls* can still be traced:—in Sātgāon (1) Purah (the modern Boro, in which lies Howrah town), (2) Bāliā, (3) Muzaffarpur, (4) Khārar (the modern Khalor); in Sulaimānābād, (5) Basandhari, (6) Bhosat (the modern Bhursut), (7) Dhārsā; and in Mandāran, (8) the great *mahāl* of Mandalghāt.* Judging from the location of these *mahāls*, the original *sarkārs* were

* *Ain-i-Akbari*, Jarrett, II, 140-1.

Sātgāon and Mandāran, which were separated by the old Dāmodar; and *sarkār* Sulaimānābād was made up of portions of them, e.g., in this district Bāliā, Basandhari and Dhārsā were detached from Sātgāon, and Bhosat on the west of the Dāmodar from Mandāran. *Sarkār* Sātgāon had a large general revenue from dues on ports and *hāts*, and a small one from vegetable markets and timber yards, of which a portion would have been realized from the area now comprised in the district of Howrah.

A few local details of the district at this early period of its history may be gathered from an old Bengali poem and from the old maps of Gastaldi and De Barros. The Bengali poem of Bipradāsa, dated 1495 A.D., describes the voyage of a merchant called Chānd Saudāgar from Burdwān to the sea.* Chānd went by Ariādaha on the east and Ghusuri on the west, and then rowing along the eastern bank passed by Calcutta, and at Bator worshipped its presiding goddess Betāi Chandī. Ghusuri, a place not mentioned in any other old work, is now the northernmost portion of Howrah city, and Bator is a part of the city south of Sibpur. In the old maps we find two more places called Pisacoly (De Barros) and Picalda (Gastaldi), or Pisolta (De Barros). Pisacoly (Bengali Pichhākuli ?), which is shown as a place between the mouths of the Dāmodar and Rūpnārāyan, has not yet been identified, and does not appear in maps published in the second half of the 17th century. Pisolta has been identified with the modern village of Pichhaldaha,† 2 miles north-north-west of Fort Mornington Point in the extreme south of the Uluberiā subdivision. Here boats used to cross the Rūpnārāyan,‡ and it must formerly have been a trade centre of some importance; now a *hāt* (market) is held there.

EUROPEAN TRADE. The first mention of any place in the district by a European writer occurs in the journal of the Venetian Cesare Federici, who left an interesting account of Bator. Cesare Federici visited the place about 1578 and described it as follows:—"A good tide's rowing before you come to Satagan you shall have a place which is called Buttor, and from thence upwards the river is very shallow, and little water. Every year at Buttor they make and unmake a village with houses and shops made of straw, and with all things necessary to their uses, and this village standeth as long as the ships ride there, and till they depart for the Indies; and when they are departed, every man goeth to

* H. P. Sāstrī, Proc. A.S.B., 1892, p. 123.

† C. R. Wilson, J.A.S.B., 1892, p. 112.

‡ It is mentioned in the 17th century biographies of Chaitanya.

his plot of houses and then setteth fire on them, which made me to marvel. For, as I passed up to Satagan, I saw this village standing with a great number of people, with the infinite number of ships and bazars, and at my return coming down with my captain of the last ship, for whom I tarried, I was amazed to see such a place so soon razed and burnt, and nothing left but the sign of the burnt houses."*

From this account it is clear that Bator was a rendezvous for trading ships unable to proceed higher up the shallow reaches of the river, and that what is now called a *hāt* or periodical market was held there. The centre of this trade was Sātgāon, from which were exported in the 16th century "rice, cloth of Bombast of diverse sorts, Lacca, great abundance of sugar, mirabolans, dried and preserved, long pepper, oyle of zerzeline, and many other sorts of merchandise." The same impression of Sātgāon as a thriving port fed by numerous subsidiary marts is gathered from the account of Ralph Fitch (1586). "Satagam is a fair city for a city of the Moors, and very plentiful of all things. Here in Bengala they have every day in one place or other a great market, and they have many great boats, wherewithal they go from place to place and buy rice and many other things."

This trade, originally monopolized by the Portuguese, was gradually shared in by the Dutch, the English and the French. As European trade in Bengal expanded, it led to an extension of cultivation and to the settlement of weavers and other artisans along the river bank, so much so that, after the capture of Hooghly from the Portuguese, a *Faujdār* had to be specially posted to Hooghly to control the growing trade along the river. The large increase in the river and sea-going traffic also attracted pirates, particularly Arakanese and Portuguese half-castes. These pirates infested the estuary of the Hooghly, but gradually became more daring, and sailed higher up. To check their raids, the Musalmān Government built, apparently about 1666, a fort on the west bank known as Tanna Fort. It is shown in Valentijn's and subsequent maps, and is thus described in the diary of the Agent, Streynsham Master, under the date 30th November 1676:—"Tannay is distant from Hooghly about forty miles by water and twenty miles by land. There stands an old fort of mud walls, which was built to prevent the incursions of the Arracanese,

* Original edition of 1587, translated in Richard Hakluyt's *Principal Navigations, Voyages, etc.*, Glasgow Reprint, Vol. V., pp. 410-411. The English has been slightly modernized, as there appears to be no particular object in reproducing the archaic forms of an old translation.

for it seems about ten or twelve years since they were so bold that none durst inhabit lower down the river than this place, Arracanese usually taking the people of the shore to sell them at Pipley."* This fort was frequently mentioned in the European accounts of the 17th and 18th centuries, and played an important part in the early struggles of the English.

In December 1686 the rupture with the Viceroy Shaista Khān led to the retreat of the British from Hooghly under Job Charnock. The refugees found temporary shelter at Sutānuti, the present site of Calcutta, but the country was up in arms and a large army was advancing against them. It was accordingly decided to fall back on Hijilī further down the river. On the way they stormed and took the fort of Tanna, an exploit laconically described by Charnock as follows:—"On the 11th February 1687 assaulted and took his fort at Tanna with the loss only of a manne's legg and some wounded."† Not satisfied with this, they plundered and destroyed everything between Tanna and Hijilī including several granaries and salt depôts belonging to the Nawāb They also seized and carried off a number of Mughal vessels, which they met in the river, and, sending several of their own ships to Balasore burned and destroyed about forty more native merchant vessels. The war was concluded in August 1687 by a treaty under which the British were allowed to move up from Hijilī and settle on a tract of land near Uluberiā, to erect magazines and construct a dock for shipping; but they were forbidden to go beyond the Tanna forts and had to restore all the ships they had seized. This treaty was received coldly, by the Court of Directors, which reminded Charnock that "it is of vanity to fancy that your prudence or subtlety procured those good terms . . . It was not your wit or contrivance, but God Almighty's good providence, which hath always graciously superintended the affairs of this Company."

EARLY STRUGGLES OF THE BRITISH.

Charnock and his little band now moved on to Uluberiā (on the 17th June), but after a short time went to Little Tanna, from which, with the permission of the Mughal authorities, they returned to Sutānuti.‡ At first Charnock had recommended that the British should make their headquarters at Uluberiā, but afterwards the Bengal Council changed their minds and reported

* *Diary of William Hedges*, Yule II, 287.

† Charnock's letter to Court, dated 10th September, 1687, Yule, II, 65; Patna Factory Letter, dated 25th June, 1687, id. II, 62.

‡ According to Broome, Charnock commenced making docks at Uluberiā for careening the ships, which by this time were greatly in need of repair, and stayed there three or four months. It is doubtful, however, whether the stay at Uluberiā was so long.

in favour of Sutānuti, as we learn from a subsequent letter referring to:—"Our Generall Letter by the *Beaufort*, and Our Diaries of that Yeare wherein we have layd downe Our reasons for the altering our opinion about Ulubarreah and pitching on Chuttanuttee as the best and fittest up the River on the Maine, as we have since experienced, and likewise been sattisfyed that Ulubarreah was misrepresented to us by those sent to survey it."* This letter was written from Madras where the Bengal Council had been forced to retire. The subsequent adventures of Charnock and his followers took place outside this district, and it will be sufficient to say that at length on 24th August 1690 Charnock arrived for the third time at Sutānuti and founded the present city of Calcutta. To those curious about such things it is a quaint reflection that Uluberiā, now a quiet provincial town, might have been the capital of India.

Six years later the existence of the infant settlement was threatened by the rebellion of Subhā Singh. One party of the insurgents laid siege to Fort Tanna, but the British, at the request of the *Faujdār* of Hooghly, sent a vessel with some guns to assist the garrison, and the insurgents were compelled to retreat.† For some years after this the district had peace, and the foundation of Calcutta assisted its development. Bator indeed declined, most of its trade being transferred to the other side of the river; but new villages sprung up, docks were opened for repairing ships, while gardens and villas were built in Howrah city as suburban retreats. Captain Alexander Hamilton, who visited Calcutta about 1706, thus described Howrah:—"On the other side of the River are Docks made for repairing and fitting their ships' Bottoms, and a pretty good Garden belonging to the Armenians, that had been a better place to have built their Fort and Town for many Reasons. One is, that where it now stands, the Afternoon's Sun is full in Front of the Houses, and shines hot on the Streets, that are both above and below the Fort. The Sun would have sent its hot Rays on the Back of the Houses, and the Front had been a good shade for the Street."‡

LAST DAYS OF MUGHAL RULE.

On the accession of the Emperor Farrukhsiyar, the Bengal Council decided to send a deputation to Delhi with a petition for the renewal of their *farmāns*. In this petition they applied for a lease of additional villages, five on the west side and thirty-three

* General Letter from the Council of Bengal to the Court, dated 30th September 1689, l.c., Yule, II. 86.

† Broome, *History of the Bengal Army* p. 28; Stewart, *History of Bengal* (1847), p. 210; C. R. Wilson, *Early Annals of the English in Bengal*, I. 147-150.

‡ *A New Account of the East Indies*, Vol. II., p. 12.

on the east side of the Hooghly. The list of villages is given in the Consultation Book of the Council under the date May 4th, 1714, and mentions "Salica" (Sālkhiā), "Harirah" (Howrah), Cassundeah (Kāsundi), "Ramkrissnapur" and "Batter" (Bator), all in *parganas* "Borrow" and "Paican" with an annual rent of Rs. 1,450.* The deputation under John Surman and Khojā Sarhad Armenian did not start till after March 1715, and after a delay of 2½ years, Mr. Surman came back with 33 *farmāns* and *hasbul-hukums*. The deputation was successful in getting orders about the *tālukdāri* of all the villages applied for, but could not secure a lease of the five Howrah villages, because the landlords were prevented by the Nawāb from parting with their lands on any terms.†

During the next 12 years the rent-roll was twice revised, first in 1722 by Jāfar Khān *alias* Murshid Kulī Khān and again in 1728 by his son-in-law Shujā-ud-din. During these revisions the zamīndāri of Burdwān received large additions, the whole of Uluberiā and a large part of the Howrah subdivision being included in it. Furthermore a strip of land on the west bank of the river from Hooghly down to Howrah was separated and raised into a distinct zamīndāri called Muhammad Amīnpur.‡ In this way the lands of Howrah district, excepting certain *kharijā mahāls*, came to be under two Hindu zamīndāris, Burdwān and Muhammad Amīnpur, as is shown in Rennell's Atlas (Plates VII and IX).

In 1741-42 A.D, the Marāthā cavalry under Bhāskar Pandit swept over Western Bengal, and forced Alī Vardi Khān to retire precipitately from Burdwān to Kātwā. The whole tract from Akbarnagar (Rājmahāl) to Midnapore and Jaleswar came, we are told, into the possession of the Marāthās.§ Mīr Habīb made himself master of Hooghly, and the Marāthās led by him overran the lands on the western side of the river and are said to have seized the Tanna Fort. The war continued till 1751, and the land suffered frequently from the incursions of the Marāthā cavalry, and also from the bands of dacoits that sprung up amid the disorganization of administration. Fort Tanna again came into

---

* C. R. Wilson, *Early Annals of the English in Bengal*, II. p. 172.

† *id.* Vol. II, 287-288, Nos. 28 and 29; J. Grant's View of the Revenues of Bengal, Appendix to *Fifth Report* (Madras Reprint, 1884), I. 486; C. W. B. Rouse, *Landed Property of Bengal* (1791), I. 104.

‡ *Fifth Report* (Madras Reprint, 1884), Grant's Analysis of the Finances of Bengal, I. 267, 322; Grant's View of the Revenues of Bengal, I, 457.

§ *Riyāzu-s-Salātin*, Bib. Ind., pp. 343-4.

prominence in 1756, when Sirāj-ud-daula advanced upon Calcutta. The British commenced hostilities by an attack on the fort, delivered by two vessels of about 300 tons and two small brigantines. As soon as they opened fire, the garrison, consisting of about fifty of the Nawāb's troops, evacuated the place. A small detachment of Europeans and lascars then landed and took possession, spiking some of the guns and throwing the remainder into the river. Next day 2,000 men arrived from Hooghly, drove the detachment to their boats and opened a heavy fire on the vessels from their matchlocks and two field-pieces which they mounted on the walls. The ships attempted to return the fire, but their light guns made no impression on the walls of the fort, and though a reinforcement of 30 men was sent from Calcutta, they were obliged to return, having failed in their attempt. The failure of this attempt subsequently cost the British dear. After the capture of Calcutta and the massacre of the Black Hole, the survivors in attempting to escape down the river were driven back by the guns mounted on the fort, and a sloop and a snow were forced ashore. Four days later they were joined by three vessels from Bombay and managed to pass the fort safely with the loss of only two lascars.*

The capture of the fort was one of the first successes of the avenging force under Clive and Admiral Watson. As soon as he heard of their approach, the Nawāb had the fort put in order, commenced building another called Aligarh on the opposite bank, and had two ships loaded with bricks ready to be sunk in the channel between them. A sloop coming up in advance of the fleet prevented the sinking of these two ships, and on the 1st January the forts were evacuated without a shot being fired.† A contemporaneous account briefly describes the action as follows:— "On the first of January, the *Kent* and the *Tyger* anchored between Fort Tanna and a Battery opposite to it, both which the enemy abandoned as the ships approached. About forty guns, some fourteen pounders and all mounted on good carriages, with some Powder and Ball were found in this Fort and Battery; and the Admiral left the *Salisbury* as a Guardship to prevent the enemy from regaining them." A letter from an officer of the *Kent*, dated Calcutta, February 1st, 1757 confirms the above

* Broome, *History of the Bengal Army*, pp. 55, 69, 70; C. R. Hill, *Bengal in 1756-7*, Vol. I. p. cxxxi.

† Broome, *History of the Bengal Army*, pp. 80, 86.

account:—"We sailed for Tanna Forts, about two miles below Calcutta the first of January; but they abandoned them on our approach. The *Salisbury* was left a Guardship there."*

The victory of Plassey made the English the virtual masters of Bengal. Mīr Jāfar, who had been raised to the throne, was within three years deposed by them, and Mīr Kāsim Alī Khān placed on the *masnad*. By a treaty, confirmed by an Imperial *sanad* dated 11th October 1760,† Mīr Kāsim assigned to the East India Company for military charges the districts of Burdwān, Midnapore and Chittagong. Howrah was included in Burdwān and thus became British territory. The only other notable event in the history of the district during the 18th century was the action with the Dutch fought in the Hooghly in 1759. At the time there were only three Indiamen in the river, which were ordered up to protect Calcutta, while the garrisons at Tanna Fort and Charnock's Battery were strengthened by the best of the British troops under Captain Knox. The Dutch fleet came up cautiously as they had no pilots. On the 21st November they anchored off Sānkrāil Reach, just out of cannon shot from the English batteries; on the 23rd, their troops landed on the western bank, and marched by land along the Saraswatī river towards Chinsura, while the vessels dropped down to Melancholy Point, below which the three English ships were at anchor. On the 24th, after some infructuous negotiations, the three English ships weighed anchor, and notwithstanding the enemy's superiority—they had seven ships and four were large vessels, each with 36 guns—boldly came alongside and attacked them. A desperate action ensued, which lasted for two hours. At length, the Dutch Commodore struck his colours, and all his captains followed his example, with the exception of the second in command, who fought his way gallantly and got clear off to Kālpī, the English ships being too much crippled to follow. There, however, he was captured by two English ships hurrying up to join in the defence. The action had been short, but fierce. One ship, the *Duke of Dorset*, was riddled through and through, 90 shot were in her hull, and her rigging was cut to pieces, but not one man was killed, though several were wounded. The English had adopted the expedient of lining their quarters with bags of saltpetre, to screen the men from the enemy's fire, an

EARLY BRITISH RULE.

* *A New History of the East Indies* (1758), by Captain Cope. Appendix VI, pp. 418, 420; *Bengal in 1756-7*, II. pp. 197, 198, III. pp. 2, 4, 7, 11, 34, 156.

† Grants' Analysis, *Fifth Report*, I. 329.

expedient which appears to have answered, though it was a dangerous one, considering the risk of fire.*

MUTINY OF 1857. During the Mutiny there was only one episode in Howrah, which is perhaps worthy of commemoration. This was the characteristic action taken by Colonel Neill, who was proceeding up country with his regiment, the Madras (1st Royal Dublin) Fusiliers. To quote from Holmes' *History of the Indian Mutiny*:—"It was arranged that a detachment of the Fusiliers should proceed up the Ganges by steamer, while Neill himself should follow with the rest by train. Arriving at the station with a few of his men some minutes before the main body, which had been unavoidably detained, he was told by the station-master that the train was already late, and would be started at once without waiting for the absentees; and, when he remonstrated, a crowd of other officials came up, and did their best to silence him. But he soon showed them what manner of man they had to deal with. Putting the station-master, the engineer, and the stoker under arrest, he waited till all the Fusiliers had arrived, and did not release his prisoners until he had seen every man safe in his place. This single incident satisfied the Christians whom Neill was hastening to succour. They knew that the right man had come at last."

FORMATION OF DISTRICT. It remains to note the administrative changes which have taken place since the district passed under British rule. In 1787, the Government, wishing to reduce the charges of district administration, amalgamated part of Hooghly with Jessore and part with Nadiā; and apparently the strip of land known as Muhammad Amīnpur was transferred to Nadiā.† After the decennial settlement, in 1795, Hooghly, with the greater part of Howrah, was detached from Burdwān and created a separate magisterial charge; but no change was made in the Collectorate. At that time thānas Bāgnān and Amtā were placed in the Hooghly jurisdiction, but Howrah city formed a part of Calcutta, its criminal cases being tried by the Magistrate and Judge of the 24-Parganas, who used to come over once a week. In 1814 thāna Rājāpur (now Dumjor), and in 1819 thānas Kotrā (now Syāmpur) and Uluberiā were transferred from the 24-Parganas to Hooghly. On 1st May 1822 the Hooghly and Howrah Collectorate was entirely separated from Burdwān. In the

---

* Broome, *History of the Bengal Army*, pp. 262-268; Grose, *A voyage to the East Indies*, 1772, Vol. II.

† Notification in the *Calcutta Gazette*, 29th March 1787, l.c. *Selections*, Vol. I, p. 185.

meantime, the city of Howrah had been growing steadily, and its increasing importance led to another change, the magisterial jurisdiction of Howrah being separated from that of Hooghly in 1843, when Mr. William Tayler was appointed Magistrate of Howrah with jurisdiction over Howrah, Sālkhiā, Amtā, Rājāpur, Uluberiā, Kotrā and Bāgnān*. For 20 years the Magistrate remained subordinate to the Judge of the 24-Parganas, but in 1864 the district was transferred to the jurisdiction of the Judge of Hooghly. Since then there have been minor changes in the boundaries of the district, but for the administration of revenue and civil justice it is still included in the jurisdiction of Hooghly.

No old remains have yet been found in this district, probably because the rivers have changed their courses so much that ancient sites, if any, have been washed away. The oldest temple appears to be that of Melāi Chandī at Amtā with a Bengali inscription said to be dated 1056 Bengali Sana, *i.e.*, 1649 A.D. In Howrah city and in some places in the interior, *e.g.*, Nārnā, Dumjor, &c., there are a few temples in the ordinary Bengali style of architecture and more or less modern. The Bhot-bāgān temple at Howrah, dating back to the end of 18th century, is somewhat peculiar, being roofed like a Bengali temple with a portico and having Tibetan figures carved on the outside. A few mosques and churches are found in the town, but none are old. The cemetery to the north of the Town Hall contains tombstones dating from 1791. ARCHÆOLOGY.

* G. Toynbee, *Administration of the Hooghly District* (1888), pp. 30-33.

CHAPTER III.

THE PEOPLE.

GROWTH OF POPULATION. IN 1872, when the first census was taken, Howrah, which then had two subdivisions, Howrah and Mahishrekhā, with a total area of 539 square miles, was treated as part of the Hooghly district. The Khānākul thāna was transferred from Mahishrekhā to the Jahānābād (now Arāmbāgh) subdivision of Hooghly after the census of 1881; and Singtī outpost with a number of villages extending over 34 square miles was added to thāna Amtā after the census of 1891. At the time of the census of 1901, the district had an area of 510 square miles; it was and is not only the smallest of all the districts in Bengal, but is smaller than many a subdivision. Allowing for these changes, the population of the district, as now constituted, was 635,878 in 1872 and rose to 675,394 or by 6·21 per cent. in 1881, to 763,625 or by 13·06 per cent. in 1891, and to 850,514 or by 11·27 per cent. in 1901. The growth of population throughout these 30 years has therefore averaged more than one per cent. annually. Part of the increase in 1881 and 1891 may be due to more accurate enumeration, but, apart from that, there has been a remarkable growth in spite of adverse influences. Between 1872 and 1891 the district suffered much from epidemics of fever, the mortality due to the virulent fever known as Burdwān fever being estimated in 1881 as 50,000. In later years the death-rate was inflated by cholera and bowel complaints in the riparian tracts until 1896, when the construction of waterworks gave the Howrah Municipality a supply of filtered water.

The increase is chiefly due to the great industrial activity in the metropolis of Calcutta, in Howrah city, and along the river bank as far south as Uluberiā. The numerous mills and other industrial concerns have attracted a large number of labourers from other parts of India, and the local inhabitants have been enriched by the trade they bring. The improvement of sanitation has helped to reduce the death-rate in the Howrah Municipality. The drainage schemes of

Howrah, Barajol and Rājāpur have made thānas Dumjor and Jagatballabhpur less unhealthy. The embankments in the Uluberiā subdivision have prevented disastrous floods, have facilitated the extension of cultivation, and incidentally have increased the habitable area. The result is a marked increase of population in all but one of the thānas, and especially in Howrah city and thānas Dumjor, Uluberiā and Syāmpur. The one exception is thāna Amtā, where the increase in 1901 was only 2·4 per cent. A part of this thāna has suffered severely from malarial fever, so much so that in 1905 a special enquiry was made into its origin and prevalence. The part west of the Dāmodar is liable to suffer from periodical floods on account of the abandonment of the embankments on the right bank. The old trade from the north, which passed largely through this thāna, has now been diverted eastwards by roads and railways; and as it is farthest away from Howrah and Calcutta, without any good means of communication beyond a small light railway, no compensating trade has sprung up.

The salient statistics of the census of 1901 are given below.

SUBDIVISION.	Area in square miles.	NUMBER OF— Towns.	Villages.	Population	Number of houses.	Persons per square mile.	Variation between 1891 and 1901.
Howrah ..	173	2	365	431,257	101,600	2,493	+17·73
Uluberiā ...	337	...	1,086	419,257	88,447	1,244	+ 5·52
DISTRICT TOTAL...	510	2	1,451	850,514	190,047	1,668	+11·38

DENSITY OF POPULATION.

For the last thirty years the density of population has been greater than in any other district in Bengal, rising from 1,246 per square mile in 1872 to 1,668 in 1901. Even excluding the urban areas of Howrah and Bally, the density (1,351 per square mile) is still greater than in any district in the Province. The villages tend to be semi-urban in character, every thāna supporting more than 1,200 persons to the square mile. The population is most dense in thāna Dumjor, which adjoins Howrah city on the west and has a density of 1,825 per square mile, the highest in any rural area in Bengal. This figure is all the more remarkable because part of this thāna lies waste and is uninhabited, being covered with marshes and intersected by creeks. The population in Howrah city itself has nearly doubled in the last thirty years, and in 1901 there were no less than 17,510 persons per square mile, or nearly half as many as in London. The number of persons per acre in this great city varies from 8 to 83, and four of its ten wards have 58 or more persons per acre. Many of the wards, moreover, contain large areas of uninhabited land, so that the figures afford no index to the density of the population in the neighbourhood of the mills, where overcrowding mostly occurs. A large proportion of the population consists of operatives in the mills, who look forward to returning to their homes as soon as they have accumulated sufficient funds. In the meantime, they live huddled together in crowded lodging-houses as close as possible to the mills and factories where they work.

"This over-crowding is not a necessary condition in Howrah, as there is ample room for building at no great distance from the centres of industry. It proceeds partly from the desire of the operatives to live as near as possible to their work, partly from their poverty, which leaves them little to spare for rent, and partly from the pressure of municipal taxation, which falls heaviest on huts and discourages the construction of new ones, unless there is a certainty of their being kept full of lodgers. The *basti* clauses of the Municipal Act enable roads to be opened out and drainage effected; but there is at present no law under which it is possible to prevent over-crowding, which sometimes attains truly astonishing proportions. Fortunately the lodging-houses are of very flimsy materials, and there is much natural ventilation, so that the effects are probably less harmful than they would be in the case of masonry buildings."* In spite of such over-crowding in Howrah city, it is noticeable that in the district as a whole the average number of persons to each house fell from 5·9 in 1881 to 4·5 in 1901. No district in Bengal has such a low proportion except Darjeeling, where conditions are exceptional.

MIGRATION. The statistics showing the volume of immigration are no less remarkable, the number of persons resident in the district in 1901 who were born elsewhere being no less than 144,620. In other words, the proportion of immigrants to the total population is 17 per cent. Among these immigrants natives of Bihār and the United Provinces bulk largely accounting for a little over 70,000 or nearly half the total number, while Oriyās number over 8,000 and natives of the adjoining districts 49,000. The foreign element is most pronounced in Howrah city, where about two-thirds of the inhabitants are immigrants,

* Bengal Census Report of 1901.

chiefly from up-country, with a marked excess of males, of whom there are two to every female. This influx of immigrants is due to the growing demand for labour in the industrial concerns, which are mainly worked by up-country coolies, while the shopkeepers, who are enriched by the trade they bring, are also for the most part foreigners. The Mārwāris form a small but not unimportant section of the mercantile community. Some of them have made their homes in the district, and have offices and residences in Sālkhiā and the northern portion of Howrah.

The district contains two towns, Howrah and Bally, which extend along the river Hooghly for about 10 miles and contain more than one-fifth of the total district population. For practical purposes, these two towns are as much a part of Calcutta as Lambeth and Southwark are of London. Since the construction of the Hooghly bridge and the extension of tram lines there has been a growing tendency for workmen, who spend their days and earn their livelihood in the metropolis, to have their homes in Howrah; while several European and Indian gentlemen of Calcutta have houses or gardens in the town or its suburbs. The railways, mills, factories, docks, iron-works, etc., afford employment to a large number of labourers, artisans and clerks, while many boatmen and *khalāsis* are employed in the ships and boats that ply to and from Calcutta. The population of Howrah city has therefore been rapidly growing, rising from 84,069 in 1872 to 157,594 in 1901. At the same time there has been a proportionate decrease in females, the males increasing from 47,213 in 1872 to 99,904 in 1901 or by more than 100 per cent., while the females increased from 36,856 to 57,690 or by 60 per cent. only. This is apparently due to the fact that the immigrant labourers do not, as a rule, bring their wives and families with them. Bally town has also been progressing, but not at the same rate as Howrah, the number of its inhabitants rising from 13,715 in 1872 to 18,662 in 1901. Here, as in Howrah, there has been a marked disproportion in the increase of the male and female population, the number of males rising from 6,885 to 11,383 and of females from 6,830 to 7,279 during the same period. This town formed part of Howrah city till 1882-83, when it was constituted a separate municipality. TOWNS.

The rural population forms 80 per cent. of the total district population and resides in 1,451 villages. None of the villages have 5,000 or more inhabitants, but 15 per cent. have 2,000 or more, and 51 per cent. contain 500 to 2,000 persons. The average population of a village is 465, which, though exceeded in several VILLAGES.

districts of Bihār, is the highest figure in the Burdwān Division. Semi-urban conditions prevail in some strips of land along the rivers Saraswatī, Kānā and Dāmodar, for they are densely populated and have a large leavening of respectable castes. In thāna Dumjor the average village population rises to 816, a very high figure considering that much of the land lies waste owing to the number of swamps and *khāls*. The density of population is, however, accounted for largely by the fact that this thāna has direct communication with Howrah town, and consequently with Calcutta, by means of a light railway. It also shares in the industrial activity of Howrah, and it has benefited from the draining of its marshes by the Howrah and Rājāpur schemes.

SOCIAL CONDITIONS. The material condition of the people has been, on the whole, improving during the last half century. The opening of railways, the erection of new mills and factories, and the establishment of numerous industrial works in Calcutta, Howrah and their suburbs have caused a great demand for skilled and unskilled labour, and have led to a steady rise in wages as well as in the prices obtained for agricultural produce. In former years a labourer or petty agriculturist could scarcely manage to supply himself with the necessaries of life, while in bad seasons, or on other occasions of distress, his destitution was extreme. Now, however, after defraying all his expenses, he manages to save something out of his earnings or from the produce of his fields. This he carefully hoards up against sickness, seasons of scarcity, and other visitations of Providence; or, as is often the case, he saves for years only to squander the more freely on wedding ceremonies and festive occasions. It is reported, however, that the middle classes, especially those who reside in the towns and have small fixed incomes, do not share in the general prosperity owing to a comparative increase in their expenditure and other causes. This is particularly the case with the middle classes of higher caste. They have appearances to keep up and traditions to maintain, and do not reduce their expenditure on social ceremonies or alter their mode of living. Disdaining manual labour, having little enterprise and less capital, they find it difficult to make ends meet, owing to the increased cost of living, which has been such a marked feature in the economic history of the Province of late years. The subject will be dealt with more fully in Chapter VIII.

Dress. The ordinary dress of a well-to-do shopkeeper generally consists of a cotton *dhuti*, or waistband, wrapped round the loins and falling over the legs as far as the knee; a *chādar*, or cotton sheet or shawl, which serves as a covering for the upper part of his body; and a pair of country-made shoes. To this he sometimes adds a *pirān*, or short coat. An average husbandman wears a *dhuti* of smaller dimensions and coarser material, and a small *gāmchhā*, convertible into a head-dress and worn as a turban when he is at work in the fields. Only the well-to-do cultivators wear shoes. The dress worn when attending office has changed during the last half century. The townsman, in his office and outdoor visiting dress, now wears trousers, a coat or *chāpkān* with a shirt inside, a pair of shoes, a shawl in the winter and a muslin sheet in other months, with a cap or *pagrī* for his head-dress. Clerks coming from the mofussil prefer a *dhuti* to trousers, and do not wear a cap with it. The women wear a *sārī* of coarse cloth for ordinary use, and of fine cloth for festivities. Among the lower classes silver ornaments are largely worn; while with those who are better off, gold has replaced silver.

The materials used for the dwelling of a well-to-do shopkeeper consist simply of mud walls and wooden posts supporting a thatched roof. His house usually comprises three to five one-storied rooms, with a shed or large verandah outside for the reception of visitors. The homestead is surrounded by an enclosure, and the cost of the whole building is about Rs. 500 to Rs. 1,000. The furniture met with in such a house consists of several kinds of brass or pewter utensils for cooking, eating and drinking; some earthen pots for cooking; one or two earthen-ware water jars; a few wooden stools, a few mats, and a *takhtposh* or two, *i.e.*, plank bedsteads of coarse construction. The dwelling of an ordinary husbandman is much smaller and less substantial, being composed simply of mud, straw, and bamboos. It usually consists of two or three rooms, and the furniture, if so it may be called, consists of a few brass and earthenware vessels, a stool or two, and a few mats for sleeping on. Some of the richer husbandmen also possess a large strong-box, in which they keep their clothes and whatever valuables they possess, such as their wives' ornaments, rent receipts, etc. In the towns brick-built houses or tiled huts are now general. An ordinary *pakkā* house, if single-storied, costs Rs. 2,000 to Rs. 3,000, and if double-storied, Rs. 3,000 to Rs. 6,000 in the towns and two-thirds of this amount in the mofussil. The number of *pakkā* houses has considerably increased of late years in the villages of thānas Dumjor and Jagatballabhpur. Houses.

In the mofussil the shopkeeper lives on rice, pulses (*dāl*), clarified butter (*ghī*), curries made of fish or vegetables, sweetmeats, milk, etc. The food of an ordinary peasant consists simply of rice and a curry made of vegetables, with occasionally a little Food.

fish. The living expenses of a well-to-do shopkeeper or clerk in the interior are from Rs. 20 to Rs. 50, and of a fairly well-to-do cultivator from Rs. 10 to Rs. 20 per month. Most of the former can get a supply of vegetables and pulses from their gardens, while fish are plentiful in the neighbouring *khāls* or tanks. The cultivators also produce their own food largely, their stock lasting for several months in the year. In the towns artizans and mechanics draw better wages, spend more, and in spite of higher prices, live somewhat better than their fellows in the mofussil. The cost of maintaining a family of five persons among this class may be taken at Rs. 15 to Rs. 35 per month. In the towns the ordinary monthly expenses of the more well-to-do classes vary from Rs. 25 to Rs. 100, if they have got no land in the interior.

Drinking. The upper and middle classes are, as a rule, sober and abstemious. In the urban tracts tea-drinking is gradually spreading among them, but coffee is almost unknown. Opium is used chiefly by old people, while *gānja* is not much used. Intoxicating liquors are also more or less tabooed by the higher classes. About 20 years ago, when the outstill system was introduced in the mofussil, there was some apprehension that liquor-drinking was spreading among all sections of the community, and Mr. Westmacott, the then District Magistrate, made a special enquiry in 1887. He found that the apprehension was, on the whole, not well founded, and that a distinction should be drawn between landholding ryots and landless labourers, even when the caste was the same. "The improvidence which permits a man to spend a large part of his income on liquor disappears with the possession of land, and my knowledge of the district of Howrah enables me to corroborate Mr. Toynbee's testimony that landholding ryots are by no means addicted to intemperance, or to the use of intoxicating liquors to any extent. The agricultural classes, however, include the landless labourers, to whom we must give a very different character."

After mentioning the Bāgdis, Bauris, Chamārs, Chandāls, Doms, Dosādhs, Hāris, Jaliyās and Kāhārs, and the lower classes of Kaibarttas and Muhammadans, as people addicted to the use of intoxicating liquor, either *tāri* or distilled spirit, he remarked:—"I have met with no evidence whatever of any loss of sobriety among the landholding ryots, or any indication that the cheapness of liquor has induced them to become consumers of it. The landless labourers, especially among the castes which I have enumerated, have, for generations, been drinkers of spirituous liquor, according to their means. The establishment of jute mills and other industries, affording increased employment to labour at high wages, has within comparatively recent years enormously improved their position, and enabled them to increase their expenditure on liquor as well as on other objects, and the growth of intemperance among them has been the subject of remark long before the establishment of outstills."

Marriage customs.

There is nothing peculiar about the marriage customs of the people. Child-marriage is the rule, but among the better classes the difficulty of finding a suitable husband is gradually raising the age of marriage. Marriages of girls between 10 and 12 years of age are becoming not uncommon, but the strong dislike among Hindus to the marriage of girls who have attained puberty prevents the age of marriage being higher. Polygamy used to be common among Rārhī Kulīn Brāhmans,* but has now disappeared, partly from economic causes, but chiefly from the pressure of public opinion. One effect of this change has been to increase the demands of the bridegroom's guardians, as a larger number of husbands are now required, where previously one would have sufficed. Widow-marriage is not allowed by the higher castes, and is only tolerated among the other castes, except the lowest. Even among them a widow who remarries is looked upon more as a household drudge, and the marriage ceremony is reduced to a mere formality.

Village life.

The old communal life of the village has almost disappeared. The villagers used to gather under some old banyan or *pīpal* tree, of which magnificent specimens still survive; while the *chandīmandapa* and, in important villages, the zamīndāri *kachhari* were also favourite resorts. Here they would discuss village politics, such as the exactions of the *gumāshta*, the visits of the police and other public officers, thefts or burglaries in the neighbourhood, etc. Local scandals added spice to the more serious talk; while business topics, such as the price of food, of grain, and of cattle, gave it a personal interest. Larger gatherings were attracted by weekly *hāts*, at which men from different villages exchanged their ideas on every subject ranging from the vagaries of the weather and the state of the crops to the latest visits of the *dāroga* or the zamīndār. Now many of the adult members of the respectable classes have migrated to Calcutta or Howrah and their suburbs, leaving only the females, the children and old men at home, but usually visiting them on Saturdays and Sundays or on holidays. *Hāts* have been mostly replaced by daily bazars in the important villages, and the cultivators sell direct to *phariās*, *i.e.*, the agents of

* A Kulīn Brāhman who died at Bally in 1839 is said to have had 100 wives.

town traders from whom in many cases they have taken advances. Newspapers are now found in the houses of the wealthier villagers, and on Sundays and holidays a few of the better educated meet in private houses to discuss not village affairs, but politics and the news of India or the outside world.

LANGUAGE. The prevailing language is Bengali, the character of which differs little from that spoken in the contiguous districts of Hooghly or the 24-Parganas. Local Muhammadans also speak this dialect in a somewhat altered form. The up-country immigrants use Hindī or Bihāri, if Hindus, and Urdū, if Musalmāns, while the Oriyās speak Oriyā. In 1901, languages of the Aryan family were spoken by 9,947 persons out of every 10,000, viz., Bengali 8,838, Hindī 1,005, Oriyā 98, and others 59. No prominent Bengali writer has been born in this district except the poet Bhārat Chandra Rai (*alias* Mukhopādhyāya), whose home was at Penro-Basantapur, *pargana* Bhursut, thāna Amtā.

RELIGIONS. The bulk of the people are Hindus, who according to the census of 1901 accounted for 7,908 of every 10,000. Of the remainder 2,059 were Muhammadans, one professed Animism, and 32 followed other religions. As in 1881 Hindus numbered 8,009 and Muhammadans 1,956 in every 10,000, it would appear that the former have declined and the latter increased in the same proportion.

Christians. In 1901 the Christians numbered 2,588 (1,568 males and 1,020 females). The majority were Europeans and Eurasians, 579 being Indian Christians. None were reported from thānas Amtā, Bāgnān and Syāmpur, and only a few from Jagatballabhpur, Uluberiā and Bally; while nine-tenths were found in Howrah city.

Christian missions. The earliest missionary work was begun by the Baptist Missionary Society in 1793 under the Serampore missionaries, and a school started by them in 1830 appears to be still in existence. The Society for the Promotion of Christian Knowledge had schools at Howrah in 1824, of which Mr. Tweddle was Superintendent, and also in the neighbourhood of Howrah at Sibpur, Sālkhiā, Ghusuri and Bally. In 1826, Mr. De Mello took charge of the schools, and in 1827 another school, having an attendance of 120 boys, was opened at Bator. In the same year we find that the Professors of Bishop's College (opened in 1824) undertook services in the Howrah church, which owed its erection chiefly to the exertions of Professor Holmes of that college. A Sunday-school was also opened by Mr. De Mello at the college, and one of those who attended it was baptized in 1830. Another school was opened by Mr. Bowyer in 1837 at Baiskāti, 12 miles north-west of

Howrah, a building being erected to serve both as a school and chapel. The same missionary had established an English school in 1830, at the suggestion of Bishop Turner, which was "intended to serve as an ultimatum to all the diocesan schools in this district; it is proposed to select from each those scholars who are the most thoroughly instructed in Bengali, and at the same time farthest advanced in English, and remove them to this institution, where the teaching will be wholly confined to the latter language." A Christian boarding school was also started about 1837.* The Roman Catholic church at Cullen Place was built in 1832, and a school for Christian girls was opened in 1857 under the supervision of the nuns of the Loreto House. The Loreto nuns were replaced in 1880 by the Daughters of the Cross, who have since then carried on their work among the native Christians of Howrah.

At present, the Church Missionary Society maintains a resident missionary, first deputed in 1904 for evangelistic work among the Hindī-speaking people, of whom there are 85,000 in the mills and factories along the riverside. The Baptist Mission also works in Howrah, and the Baptist Zanāna Mission has 4 girls' schools there. A small American Mission calling itself "The Church of God" has lately been established in Uluberiā. The Presbyterian Church also works in Howrah among Europeans, but it does not maintain schools or missions. The Presbyterians first began to work in Howrah in 1897, but the work simply meant a service in the Town Hall on Sunday evenings. In 1901 the present church was built, and in 1904 the hall adjoining the church was erected. The church belongs to both sections of Presbyterianism at present working in Calcutta. It is managed by a board consisting of a minister, session clerk and one member from the Deacon's Court of Wellesley Square United Free Church; the minister, session clerk and one member from the St. Andrew's Church Session; and four members of the Howrah church with the minister-in-charge. The latter came out in connection with the Bengal Mills and Steamers Presbyterian Association, and the church in Howrah not being able to support a minister of its own, his services as minister-in-charge were given to it. The minister-in-charge also ministers to the mills on both sides of the river from Kāmārhāti to the Lawrence Jute Mills a little below Bāuriā.

The Muhammadans, who formed in 1901 more than one-fifth of the population, are found in greatest strength in Howrah Muhammadans.

* J. Long, *Handbook of Bengal Missions*, 1837.

city, where they number 39,239, congregating chiefly in dirty over-crowded *bastis* like Tindalbāgān, Tikāpārā and Priya Mānnā's *basti.* A large proportion of them, probably the majority, are immigrants; and hence the males are in considerable excess. Outside Howrah, Muhammadans are found in fair numbers in thānas Dumjor (32,459) and Uluberiā (29,543), and also in Jagatballabhpur. A few in thāna Dumjor are immigrants attracted to the mills on the river bank; but the bulk are residents, and not a few are old settlers. The latter date back to the days of Muhammadan rule, when their forefathers settled along the river Saraswatī and round thāna Muckwā, the old Tanna fort. In thāna Uluberiā, a few are immigrants, employed in the mills at Fort Gloster and Bāuriā, but most are local people, who live scattered throughout the villages. In Jagatballabhpur again most of the Muhammadans are indigenous and have been settled for many generations along the banks of the Kānā Nadī, which was a large navigable river in the Muhammadan period. They predominate in three groups of villages, viz., (1) about Kamalpur and Sekrāhāti, (2) Dhasā, Narendrapur and Bākul, and (3) Gustiā and Pānchlā.

In this district the Muhammadans are almost exclusively Sunnis, neither the Wahābi nor the Farāzi doctrines having spread among them. Malliks, Pathāns or Saiyads are few in number and are found chiefly among the immigrants. It is curious, therefore, to find that in the census of 1901 the largest number of Pathāns were reported from such an out-of-the-way thāna as Syāmpur. Jolāhās, the weaving class, are found chiefly in Howrah city, where they are probably immigrants, but older colonies are found in thāna Amtā and at Pānchlā in thāna Jagatballabhpur. The great majority in 1901 returned themselves as Sheikhs, a generic name which in this district includes all that do not claim to be Saiyads, Pathāns, Mughals or to belong to some special caste, such as Jolāhās. Most of the Sheikhs in rural tracts appear to be descendants of low class Hindu converts, who are too poor to be admitted among the Ashraf or respectable classes, and whose origin is indicated by their features and by their acceptance of Hindu superstitions. Many of them, however, are improving their position by means of shop-keeping and their skill as artizans; and a considerable percentage of the Muhammadan shopkeepers in Chāndni and in the municipal market of Calcutta hail from thānas Jagatballabhpur, Dumjor and Uluberiā.

Animists. Animists are few in number and are confined to Oraons and Santāls, who come to Howrah in search of employment. In 1901 the Oraons were returned at 3,328, mostly in thānā Dumjor, where they were working as coolies in Shālimār station and on its numerous sidings.

Hindus. Hindus form the large majority of the people and are divided into numerous castes or semi-Hinduized tribes. Forty-nine castes were reported in 1901 as numbering more than 1,000, while the castes noted in the margin numbered more than 15,000 and therefore deserve separate notice.

Higher castes ..	Brāhman	...	52,238
	Kāyasth	...	19,225
Pastoral castes	Goālā	...	23,930
	Sadgop	...	19,152
Fishing and boating castes.	Kaibartta	...	230,508
	Bāgdi	...	72,603
	Tiyar	...	21,914
	Pod	...	19,258
	Kāorā	...	17,575

Brāhmans. The Brāhmans, as a literate caste, naturally congregate in the towns, forming one-sixth of the population of Bally and one-eleventh in Howrah, where Sibpur is their main centre. Outside the municipal area, they are found mostly in old villages along the banks of the Saraswatī, the Kānā, and the Dāmodar, but their number decreases largely, their proportion to the population varying from one-sixteenth in thāna Amtā to one-fortieth in thāna Syāmpur. All classes of Brāhmans are to be found, but the bulk are Rārhīs, as might be anticipated in a district adjoining the Rārh country.

Kāyasths. Like the Brāhmans, the Kāyasths or writer caste congregate largely in Howrah city. In the rural thānas they are found chiefly in the older villages along the three rivers named above. The bulk belong to the Dakshinrārhī section.

Sadgops. The Sadgops, a caste found almost exclusively in Western Bengal, are mostly inhabitants of thānā Dumjor, but there are a few in Howrah city and thāna Amtā. They occupy the western border of the Division from Bīrbhūm to north-west Midnapore, and would appear to have migrated south through thānas Goghāt and Chanditalā of the Hooghly district. Their prevalence in the uplands is due to pastoral habits, and lends support to the current tradition connecting them with the caste of Gops or Goālās. They have now mostly taken to agriculture, and have thereby raised themselves to a higher caste, just as the Chāsi or cultivating Kaibarttas are now trying to do.

Goālās. The Goālās or herdsman caste form a not inconsiderable part of the population. The up-country Ahīrs, who are included in the number, are mostly found in Howrah city, and the local Goālās in thānas Dumjor, Jagatballabhpur and Amtā. They live along the three older streams, evidently attracted by the pasture lands on their high banks. A considerable number of the Goālās have now taken to agriculture, and have grown prosperous.

Kaibarttas. In a lowland district, such as Howrah, liable to be flooded, and cut up by rivers and creeks, the chief autochthonous tribes or castes would naturally consist of fishermen and boatmen, and this accounts for the fact that the predominating castes are Kaibarttas, Bāgdis, Tiyars and Pods.

The Kaibarttas are by far the largest caste, accounting in the Uluberiā subdivision for about half the total number of Hindus. Originally a non-Aryan tribe, they have been traced to a very early period, being mentioned as Kevarttas in the *Vājasaneyi-Samhitā*, Kaivarttas in the Epics and the *Manu-Samhitā*, and as Kevatas in a pillar-edict of Asoka. Not improbably they held the old kingdom of Tāmralipti, and they still continue to be the great caste of eastern Midnapore. They seem to have consisted originally of a congeneries of tribes, which coalesced owing to similarity of functions, but were still kept separate by the prohibition of intermarriage. As land was gradually reclaimed from the waste and came under settled cultivation, they took more and more to agriculture. The cultivating portion gradually drew away from the rest and set up as a higher caste with degraded Brāhmans for priests. Their power, wealth and number eventually secured for them, in the districts where they predominated, a higher social status and an acknowledgement that water might be taken from their hands (*jalācharaniya*) by Brāhmans and other higher castes. At the last census seven-eighths returned themselves as cultivating Kaibarttas or Māhishyas. The fishing (Jaliyā) Kaibarttas occupy a very low position; and in Eastern and Northern Bengal, Bihār and Orissa, all Kaibarttas and Kewats still rank very low in the social scale.

Bāgdis.

Bāgdis are found in large numbers in thānas Amtā, Jagatballabhpur and Dumjor. Originally fishermen, they have now mostly become agricultural labourers or *pālki*-bearers. They seem to have consisted originally of several tribes, as the period of mourning varies among them, in some cases lasting 31 days as among other Sudras, in others 13 days and even 11 days, as among Brāhmans. They are found chiefly in Western Bengal, from which apparently they migrated into the districts of Nadiā and 24-Parganas. In Howrah district their distribution seems to show that they came from the north-west or north. The name is connected with the tract called Bāgri in the north-west of the Midnapore district; but it is uncertain whether this name was given to that part of the country in consequence of its having been inhabited by Bāgdis, or whether the latter took their name from the country. They are held to be impure, the Tentuliā section alone being held to be a little higher and thus able to give Ganges water.

The Tiyars are found chiefly in thānas Dumjor, Jagatballabhpur and Amtā. Fishermen and boatmen, they hold a very low rank, their touch defiling. The name Tīvara is found in the *Brahmavaivarta-purāna*, but means there a hunter. In the mediæval Sanskrit dictionaries, however, it meant fisherman — Tiyars.

The Pods are found chiefly in thanā Dumjor and a few in thānas Uluberiā and Syāmpur. They form the great race-caste of the 24-Parganas and would appear to have spread across the river Hooghly into Howrah. Originally a fishing caste, a large number have become agriculturists or petty shopkeepers. The latter now claim to be a higher caste under the name of Padma Rāj, but the claim is not usually allowed. Their touch defiles, and they rank very low. Some of them, like the Doms, worship Dharmarāj, a village deity with a Buddhistic veneering. — Pods.

All the fishing castes mentioned above, the Jaliyā Kaibarttas, the Bāgdis, the Tiyars and the Pods, are regarded as impure. Their touch defiles. and they may be served by washermen, but, as a rule, not by barbers or degraded Brāhmans. They generally abstain from beef, pork and fowls.

The Kāorās are found in fair numbers in all the mofussil thānas except Syāmpur. They rank among the lowest castes, having nearly the same status as Doms or Chamārs but being slightly higher than Hāris. They take prohibited food and are not served by washermen, barbers or degraded Brāhmans. They seem to have overflowed into Howrah from the 24-Parganas, and as a rule rear pigs or work as labourers, but a number of them are village *chaukīdārs*. — Kāorās.

From the preceding account it will be seen that in this district the percentage of higher castes, such as Brāhmans, Baidyas and Kāyasths, is much smaller than in most regulation districts of the Province. The bulk of the Hindu population consists of low castes, whose Hinduization is not yet complete. Among these low castes traces of old Animistic beliefs can still be observed, especially in the Uluberiā subdivision, where the villages are farthest from industrial centres, contain a smaller number of Brāhmans and other high castes, and have been colonized in comparatively recent times. — SOME POPULAR BELIEFS.

Animism can be traced not only in customs and folklore, but also, and far more clearly, in the worship of godlings or village deities (*grām devatā*). This worship plays an important part in the domestic life of the people, and in the religious beliefs of the females. Such religious beliefs die hard, and in spite of centuries of Brahmanical teaching, still survive, though in very much modified forms. There are several distinct indications of the Animistic basis of this worship. Firstly, the godlings are spirits invoked in water pots or materialized into a rudely carved bit of stone. Secondly, the persons who officiate at their worship are not Brāhmans but members of the lower castes. Thirdly, they are propitiated by sacrifices of animals, even of such forbidden animals as fowls or hogs. Fourthly, they are worshipped not for the sake of any spiritual or intellectual benefit in this or a future life, but solely in order to obtain immediate material benefit, such as protection against illness and calamities, success in any undertaking, etc. In the process of Hinduization these features have become obscured, and have more or less disappeared in advanced villages; but in the remoter villages, and among the lowest castes, they can still be found. In some instances, such as in the worship of Dharmarāj and Satyapīr, Buddhistic and Musalmān influences are traceable; but they too have been largely modified by the surrounding Hinduism. A brief account of the principal godlings in this district is given below.

Dharmarāj. One of the most interesting is Dharmarāj, who is usually represented by a stone under a tree, daubed with vermilion, and is worshipped by a priest of the lowest castes, Dom, Pod, or occasionally Bāgdi. He is credited with powers of healing, and his priests supply medicines, while women worship him in the hope of having children. The offerings are pigs, fowls and *pachwai* beer, also rice and milk. No special day is fixed for the worship, but the favourite days are the summer full-moon days in the months of Baisākh and Jyaistha. This worship is known to be centuries old, being mentioned in early Bengali literature. The *mantras* are contained in the *Hākanda-purāna*, while special poems named *Dharma-mangala* were composed in his honour by Mayūrabhatta, Rūparām and Ghanarām. These poems connect the god with Mayanā fort in east Midnapore and Dhekur fort on the bank of the Ajai river in Bīrbhūm. As the worshippers become more and more Hinduized, the sacrifice of animals is gradually giving way to offerings of rice and milk, while the image is enshrined in a temple instead of under a tree.

Dharmarāj is represented either as Yama (god of death) or as a son of Brahmā, the latter representation being explained by a quaint tradition. It is said that when Brahmā wished to create the world, he could not imagine how he would be able to protect it, and thereupon Dharma sprang into being from his right breast. Another legend relates that Dharma had a quarrel with Nārāyan and cursed him, saying that he would be worshipped with *tulsi* leaves on which dogs make water. Nārāyan retorted with another curse, telling Dharma that he would receive worship at the hands of low caste men. It has been suggested that Dharma worship is a survival of Buddhism. In support of this theory it is pointed out that Dharma is meditated upon as *shūnya mūrti* or void, that the ceremonies and fasts in his honour all take place on the full-moon day of Baisākh, the birthday of Buddha, and that in many places Dharma is represented by a tortoise, a miniature representation of a stūpa.* Possibly Dharma worship received a veneer of Buddhism when Buddhism flourished; but the arguments are hardly sufficient to establish the proposition that it is a relic of Buddhism itself. On the contrary, animal sacrifices and the use of liquor would have been abhorrent to Buddhism proper, even in its latest Tāntric variety. There appears little doubt that the worship is substantially Animistic, though it has been in modern times largely modified by Hinduism.

Bānkurā Rai. Some of the godlings are invoked to protect their votaries against wild animals, tigers and snakes. The gods of tigers are Dakshin Rai, Kālu Rai and Bānkurā Rai. They are worshipped as spirits in water-pots or as stone images, rudely carved into the form of an armed male seated on a tiger, which are placed under trees or housed in huts or temples. No special time is fixed for their worship. Goats are sacrificed, with offerings of rice and sweets. Occasionally a low caste priest, but usually a Brāhman, officiates. These godlings are recognized as sons of Siva, and are mentioned, especially Bānkurā Rai, in old Bengali poems.

Manasā. Manasā is the godling of snakes, whose worship is widespread in this district on account of the number of snakes it contains and the dread of their bite. She is represented either by the *manasā* plant (*Euphorbia Nerifolia* or *Ligularia*) or by a bit of stone, which is rudely carved into the form of a female seated on a snake, or it may be, by a shapeless block smeared with vermilion. The plant or stone is generally found under a tree, preferably an *aswattha* tree, or is housed in a hut, a room, or occasionally a small brick temple. The officiating priest is sometimes a man of low caste, *e.g.*, a Kaibartta at Srīkrishnapur, and a Bāgdi or Hāri at Jaypur in the Uluberiā subdivision, but more frequently he is a Brāhman. The offerings consist of rice and other articles, but on important occasions goats are sacrificed. The goddess is said to be particularly fond of two plants, the *raktajavā* (*Rosa*

* Bengal Census Report of 1901, page 204, paragraphs 383-84.

Chinensis) and the *durbā* grass. She is especially worshipped on the last days of the months of Srāban and Bhādra (August and September), a season when snakes are forced out of their holes by rain and are a very real danger to the bare-footed wayfarer. The Goālās, who graze cattle in the open country and are therefore particularly liable to snake-bite, besides losing many cattle, worship the goddess under the name of Rākhāl manāsa. A *manāsā* plant is set up under a tree, and a special festival takes place on the last day of Paus, *i.e.*, in the middle of January. The cowherd boys go round begging and collect money for the offerings, the ceremony itself being conducted by a Brāhman.

Accordingly to tradition, Manasā was the sister of the snake Vāsuki, wife of the sage Jaratkāru and mother of the sage Astik, of whom a long story is told in the Adiparva of the *Mahābhārata*. She is repeatedly mentioned in old Bengali poems, while special poems were composed describing her efforts to extend her worship, and the punishment awarded to the unbelievers. The story of Chānd Saudāgar and his daughter-in-law Behulā has been versified by Bipradāsa (1495 A.D.), Kshamānand and others.

Panchānan.

For the prevention or cure of illness worship is offered to several godlings, *e.g.*, for children's illness Panchānan and Sasthī, and for other ailments, Sītalā, Olā-Bibi, and Ghantākarna. Panchānan (Panchānanda or Pānchu Thākur) is worshipped either as a spirit in a water-pot, or is represented by a clay or stone image riding a goblin, which is placed under trees or in a petty temple. He has sometimes a priest of the lower castes, *e.g.*, a Kaibartta at Dānkha and a Bāgdi at Jaypur in Uluberiā subdivision, but more often a Brāhman. Rice, sweets and flowers are offered to him with clay horses; and when the villagers think he is much displeased with them, a goat is sacrified. If several children die, he is propitiated in order that he may spare the lives of the children born after them, and the latter are called Pānchu or Pānchī. The number five is sacred to him; and the children are believed to be free from illness for five years after birth, if his worship is observed. He is also propitiated for the cure of certain special ailments of children, *e.g.*, when they get a crick in the neck. The tradition runs that he was the son of Siva by a Koch woman, and that, on account of his low birth, none paid him reverence until he was made master of eight diseases.

Sasthī.

Sasthī is a benignant goddess who presides over the health and well-being of children. She is worshipped at home in a water-jar with a branch of the banyan tree, and with offerings of sun-dried rice, sweets, curds, fruit and flowers, 6 days, 21 days and

31 days after the birth of a child; a Brāhman officiates. She is worshipped by Brāhmans on the 21st day in the case of a male and on the 31st day in the case of a female child; but Kāyasths worship her on the 31st day whether the child is male or female. The ceremony on the 21st day is often performed outside the house under a banyan tree, under which is a representation of the goddess, viz., a stone daubed with vermilion or a clay image seated on a cat surrounded by little images. Her blessings can be invoked on any sixth day in the light half of a month, when mothers fast and offer her rice and other articles through a Brāhman. Her chief festival is on the *bana-sasthī* day of the month of Jyaistha (May-June) Fans in hand, the village women go to the banyan tree, taking bamboo-leaves tied with saffron-coloured threads. A Brāhman officiates as priest and gets the rice, fruit, etc., offered. The women take back the threads and tie them round their children's wrists to ensure their health. Sasthī is probably a relic of the old Vedic Animism. According to tradition, she is a daughter of Brahmā and wife of Skanda, the general of the gods. She brought to life the dead son of king Priyabasta, who in gratitude promised to extend her worship on earth.

The goddess Sītalā is believed to have power to produce and disperse infectious diseases, such as measles, chicken-pox, and above all small-pox; hence she is also called Basanta-chandī. Among the higher castes a Brāhman officiates as priest; but Kaibarttas and members of other low castes officiate for the castes to which they belong. She is represented as a spirit in a water-jar, as a simple block of stone or an image under a banyan or *bakul* tree, or is housed in a small temple. The image is one of a naked female riding an ass, with an winnowing-fan on her head, with spots on her cheeks like pox pustules, and holding in her hands a vessel and a broom; the latter is symbolical of her power to sweep away diseases. Rice, fruit and sweets are offered to her with goats or sheep in special cases. *Bātāsā* is said to be her favourite sweetmeat. Sītalā.

When an epidemic of small-pox or even cholera breaks out, the women resort to her shrine, pour water on the roots of the tree or on the temple verandah, and burn lights before her in the evening, accompanied by blowing of conch-shells. A party of men, usually of the low castes, are hired to sing her praises for three days. At the end of this time there is a *pūjā*, and sweets, etc., are distributed among the villagers, generally by the woman that cleans the place. Low caste men, such as Bāgdis, Doms and Chandāls, sing from door to door, and beg for alms, carrying a little clay figure of Sītalā in a basket. According to tradition, she is the daughter of Sāvitrī by Brahmā, and is the chief of seven sisters, mistresses of contagious diseases. Her worship is an old one, being referred to in early Bengali literature.

Olā-Bibi. Olā-Bibi, or as Hindus prefer to call her Olāi-Chandī, is propitiated in epidemics of cholera (Bengali *olā-uthā*), chiefly by low caste Hindus or Muhammadans, from whom the priests are recruited. A number of these men beg from door to door, gather rice and pice, and then go to her shrine. She is usually represented by a water-jar under a *nim* (*Melia Azidarachta*) tree. Rice, sweets and fruit are offered, and goats are sacrificed. After the *pūjā* is concluded, the people return home, playing on the *dhol* and singing songs. The employment of a Muhammadan as priest is peculiar, and the present form of worship must be post-Muhammadan.

Ghantā-karna. Ghantākarna (*i.e.*, the bell-eared) is the godling of skin diseases. He is worshipped on the last day of Phālgun for the prevention of itch, eczema, etc., which are common in the beginning of the spring. The ceremony takes place before the front door of the house and is finished before sunrise. Ghantākarna is represented by a lump of cow-dung placed on a blackened old earthen pot, into which are put a few cowries dyed with vermilion. An old woman recites *mantras*, which are repeated by other women, and offers rice, *dāl* and fruit with *ghentu* flowers (*Clerodendron infortunatum*) and *durbā* grass. When the offerings have been made, the children break the pot to pieces with sticks According to tradition, Ghantākarna was a devoted servant of Siva and was rewarded with the power to cure or prevent skin diseases.

Jwarāsur. Jwarāsur (*i.e.*, the fever-demon) is invoked in individual cases to grant recovery from fever and by the villagers generally during epidemics of malarial fever. He is worshipped by the lower castes with the aid of a Brāhman. Besides the usual offerings of rice, sweets and fruit, goats are sacrificed in special instances.

Satya-Nārāyan. Satya-Nārāyan is a godling whom all classes of Hindus worship in order that they and their families may prosper. He is worshipped on the evening of the full-moon and by many every month, a Brāhman acting as priest. The *thākur*, as he is called, is represented by a drawing on a wooden seat with a few loops, called *mokāms*, and a post at each corner, called *tīr*. The offerings consist of flour, molasses or sugar, and milk (each weighing five *pawās*), betel-leaves and nuts (25 each) with 32 plantains. This is known as *kachchā sirni*. Five *pawās* each of *pakkā sirni* sweets, *sandesh* and *bātāsā* are added. The priest worships Nārāyan and then repeats the story of the god. The articles offered are mixed and made into a jelly, part of which is distributed among the worshippers present, and the rest is sent to neighbours.

The worship smacks strongly of Muhammadanism. The absence of any image, the use of words like *sirni*, *mokām* and *tīr*, the five loops in the drawing, and the recurrence of five as a number in the offerings, all indicate Musalmān influence. Legend, moreover, relates that Nārāyan appeared in the guise of a *fakīr* or Musalmān ascetic, and that objection was at first raised to his worship because he was a Yavana. Satya-Nārāyan would thus appear to be a variant of Satyapīr, a deity worshipped by the lower class of Muhammadans and evolved after the establishment of Islamic rule in Bengal.

Another godling of disease is Subachanī, who if duly propitiated will restore health to the sick. She is worshipped in a water-pitcher by a Brāhman priest, with the usual offerings of rice, milk, sweets and fruit. But the chief peculiarity of the worship is that the priest draws 21 ducks, one of which is one-legged. The story is that a man ate up as many ducks and was imprisoned for this grave offence, but was released on worshipping Subachanī. In some places, a part of the offerings is given to a Musalmān. Subachanī.

Mangal Chandī is another deity represented by no image, but worshipped as a spirit in a water-pot. The worship takes place on Tuesdays in the month of Jyaistha. Tradition runs that the childless king Anga obtained issue by worshipping this deity. Mangal Chandī.

Hu is worshipped on the last day of the month of Kārtik and on the following Sunday in the month of Agrahāyan. Tradition relates that a poor Brāhman obtained wealth in consequence of his two daughters worshipping this deity. According to some the sun god, and according to others Durgā, is worshipped in the form of Hu; but the name appears to point to a non-Aryan origin. Hu.

It is somewhat refreshing to turn from these survivals of primitive Animistic beliefs to one of the latest developments of Hinduism—the Rāmkrishna Mission, which has its headquarters at Belur in this district, and was founded in 1897 by the disciples of Rāmkrishna Paramhansa with Swāmī Vivekānanda as their head.* RAMKRISHNA MISSION.

* This history of the Mission has been compiled with the help of a note kindly sent, on behalf of its Secretary, by Swāmī Sivānanda of Belur.

Rāmkrishna Paramhansa was the son of Khudirām Chattopādhyāya (Chatterji), a member of a respectable Brāhman family, and was born at Kāmārpukur in the Hooghly district in 1834. At an early age he is said to have displayed deep religious fervour and to have had fits of religious ecstasy. On being invested with the sacred thread, he studied for some time in a *tol* or Sanskrit school kept by his eldest brother, Rāmkumār, at Thanthaniā in Calcutta. In 1853 the late Rānī Rāshmanī of Jaun Bazar, Calcutta, built the well-known temple of Kālī at Dakshineswar, 6 miles north of that city, and Rāmkumār was appointed its priest. Rāmkrishna went with him to Dakshineswar, and there for 12 years practised *yoga* (meditation on and rapt communion with God) under a big banyan tree, which is still pointed out to the visitor. His asceticism and religious fervour, his poetical and mystical view of life, combined, however, with homely common sense, began to attract attention; Keshab Chandra Sen of the Brāhmo Samāj being the first to bring him to the notice of the educated classes of society in Calcutta. He found many admirers, and died of cancer in the throat in 1886. Further details will be found in *Rāmakrishna : His Life and Sayings*, by Professor Max Müller, published in 1898, and in *The Life of Rāmkrishna* by Dr. Ram Chandra Dutt.

Rāmkrishna left a small body of disciples, who practised asceticism in a monastery at Baranagar in the 24-Parganas, in the Himālayas and at different places of pilgrimage in India. The greatest of these disciples was Swāmī Vivekānanda, originally known as Narendra Nāth Dutt, the son of an attorney of the High Court. Born in Calcutta in 1863, he was educated at the General Assembly's Institution and graduated at the Calcutta University in 1884. He became a disciple of Rāmkrishna and adopted the life of a devotee in 1886. In 1890 he visited Madras, and in 1893 he was sent by the Rājā of Rāmnād as a representative of Hinduism to the Parliament of Religions held at Chicago, where his exposition of Vedānta doctrines made a great impression. For three years after this he travelled in America, expounding the doctrines of *yoga* and Vedāntism, and in 1896 he visited and lectured in England. On his return to India in 1897, Vivekānanda founded a *math* or monastery at Belur, and died, a comparatively young man, in 1902. The last five years of his life were years of great activity, for he made a tour through Almorā, Kashmir, Lahore and Madras, preaching and lecturing; he again visited England and the United States, founding a Vedānta Society in San Francisco; and he organized the work of the Rāmkrishna Mission in India.

The Mission work is now carried on by a band of advanced indus, with whom are associated some Americans of the United States, such as Sister Niveditā. The nature of the work which is being done in India may be gathered from the following brief resumé. At Belur, the headquarters of the Mission, Brahmachārins (or disciples) are trained. In Calcutta a Bengali magazine, the *Udbodhan*, and theological books are published. At Bhābdā in Murshidābād there are an orphanage and school, at which pupils are given a general and technical education. At Benāres there is a school for training Brahmachārins, and a home of relief or hospital At Māyāvatī (Almorā) an English magazine, the *Prabuddha Bhārat*, and theological books are published. At Kankhal (Hardwār) there is a home of service (*sevāsrama*), *i.e.*, a hospital for the poor. At Madras there are free schools for poor boys and girls, lectures are given, theological classes are held, and a magazine, the *Brahmavādīn*, and theological works are published. At Bangalore theological classes are held, and the doctrines of the sect are preached. The Mission also gives relief to the distressed in time of plague and famine. In 1908, for instance, members of the Mission, at the request of the Collector of Purī, started relief operations on their own account in the famine-stricken area in and round the Chilkā Lake, rendering Government relief measures unnecessary in the 26 villages with which they dealt.

The doctrines of the Mission are dealt with in the *Rāmkrishnakathāmrita* (*i.e.*, the nectar of the story of Rāmkrishna), Parts I—III by M.; while their Vedāntic aspect is expounded in the works of Swāmī Vivekānanda. A collection of Rāmkrishna's sayings has also been published by Max Müller and by the late Pratāp Chandra Mazumdār of the Brāhmo Samāj. Rāmkrishna himself appears to have been a mystic and devotee, described as gentle in thought and deed, who favoured exposition by means of parables and allegories. As regards his doctrines, Max Müller writes:—"Rāmakrishna himself never claimed to be the founder of a new religion. He simply preached the old religion of India, which was founded on the Veda, more particularly on the Upanishads, and was systematised later on in the Sūtras of Bādarāyana, and finally developed in the commentaries of Samkara and others. Rāmkrishna was in no sense of the word an original thinker, the discoverer of a new idea or the propounder of any new view of the world. But he saw many things which others had not seen, he recognized the Divine Presence where it was least suspected, he was a poet, an enthusiast, or, if you like, a dreamer of dreams. But such dreams also have a right to exist, and have a claim on our attention and sympathy. Rāmakrishna never composed a philosophical treatise; he simply poured out short sayings, and the people came to listen to them, whether the speaker was at the time in full possession of his faculties, or in a dream, or in a trance." As regards these sayings, Max Müller writes:—"To my mind these sayings, the good, the bad, and the indifferent, are interesting because they represent an important phase of thought, an attempt to give prominence to the devotional and practical side of the Vedānta with other religions." Elsewhere he says that Rāmakrishna was deeply imbued with the spirit of the Vedānta philosophy and that that philosophy was "the very marrow and bones of Rāmakrishna's doctrine."* According to Swāmī Sivānanda, Rāmakrishna "realized that all existing religions are different paths leading to one God. All the paths are equally right, and every sincere seeker is sure to attain God, whatever may be the path he chooses for himself."

The same doctrine was expounded by Swāmī Vivekānanda at the Parliament of Religions, where he said "that it was a Hindu principle to recognize all faiths as expressions of truth, and that from his earliest boyhood he had repeated a sacred text, used daily by millions in India, which says that as the different streams having their sources in different places, all mingle their water in the sea, so the different paths which men take through different tendencies, various though they appear, and crooked or straight, all lead to the one Lord."† Probably, however, it was not Vivekānanda's advocacy of an universal religion that appealed to Indians, so much as his forceful character and the impression he made on the patriotic spirit of young Hindus. To quote from an article in a recent number of *The International Review*:—"He returned to India in triumph to be hailed as the prophet of new India, as one who had dared to assert the spiritual wealth of ancient India in face of the western world. He at once became the hero of the young generation—not unnaturally so. His character and his career embodied many of the qualities which were felt to be lacking amongst his countrymen. A manliness, a self-reliance, even an aggressiveness were felt to be his, which were very different from the proverbial weakness and subservience of the "mild Hindu." The spirit of Vivekānanda may stand for the spirit of the new era in India. We find his name repeatedly quoted to-day as the representative of Indian national aspirations. His is the religion of the nationalists—the cult of India—the bold assertion

* *Rāmakrishna: His Life and Sayings*, pp. 11, 12, 70, 94, 97.

† *The World's Parliament of Religions*, Vol. I, pages 242, 243.

of India's right to stand among the nations as the mother of illumination and light. At the same time he is broadly tolerant, nay, universal in his acceptance of the other world-religions. All, he claims, are contained in Vedānta"

Speaking generally, the tenets of the sect are Hinduistic, and on the philosophical side have a Vedāntic basis. Socially, the Mission represents advanced Hinduism, having no objection to the use of meat, to travel in foreign lands, or to the admission of non-Hindus into its ranks. Swāmī Sivānanda describes the general object of the Mission as being to "propagate the principles propounded by Srī Rāmkrishna Deva, and illustrated by his own life, for the benefit of humanity, and to help mankind in the practical application of those principles in their spiritual, moral, intellectual and physical needs."

At the census of 1901 Rāmkrishna's followers returned themselves as Hindus, and no statistics are available to show their number. The professed disciples are either laymen or celibate ascetics, who prefer to dress in orange-coloured robes. The latter conduct most of the practical work of the Mission, such as the hospital, the school, the orphanage, the training of the Brahmachārins, and the delivery of theological lectures. On them, too, falls the brunt of the work in times of famine, in epidemics, and in crowded pilgrimages. On the birth *tithi* of the founder in February a fair is held at Belur, and in August another fair is held at Kānkurgāchhi in the 24-Parganas, where his ashes were buried. Both these fairs are largely attended.

CHAPTER IV.

PUBLIC HEALTH.

GENERAL CONDITIONS. THE climate of the district leaves much to be desired from an hygienic point of view. The land is low-lying, intersected by rivers and creeks, and studded with marshes, stagnant pools and silted-up river channels. Humidity is high, the rainfall is heavy, and the heat, though tempered to some extent by sea-breezes, is enervating. The result is that by August and September the weather is relaxing, water is muddy, and vegetation is rank. From September onwards, with the gradual cessation of the rains, fever and bowel complaints become common, the mortality being highest in December. It decreases from January till March, after which cholera, aggravated by bad drinking water in the hot weather, frequently breaks out. On the whole, however, the health of the people of Howrah is much better than in the adjoining district of Hooghly, the Ghātāl subdivision of Midnapore, and the districts on the other side of the river Hooghly, such as Nadiā, Jessore and the 24-Parganas.

Generally speaking, the climate is better in the south than in the more water-logged tracts to the north. Of the rural thānas Syāmpur is the healthiest, in spite of periodical epidemics of cholera, while Amtā is the most unhealthy, suffering in the north and north-west from a virulent form of malarial fever. The Dumjor thāna, once a fever-stricken area, has been much improved by the draining of its marshes. Now the feverish tracts lie chiefly along the thickly populated banks of the old, silted-up Saraswatī in thāna Dumjor, the Kānā Dāmodar in thāna Jagatballabhpur, and the Dāmodar, now much reduced in volume, with its old bed on the west in thāna Amtā. The death-rate in the municipalities of Howrah and Bally is higher than in the interior, as will be apparent from the marginal table giving the death-rate per mille for 1907 and the previous quinquennium. The difference may be partly

		1902-06.	1907.
Howrah	...	41·91	37·74
Bally	...	66·06	42·98
Rural area	...	30·07	33·53

due to better reporting in the municipalities; but the excess is so marked that it may fairly be ascribed mainly to the insanitary conditions of an overcrowded town life. Bally suffers especially from fever and bowel complaints, Howrah from cholera, dysentery and diarrhœa. Since the introduction of water-works in 1896, the mortality from cholera has considerably decreased in the latter town; and it is expected that the death-rate will decrease still further on the completion of the new drainage scheme, which is now being carried out.

The present system of reporting and compiling vital statistics was introduced in 1892, and it would be of little use to compare the results with the unreliable figures reported for previous years, *e.g.*, the number of deaths reported in 1871 and 1872 represented a mortality of only 4·6 and 4·5 per mille respectively—obviously impossible figures. Under the present system, compulsory registration is in force in the towns, *i.e.*, parents, guardians or the persons directly concerned are required to report births and deaths to the town police. In rural circles each village watchman is provided with a pocket book, in which he is required to have all births and deaths that may occur within his jurisdiction recorded by the village *panchāyat*; these are reported on parade days at the police stations and outposts, which are the registering centres. The statistics thus obtained are compiled and classified by the police, and submitted monthly to the Civil Surgeon, who prepares the figures for the whole district for inclusion in the annual report of the Sanitary Commissioner. The statistics are checked from time to time by superior police officers and by Inspectors and Sub-Inspectors of Vaccination. VITAL STATISTICS.

In the towns, the higher level of intelligence and the fear of legal penalties tend to make registration and the classification of diseases more accurate than in the rural tracts. In the latter the reporting *chaukīdār* is generally illiterate, and vital registration is less correct, the chief defects being that still-births are very often omitted, while births of females and births in outlying parts, and among the lowest castes, are overlooked. Deaths are more carefully recorded, but the causes of death, except cholera and small-pox, are hopelessly confused, the bulk being classified under the general head of fever. Still the figures can be accepted so far as concerns the relative healthiness or unhealthiness of different years and the approximate growth of the population.

The returns from 1892 to 1907 show that the birth-rate is generally above 30 per mille, falling below it only in 1892, when registration was imperfect, and rising to above 36 per mille in four years, viz., 1897, 1899, 1900 and 1904. The birth-rate Births.

for the district would be still higher but for the two towns. In Howrah the birth-rate was lower than 25 per mille in eight years, falling below 20 per mille in three years, and rose above 30 per mille only in 1897, when it was 31·17 per mille. In Bally registration is not so good as in Howrah, and the variation in the reported birth-rate is extraordinary, being 19·82 in 1892, 13·17 in 1894, 39·54 in 1903 and 59·74 in 1904; but in nine years it was lower than 22 per mille. The low birth-rate in the towns is apparently due to the preponderance of males over females among the large immigrant population and partly also to the habit of sending away females before confinement to their homes in the country.

Deaths. The death-rate for the district during the same period was never below 25 per mille, and it was above 30 per mille in eleven years, rising to 37·71 per mille in 1900. Since 1899 the mortality has continued to be heavy, never falling below 30 per mille, a result due largely to the high death-rate in the towns. The highest mortality was recorded in 1900, when a death-rate of 60·50 was returned for Howrah and of 43·53 per mille for Bally, but these figures were probably misleading, being calculated on the census figures of 1891. Still, in the year after the census (1902), when the new figures were available, there was a death-rate of 35·26 per mille in the district as a whole, Howrah returning 47·43 and Bally 37·40 per mille, both calculated on the new figures. Fever, as usual, is the commonest cause of death, though the mortality due to it appears to have decreased slightly during the last six years. No perceptible change is observable in the proportion of deaths from cholera or bowel complaints. The unhealthiest months are November, December and January, the worst being December.

Infantile mortality. Infantile mortality is high, though not as high as in other districts. No less than 20 per cent. of the children born in the district die within twelve months of their birth, and according to the statistics for 1901—06, 11 per cent. more die within the next four years. More male infants die than females, and the feverish months of September to December are especially fatal. The Indian mother is usually a good nurse; but poverty and early marriage produce a weak mother and sickly child, while the child's chances are minimized by want of sufficient nourishing food and clothing, and by the mother's ignorance of infantile diseases.

DISEASES. The mortality attributed to fever is inflated by the fact that the ignorant *cahukidārs* often report deaths under this head that are really due to respiratory diseases, dysentery and diarrhœa, etc. But there can be little doubt that fever is responsible for a large proportion of the deaths, the experience of 16 years (1891—1906) showing that out of an average death-rate of 31·03 per mille, fever accounted for no less than 14·45 per mille or nearly half. The mortality is far less, however, than in the remainder of the Burdwān Division or in the Province as a whole, the average for Howrah during 1902—06 being only 13·91 per mille, as compared with 21·79 and 21·86 per mille respectively. Fever prevails after the rains from September to January, and is chiefly prevalent in those parts of Howrah and Bally where shallow pools abound, and elsewhere in the tracts which are water-logged and covered with effete water-courses and stagnant ponds. The highest death-rates were reported in 1899 and 1900, after which there was a slight but steady fall to 12·09 per mille in 1906, this being the minimum. **Fevers.**

As regards the types of fever prevalent, Lieutenant-Colonel F. J. Drury, I.M.S., Civil Surgeon of Howrah, wrote as follows in 1906:—"In my opinion the fevers of the Howrah district are mainly malarial. In 1864 a Board appointed to inquire into an epidemic of fever in the districts of Burdwān and Hooghly (which then included Howrah) expressed the opinion that the prevailing fever was immediately caused by malaria. The Sanitary Commissioner of Bengal in 1870 expressed a similar opinion, and after examining the many supposed causes of the prevalence of malaria, attributed it mainly to insufficient drainage, the partial or complete obliteration of rivers, and the pernicious state of soil, air and water, which is thereby produced. On consulting a number of annual sanitary reports, I find that during the past 14 years all the Civil Surgeons are of opinion that the fevers of the district are malarial, while not one of them suggests any other cause. This prevalence of malaria is generally said to be caused by the defective drainage and water-logged condition of the district; and it is almost invariably noted that the fever mortality is highest in the three or four months succeeding the cessation of the rains. I have only one record of an investigation into the prevalence of malaria in a part of the district, viz., a report on its prevalence in the village of Raspur near Amtā by Captain Ross, I.M.S., Deputy Sanitary Commissioner. In the autumn of 1905 there was a heavy mortality from fever along the banks of the Dāmodar in the neighbourhood of Amtā. This outbreak was attributed by the villagers to flooding of the adjacent lands. Captain Ross visited Raspur and considered the question in the light of modern views as to the causation of malaria. He rejected the opinion that inundation of the land was the cause of the malarial fever, and attributed it to the presence in the village of a great number of small *dobās* surrounded by bamboo clumps and dense undergrowth. These *dobās* form an ideal breeding ground for the anopheles mosquito, which carries the germs of malaria from the sick to the healthy. The same kind of conditions are found in many of the villages of the district, and on the introduction of a case of malarial fever into a village the disease is likely to spread."

Burdwān fever.

Formerly the severe type of fever known as Burdwān fever prevailed in the northern parts of three thānas, viz., Amtā, Jagatballabhpur and Dumjor. From the special reports submitted to Government in 1874 it appears that in this district the epidemic broke out first in 1861 in the tract round Howrah and then advanced north-westwards, attacking certain villages but leaving others untouched. In 1866 the epidemic had reached Amtā, and in 1868 spread along the right bank of the Dāmodar, attacking, though with less violence, the villages that had till then been unaffected. By 1874 its violence had more or less been spent in the district. The mortality appears to have been heaviest in the tract on the left or east bank of the silted-up river Kānā.

Small-pox.

Small-pox appears every year, but is rarely epidemic or widespread. It was only in 1906 that the death-rate rose over one per mille, the incidence being highest in March and April. The town of Howrah suffered rather severely, having a death-rate of 3·43 per mille; but the villages in the interior were comparatively immune.

Cholera.

Cholera is endemic in this district, the average death-rate during the 15 years 1892—1906 being 3·73 per mille, while in 1907 the death-rate rose to 7·38 per mille, the maximum recorded. There are two seasons in which cholera breaks out, the first in December and January, and the second in April and May, both in consequence of bad drinking water. Of the rural areas, Syāmpur thāna suffers most, apparently on account of the difficulty of getting good drinking water after the rains. Howrah city returns the largest mortality, the reported death-rates in 1895 and 1896 being as high as 11·10 and 9·58 per mille respectively. In 1896 the new water-works were opened; and a supply of filtered water being available, the mortality dropped to 3·38 in 1897, and to 0·96 and 1·63 in the next two years. In 1900 there was a rise to 4·53 per mille; and the rise was more or less kept up during the next seven years. The rise is probably connected with the large influx of coolies from Bihār and other places up-country. These coolies live huddled together in insanitary *bastis*, often do not drink pipe water, and eat the coarsest kinds of grain.

Far more deaths are caused by dysentery and diarrhœa, the average mortality in 1892—1906 being over 4·46 per mille. The death-rate is fairly persistent, varying only from 3·81 to 5·69 per mille, and the highest incidence of mortality is in December and January. Both the towns show the largest mortality in the district. In 1900 and 1901 Howrah had a death-rate of 10·55 and 7·11 per mille respectively; and in 1903 and 1904 the mortality in Bally was 10·66 and 10·82 per mille. The district has long been one of the four areas in Bengal conspicuous for the high death-rate under this head, the others being Orissa, Hooghly, and parts of Patna and Sāran; and a special inquiry was therefore made in 1905-06 by Captain W. C. Ross, I.M.S., Deputy Sanitary Commissioner. Dysentery and diarrhœa.

Briefly the results of this inquiry, so far as Howrah is concerned, are as follows:—(1) Dysentery is prevalent, but it is not of a severe type, and does not constitute an important cause of death. (2) Diarrhœa is the heading under which most of the dysentery and diarrhœa deaths are returned. (3) A large number of the deaths from diarrhœa are due to terminal diarrhœa in cases of fever (*Trypanosomiasis*?); this is the principal factor of error and greatly magnifies the dysentery and diarrhœa death-rate. (4) A number of the deaths returned under dysentery and diarrhœa are really due to cholera (atypical and lingering cases). (5) Infantile diarrhœa and acute infective diarrhœa are remarkable for their rarity, but simple diarrhœa in old age causes a considerable number of deaths. (6) Of bowel complaints, cholera is the only disease which causes a large number of deaths, cholera being endemic in the district.

Regarding the nature and causation of dysentery and diarrhœa in Howrah, Captain Ross remarked:—"Most of the deaths under diarrhœa and dysentery were those of old people, and on going into a number of individual cases I found that there was a remarkable resemblance in the clinical history of each case. A man or woman, generally over 50 years of age, has fever of a quotidian, or sometimes double quotidian, type for two or three months. The spleen is invariably enlarged, and later the liver generally becomes enlarged; emaciation and anæmia are always present and progressive; often there is œdema of the feet and ankles, etc., jaundice frequently supervenes, and the case ends in death with a terminal diarrhœa of two or three weeks' duration. This disease appears to be exceedingly common in Howrah district, and in my opinion the clear clinical picture it presents compels me to diagnose it as *Trypanosomiasis*. Further, in this connection, I was informed by the medical men at Amtā that this disease, with exactly the same clinical history, is very common there and affects young children especially, and also the very old, though no age is exempt. In young children jaundice is always a prominent symptom, and diarrhœa, though often present near the end, is not usually severe; death is generally due to progressive weakness caused by fever and wasting. In adults, and especially in the very old, life lingers longer, and generally death ensues from the additional weakness caused by diarrhœa. No cases amongst children recover, and very few cases amongst adults. The condition is most fatal, and causes a very large number of deaths.

"Although dysentery is not a large prominent factor in the death returns, yet it is more prevalent as a disease than in other districts which are less low-lying and better supplied with good water. Both the prevalence of dysentery and the large mortality from cholera are directly due to the exceeding badness of the water-supply. I saw no wells anywhere during my tour. The tidal rivers are filthy and polluted to a degree, and yet they are largely used for drinking and all other purposes. Otherwise, the water used can only be obtained from *dobās.* Tanks are few and far between, but *dobās* are at every door. The water in these is used for all purposes, and must frequently be directly contaminated from cases of cholera and dysentery. It is muddy and dirty, and smells very badly owing to the number and nature of the uses to which it is put. In fact, a *dobā* is little more than a cess-pool diluted. The first sanitary necessity of the district is the construction of a *pakkā* well in each village to be reserved for drinking and cooking purposes. Until this is done, the death-rate from cholera must continue. The people are neither so stupid nor so bigoted as the Oriyâs, and will use wells gladly if they are made. So at least I was assured both by the people and by the local officers. Where there is a clean tank, as at the Amtā court, people come from long distances to get good water for drinking, and nearly all the people in the town take water from it. The result is that cholera has no hold in Amtā, and only a few cases have occurred recently owing to importation from neighbouring villages where it is epidemic."

Plague. Plague was detected first in 1900, and has not yet been virulent, the number of deaths being generally below 200 per annum. The only exception was in 1905, when 1,277 persons died, the vast majority (1,151) being in Howrah city. The disease, as a rule, makes its appearance in November, and cases continue to occur until the hot days of April. The people seem to appreciate the benefit of cleanliness and disinfection, and readily disinfect their houses or ask the municipality to do so. They have also learnt the value of evacuating infected houses, but segregation and inoculation are not looked upon with favour and are seldom practised.

VACCINATION.

Though small-pox occasionally breaks out in an epidemic form, the district is, as a rule, comparatively free from its ravages. Vaccination is compulsory in the two towns of Howrah and Bally, the Act having been extended to the former in 1882 and to the latter in 1884. Here the prejudice against vaccination has died out, but in the rural tracts it still lingers, though the general attitude is one of mild indifference. The chief objectors are Musalmāns and the lower castes of Hindus, but, in spite of this, vaccination is making good progress. In 1907-08, 20,589 primary vaccinations were performed, of which 20,506 were successful, while the average annual number of persons successfully vaccinated during the previous five years was 22,432 or 33 per mille. Anti-septic vaccination has been introduced, and in most instances prepared lymph has been substituted for arm-to-arm vaccination as being more efficacious.

In the last quinquennial report for the Burdwān Division (1900-01 to 1904-05) the Commissioner remarked :—" In Howrah a large number of factory operatives are vaccinated every year. A large number of infants are also vaccinated annually, but the proportion is still below 500 per mille. The general condition of health, opposition from parents, and the inability of the vaccinators to finish the entire area of the district account for the low rate of infant vaccination. The Civil Surgeon reports that the people object to the vaccination of infants under six months, but most of the Hindus are willing to have children above six months vaccinated, while Muhammadans generally object to vaccination at any age. The repugnance to vaccination is gradually dying out, though opposition in some form or other is still experienced and is shown more by Muhammadans ; but generally the attitude of the people is more tolerant than before."

SANITATION.

As regards the progress of sanitation, the following remarks of the Commissioner may be quoted :—" The great sanitary need of the district of Howrah is the improvement of drainage, filling up the numerous unhealthy tanks, and the removal of excessive vegetation from the vicinity of dwelling-houses. In the town of Howrah drainage works are in progress, though it will take some years to bring the work to a completion. The water-works have removed all difficulties about good drinking-water. Very little has been done to fill up the large number of unhealthy tanks: the work is progressing slowly for want of funds. The town of Bally has its natural drainage towards the paddy-fields in the west. The people obtain their supply of drinking-water from the river Hooghly. As in Howrah, there are numerous unwholesome tanks, which the municipality with its limited resources can hardly be expected to fill up. A large tract of the country in the Uluberiā subdivision is liable to submersion almost every other year owing to the zamīndāri embankments not being kept in proper repairs. This has two divergent effects. At first the flood-water cleanses the country, and cholera disappears. But after the floods are over, large collections of stagnant water remain and fever becomes rife."

Village sanitation. Village sanitation is in its infancy, and the general sanitary principles which should govern a communal life under modern conditions are but little known or understood. Domestic cleanliness is fairly well attended to, but drinking water is taken from polluted tanks and ponds, or, less often, from wells, which are not cleansed; from tidal rivers or creeks, which are often contaminated by dead bodies and other organic matter; and in the south from the canal. The people defœcate in the fields and gardens, while the paths and drains are often in a filthy condition. There are, moreover, no conservancy arrangements for removing dirt and excreta. Tanks are still dug or old tanks re-excavated by private charity, but their number is becoming fewer. The District Board, however, has sunk a few tube or double ring wells, and to a certain extent has tried to cleanse jungles and drains. Lately, a burning *ghāt* has been built at Dumjor, and some of the tanks are being set apart for drinking purposes. The large drainage schemes of Rājāpur and Howrah have helped to drain many of the big marshes of thāna Dumjor, and have thus materially improved its sanitation. A smaller scheme for draining the feverish tract comprised in Amtā thāna was proposed thirty years ago, but is still under consideration.

Urban sanitation. The insanitary conditions prevailing in the villages were until comparatively recent years intensified in the towns, especially in Howrah with its large immigrant population. In 1889 the Sanitary Commissioner inspected the municipality and remarked:—"Of all the large municipalities in Bengal which I have inspected—and I have inspected nearly all of them—Howrah is without exception the dirtiest, most backward, and badly managed municipality I have seen." In 1893 the Sanitary Commissioner, after inspecting the municipality, expressed his agreement with the above remarks of his predecessor and added—"Generally speaking, the sanitary condition of the town of Howrah is most deplorable. On every side one is met by violent breaches of ordinary hygienic laws. I have never, in fact, seen a town in such a dangerously insanitary condition, and I should be very sorry to live in it myself." Since then there has been a remarkable improvement, though the sanitation of this great city is a very difficult matter on account of its low-lying situation, its very rapid growth, and past neglect in laying out and properly supervising its building sites. The general level of the town is very little above ground water level even in the hot weather, and during the rainy season the ground is water-logged. Ponds and tanks abound even in the most crowded parts, are nearly all filthy, and on account of their number, size and depth, will take years to reclaim, though the work is being gradually undertaken. A very large proportion of the holdings are tiled huts, many of which are built on the insanitary, ill-ventilated plan commonly found in Bihār; and even the narrow gullies which exist between the huts are closed up so as to secure greater privacy, thus still further hindering ventilation and serving as receptacles for filth.

It remains to note the improvements effected in meeting the most pressing sanitary wants of the town, viz., (1) a filtered water-supply; (2) a good drainage system; (3) an improvement of the *bastis*; and (4) better conservancy arrangements for the disposal of filth and night-soil.

Water-supply.

A filtered water-supply has been provided by means of system of water-works. The head-works are at Serampore, 12 miles higher up the river, where water is pumped from the Hooghly into four settling tanks, being then passed into four filter beds, and thence through a filtered well into a large water reservoir. From this reservoir the water is conveyed by pipes to Howrah and pumped up to three wrought-iron reservoirs, which hold 448,000 gallons. From the latter water is distributed through 461 miles of iron pipes to the different roads and lanes. In 1907-08 the monthly average of river water pumped into the settling tanks was over 70,753,000 gallons, and of filtered water pumped into the elevated reservoirs 61,658,000 gallons. The daily average of filtered water sent into Howrah was 2,021,000 gallons, and there were 4,221 house-connections. Outside the town, water is supplied to the East Indian Railway works at Bāmangāchi and Liluāh. Most of the mills also get their supply of drinking water from the water-works, and a few from Calcutta. Some use jewel filters, three obtain water from tanks, and others from wells reserved for the purpose In the Delta Jute Mills the river water is pumped into a settling tank and thence into an iron tank, from which it is distributed to the lines in pipes.

The water-works were opened in 1896, the original cost being Rs. 13,94,500, which has been increased to nearly 17 lakhs (Rs. 16,70,310) by subsequent additions and alterations The maintenance charges averaged in the next nine years Rs. 54,821, and in 1906-07 amounted to Rs. 50,728. The cost of maintenance works out to a little over one anna per 1,000 gallons supplied; but the actual cost, including capital outlay, is about 3½ annas per 1,000 gallons. Analysis shows that the water has a high standard of purity.

Drainage. Howrah is situated on comparatively high land on the west bank of the Hooghly, the general slope of the land and the consequent flow of drainage being away from the river with a natural outfall in the south-west corner of the town. The actual watershed of the town extends from north to south along a line about 400 feet to the west of the Grand Trunk Road. Drainage on the east side of this line falls into the Hooghly and on the west into *jhils* and low-lying land, eventually overflowing into drainage channels, which empty themselves into the river on the south-east.

There was till recently no regular system of drainage. Most of the drains were *kachchā* drains without any proper alignment, in which the sewage collected and stagnated, and the few *pakkā* drains were wrongly constructed. A regular scheme has now been prepared for the effective drainage of the whole town at a cost of about 10 lakhs. For this purpose the town has been divided into several sections, viz., the northern foreshore, the southern foreshore, the central section and the Sibpur section. In two of these (Sibpur and the southern foreshore) the new system has been introduced, and the rest of the work is expected to be finished in six more years, the cost being met by loans from Government. When first the work was undertaken, the opposition was so great, that work done during the day was sometimes torn up at night ; but the results achieved have not only shown the people how much more sanitary their abodes have become, but also have considerably enhanced the value of the land as building sites Any one, it is said, who was previously acquainted with the localities which have been drained, and will compare them now with other localities which have not been drained, cannot but be greatly struck with the vast improvement effected. The former have clear running streams, and a total absence of insanitary cesspits. The latter have their *kachchâ* drains filled to overflowing with a black sweltering sewage-laden liquid, beneath which, in many cases, are deposits of most offensive sludge; while the neighbourhood is full of filthy cesspits, the contents of which overflow and soak into the ground or find their way into neighbouring tanks.

Bastis. The filthy overcrowded *bastis*, which were once the reproach of Howrah, are being gradually opened up by new roads and connected with the new drains, where possible. A set of bye-laws has also been framed for the construction of new huts, and more attention is being paid to their lighting and ventilation. Situated in the midst of nearly every group of huts are shallow ponds formed by the promiscuous excavation of earth for house-building. In the dry months they become breeding grounds for mosquitoes and are frequently used for the purposes of nature. In the rains refuse and debris are washed into them and make them obnoxious. A considerable number of them have now been filled up, but there are so many that the work will take many years to complete. Still the municipality has been and is making steady progress in improving the sanitary condition of the *bastis*.

Conservancy. Night-soil and sullage water are removed in covered carts and buckets to depôts, and thence taken to three trenching grounds. The main portion is conveyed in wagons by a sewage steam tramway to the Belgāchiā trenching ground; and about 25,000 gallons of liquid matter are disposed of daily in biological filters, the deodorized effluent being used to irrigate land with crops of *dub* grass. Sewage is also disposed of in septic tank installations in the Howrah Iron Works, Bally New Mills, and Fort Gloster Jute Mills, the installation in the mills last named being the first set up by any factory in Bengal. Three burial grounds have been provided for Musalmāns and three burning *ghāts* for Hindus. A fine burning *ghāt* (Jagat Banerji's *Ghāt*) was built at Sibpur in 1903 at a cost of Rs. 13,000 raised entirely by subscriptions.

Private sanitary works. In 1893, an iron bathing *ghāt* was erected in Howrah by Bābu Khīrod Prasād Pāl at a cost of about Rs. 15,000; and in 1894, a large public bathing *ghāt* was constructed in the Bally municipality through the liberality of Bābu Chunī Lāl Khetrī of Calcutta at a cost of Rs. 7,000.

MEDICAL INSTITUTIONS. At the beginning of the present century there were seven dispensaries in the district, but one of them, the Singtī Duke Charitable Dispensary, has since been closed. The following is a brief account of the public medical institutions of the district.

The premier medical institution is the Howrah General Hospital, which was opened in 1861. At present it consists of a large block of wards for European cases, a block for Indian male cases, a dispensary and a small block for Indian females. It is undergoing a large scheme of reconstruction, which will greatly increase its accommodation and usefulness ; and it will soon consist of an European general block, European infectious block, Indian male surgical block, Indian male medical block, a large block for Indian female cases, and nurses' quarters. There are now 95 beds for male and 24 beds for female patients, and in 1907 altogether 2,116 indoor patients and 13,979 outdoor patients were treated, representing a daily average of 65 and 105 respectively. In that year a bequest of Rs. 25,000 made by the late Bābu Devī Prasād was utilized for the improvement of the Indian ward.

The Beames Charitable Dispensary at Bally is almost entirely maintained by the municipality. In the rural tracts there are four public dispensaries, viz., (1) at Amrāgorī, the Amrāgorī Hāzrā Dispensary maintained partly by the District Board and partly from the interest on a fund of Rs. 19,000 raised by subscriptions ; it is so called after Bābu Iswar Chandra Hāzrā ; (2) at Syāmpur, maintained partly from private subscriptions, but chiefly by the District Board; (3) at Uluberiā, maintained by Government, the Local Fund and private subscriptions ; and (4) at Amtā, maintained by the District Board and private subscriptions. The dispensaries at Uluberiā and Amrāgorī alone have accommodation for indoor patients, the former having six beds for males, and the latter four beds for male and two beds for female patients. All the others treat only outdoor patients. In 1907 the largest number of patients was treated at the Amrāgorī dispensary, viz., 6 540, the daily average being 42·40.

The *Kavirāji* or native Hindu system is still much in vogue ; and the patent medicines advertised in papers are fairly popular. The homœopathic system has also many advocates and is largely resorted to for children's ailments or chronic illness. The allopathic system is, however, most favoured by the well-to-do classes, especially for surgical operations. The efficacy of quinine for the treatment of malarial fever is now pretty well understood. Among the lowest classes, however, the worship of Sītalā during epidemics of small-pox, of Olā-Bibi in cases of cholera, and of Sasthī and Pānchu Thākur for children's illnesses is still common ; while simple compounds of vegetable drugs, administered by elderly females or old men, are generally resorted to for a number of diseases.

CHAPTER V.

AGRICULTURE.

GENERAL CONDITIONS.

OF all the districts in Bengal, Howrah is the least dependent on agriculture for the support of its population. It is practically a metropolitan district, a large proportion of its inhabitants obtaining employment in the adjoining city of Calcutta and in the numerous industrial concerns along the Hooghly. These concerns are situated in the long riparian strip of high land which stretches from the Bally *Khāl* on the north to the mouth of the Dāmodar on the south. It contains the populous city of Howrah and the town of Bally, and below them are numerous mills, brick-fields and scattered homesteads. Even in the interior the villages are tending to be semi-urban in character, and the villagers contribute largely to the artisan class.

Conditions are, on the whole, favourable to cultivation, as there is a rich alluvial soil which receives periodical deposits of fertilizing silt from the overflow of the Dāmodar and Rūpnārāyan. In the south, the land between those rivers lies very low and has to be protected from floods by embankments. In the north the country is cut up by numerous *khāls* or creeks, and there are many *jhils* or swamps, so that a large area lies waste and unculti-vable. Elsewhere there are wide stretches of low rice lands with *āus* rice or jute, sugarcane or orchards on lands of a slightly higher level. On a part of the latter pulses are grown after the reaping of *āus* or jute, and along the *jhils* spring rice crops are raised. In the south the land is almost exclusively sown with winter rice, which is followed by *khesāri* pulse on some of the higher lands. On the alluvial accretions called *chars*, which form in the rivers, vegetables, oil-seeds, and, occasionally, tobacco are grown after the rains are over.

RAINFALL.

The annual rainfall averages 56·95 inches, though there are extraordinary variations, the fall, for instance, being 35·7 inches in 1895-96 and 78·6 inches in 1900-01. As a rule, it is over 50 inches, and this is amply sufficient for the crops : indeed, the land being low and intersected by watercourses, 40 inches will suffice, if only the distribution is seasonable. An ideal rainfall from the cultivator's point of view would be as follows.

A few showers in February and April are hailed with delight because they soften the ground for ploughing. Then should come sunny weather in May, followed by heavy rains in June and July, with lighter showers in August. The period from the middle of August to the middle of October is the most critical for the rice crop. Heavy rains in the latter part of August cause high floods, which submerge the unembanked lowlands, and if prolonged destroy their crops; while heavy rain in the first half of September soddens the ears of rice and prevents their development. The most anxious period, however, is when the plant is ripening, *i.e.*, from the middle of September to October. Fair showers are then absolutely necessary, otherwise the crop withers away. In flooded areas, the loss of the rice can be compensated for by a good *rabi* harvest or in very low lands by the spring rice; but if the crops fail in October, the loss can hardly be made good, because the ground is too hard for spring rice and it is too late for *rabi* sowing. Rain in the early winter (November-December) is unwelcome, because it hampers the cutting of the crops and is apt to make them rot on the ground.

The effect of rainfall on the crops at different parts of the year is popularly expressed by a number of pithy sayings known as *Khanār bachan*, *i.e.*, the words of Khanā. For example, *Yadi barse Aghane, Rājā jān māgane. Yadi barse Māgher shesha, dhanya rājā, dhanya desha. Yadi haya Chaitramāse brishti, tabe haya dhāner shrishti. Jyeshthe shukho Ashāre dhārā, shashyer bhār nā sahe dharā. Chaitre kuyā Bhādre bān, narer munda garāgari jān.* "If it rains in Aghan (November-December) the king goes out to beg. If it rains in the end of Māgh (February), blessed is the king, blessed is the land. If it rains in Chaitra (March-April), paddy is grown. Dry weather in Jyaistha (May-June) and heavy rain in Asārh (June-July) make the earth groan with the weight of the crops. Mist in Chaitra and floods in Bhādra (August-September) make (dead) men's heads roll on the ground." These sayings seem to date back to a time when floods were much dreaded, as adding great personal distress to the loss of the crops.

IRRIGATION. Irrigation is practised, but not on an extensive scale, for the rainfall is abundant, and the lands lie low, with a very gentle, almost imperceptible drainage slope. Winter rice, the staple crop, being ordinarily raised on lands below or at flood-level requires no irrigation except in exceptional years of drought; while jute, the second crop of economic importance, grows and is cut in the rains, when there is ample moisture. In fact, artificial irrigation is required only for certain special crops, such as sugarcane, potatoes, brinjals, betel-leaf and spring rice, the cultivation of which either takes place after the rains or is spread over several seasons.

The sources of irrigation are partly natural, such as rivers, creeks and swamps, partly artificial, such as canals, drainage channels, tanks and wells. The important winter rice crop usually receives a sufficient supply of water from the overflow of the rivers, but water from the canal and from the drainage channels is also used for its irrigation. It is taken in from the Hooghly at spring tides, and is held up by means of lock-gates in the canal, as well as in the drainage channels, being supplied to the cultivators, on application, by the Public Works Department. Otherwise, irrigation direct from the rivers and creeks is rare, unless the fields to be watered are nearly on the same level. Occasionally, however, some of the smaller creeks are dammed up, thus raising the water-level and impounding a supply for the dry months. The spring rice is also often irrigated from swamps, on the banks of which it is grown. Sugarcane and betel-leaf are generally irrigated from adjoining creeks or tanks, as they require a large supply of water. Well irrigation is not much practised, though the water-level is only a few feet below the surface. Well water is used chiefly for orchards and homestead lands, and is supplemented by the supply drawn from pools, tanks and ditches, most orchards having a pool or a tank attached to them, which furnishes the water wanted after the rains.

There is comparatively little canal irrigation. Ordinarily an ample supply of water can be had from other sources, and in the summer, when the latter sources dry up, the canal also contains very little water. There is, however, a considerable demand for canal water just after the rains, if the monsoon has been deficient in strength. The drainage channels, which traverse lands on a very low level, are probably of more use, because in years of scanty rainfall water can be brought along them from the Hooghly river in the critical months of September and October.

Water is raised from wells by means of buckets or earthen pots with a rope, which occasionally is put round a pulley on a wooden bar fixed on supports. In the fields the usual mode of raising water is by a *dongā* or canoe-shaped piece of wood scooped out inside. At each end a man holds a rope; and having dipped the *dongā* in the water, they swing it up into a channel leading to the fields. Water can be raised in this way two or three feet

Water-lifts.

only. If the water has to be raised higher, the men stand on a fixed frame raised above the water and have longer ropes tied to the *dongā*, or draw up water in pots. The up-country *lāthā* is also occasionally seen in gardens near the towns.

SOILS. The soil throughout the district is alluvial and varies from sand in the river beds to sticky clay in the interior along the silted-up streams and mud in the swamps. Clayey and deep loamy soils prevail in the north, and lighter loams in the south, where the deposits are more recent. The cultivators have a long list of names for different classes of land, judged from various points of view, for they classify the soil according to its level, composition or yield. As regards level, it is called *jalā* when below water-level (*i.e.*, usually *sāli* or paddy land), *sunā* when above water-level, and *dāngā* at a higher level. On the highest levels there are *bāstu*, or homestead land, and *ulbāstu*, or land immediately round the homestead. According to composition, the soil may be *bele* or sandy, *entel* or clayey, *penko* or muddy, *dhasā* or marshy, and so forth. According to yield, the *sāli* and *sunā* lands are divided into *āwal* or first class, *doyam* or second class, *seyam* or third class, *chāhāram* or fourth class, and so on, the terms being relics of the old Musalmān classification.

PRINCIPAL CROPS. The following is a statement prepared by the Agricultural Department showing the normal areas under the principal crops and the percentage of those areas to the normal net cropped area:—

Name of crop.	Normal acreage.	Percentage on normal net cropped area.	Name of crop.	Normal acreage.	Percentage on normal net cropped area.
Winter rice ...	125,200	50	Summer rice ...	6,500	8
Sugarcane ...	8,500	3	Other *rabi* cereals and pulses ...	11,200	4
			Other *rabi* food-crops	7,600	3
Total *aghani* crops	133,700	53	inseed ...	2,000	1
			Rape and mustard	2,300	1
			Til (*rabi*) ...	1,200	...
			Other oil-seeds...	100	...
Autumn rice ...	18,500	7	Other *rabi* non-food crops ...	1,500	1
Maize	300	...			
Other *bhādoi* cereals and pulses ...	1,800	1	Total *rabi* crops	32,400	13
Other *bhādoi* food-crops	2,700	1	Orchards and garden produce ..	34,500	14
Jute	56,900	23			
Til (*bhādoi*) ...	300	...			
Total *bhādoi* crops	80,000	32	Twice-cropped area	30,000	12

According to the statistics for 1907-08, out of a total area of 326,400 acres, the area not available for cultivation is 52,400 acres, culturable waste other than fallow accounts for 16,000 acres, and current fallows for 15,600 acres; while the net cropped area is 242,400 acres.

Rice. Rice forms the staple crop of the district, being grown on a normal area of 150,000 acres or 63 per cent. of the total area. It is a food-grain especially suited to low moist lands receiving an abundant rainfall, such as those which make up the greater portion of Howrah. An immense variety of different kinds of rice are grown, but the crops may be grouped under three main heads according to the harvest seasons, viz., *boro* or spring, *āus* (literally *āsu*) or autumn, and *āman* (or *haimantik*) or winter rice.

Boro and *āus.* *Boro* rice is transplanted along the banks of marshes, or in very low lands which remain wet till summer. Ploughing is not required. It is sown in January and reaped in April and May. This class of rice includes only coarse varieties, and only a small quantity of land can be found fit for its cultivation. *Aus* rice is sown, chiefly broadcast, on *sunā* lands and preferably loamy soils. It is sown in May and reaped in August and September, being often followed by a second crop of pulses. This crop also yields coarse varieties of rice. Formerly *āus* was a fairly large crop, but it has been replaced by jute, which pays the cultivator better. In the sayings of Khanā we find several references to the autumn rice crop:—*Auser bhui bele, pāter bhui ātāle. Vaishākher prathan jale, āus-dhān dwigun phale. Aus-dhāner chāsh, lāge tin māsa.* "The soil of *āus* is sandy, that of jute clayey. In the first rains of Baisākh (April-May), *āus* paddy yields double. The cultivation of *āus* paddy takes three months."

Winter rice. *Aman* rice is the great crop of the year. It is grown on lands lying below flood-level, except where water lies so deep as to preclude cultivation. The land which gets the right quantity of water and most of the detritus washed off the upper lands is naturally the richest, and is therefore called *āwal* or first class land. It forms the deepest or nearly the deepest part of the fields, while above and below it is *doyam* or second class land. In a year of excessive rain the upper *doyam*, and in a year of drought the lower *doyam*, will be as good as *āwal*; but in a year of average rainfall the *āwal* will be better than either. Above and below the *doyam* are the zones of inferior *seyam* and *chāhāram* soils.

In the north the ground is frequently manured with cow-dung (50 baskets to a *bighā*) except in the lower lands, where manure would be dissipated in the water. After manuring, ploughing begins, as soon as the ground has been sufficiently softened by rain, towards the end of winter or in the beginning of spring. There are generally four ploughings before sowing or planting. The clods are then pulverized by drawing a *mai* or harrow over them. *Aman* rice may be sown broadcast, but is more usually sown in a nursery and transplanted into the fields. It is sown in May and June, and is transplanted in the rains, chiefly in July and August. It cannot be sown broadcast if the ground dries up early, or does not dry up at all, or has been newly broken up. The usual quantity of seed used is 16 seers to a *bighā*. The labour required for transplanting varies according to the distance of the fields from the village, the depth of water and other circumstances, but on the average it takes a man five days per *bighā*. Harvesting begins on high lands in November or December, and is mostly finished by the end of January. On the lower grounds it continues till the end of February and sometimes till the middle of March.

The reaping is easy enough till the low lands are reached after the *āwal*. The *doyam* may be got in dry, but *seyam* and *chāhāram* have generally to be reaped in water. In dry reaping the straw with the paddy is laid in bundles on the fields in order to dry it, and after two or three days is carried home for threshing. In wet reaping the heads of the stalks above water are generally cut and then carried to a dry spot for drying. Paddy reaped dry is usually threshed by beating the bundle against boards till all the grain is separated. The bundles of straw (*khar*) are then stored for sale or use. Paddy reaped wet is trampled out by oxen. The straw (*pāl*) is sour and useless, except for feeding cattle. After threshing the paddy is winnowed and stored in thatched granaries with split bamboo walls (*marāi*).

The outturn naturally varies according to the nature of land, timely or untimely weather, and the care given to cultivation. On an average the outturn of *sāli āwal* rice per *bighā* is estimated at 7 to 10 maunds of paddy and one *kāhān* of straw; and of *sāli doyam* at 5 to 8 maunds of paddy and the same quantity of straw. Some of the best lands, if manured, have been known to yield 12 maunds per *bighā*, but such a heavy yield is very rare. Generally speaking, the outturn, taken at the rate of eight maunds of paddy and one *kāhān* of straw, would be worth in the selling season not more than Rs. 26 (24+2).

Pulses. After rice, pulses are the most important of the food-grains. Gram is not grown, but other pulses, like *khesāri*, *mūng*, peas and *masuri*, are favourite second crops. *Khesāri* or *teorā* is sown on low rice lands when the *āman* is damaged by floods or has a poor outturn. It is sown broadcast in October, grows slowly until the winter rice is harvested, then shoots up rapidly, and is gathered in February and March. It costs little to cultivate, but the yield is not large if the rice crop is good. It is a grain which the well-to-do eschew, but owing to its cheapness, is much used in the form of *dāl* by the poorer classes. The other pulses form the main cold-weather crops on *sunā* lands. They are sown in October and November after ploughing and are reaped in February and March. The ploughing is more carefully done, the seeds cost more, and the outturn is more valuable. They furnish the *dāl* eaten by the higher classes.

Oil-seeds, such as linseed, *til*, rape and mustard, are cold-weather crops grown only in small plots on high lands round the village sites and on the river *chars*, which are periodically fertilized by new silt. Oil-seeds.

Next to rice, jute is the chief crop, especially in the north. It has largely replaced *āus* rice, and in 1907-08 it was grown on 65,000 acres, or one-fourth of the net cropped area. In most villages in the Sadar subdivision it is raised on *sunā* lands that are not occupied by sugarcane, vegetables or orchards. The ground is usually manured with cow-dung or rich muddy earth dug up from tanks or ditches. After the first showers in May, the ground is ploughed up, and the seed (about two seers per *bighā*) is sown. The fields are then weeded twice or thrice before the heavy rains begin. In August and September the jute is cut, stripped of its leaves, carried to water in bundles, and there steeped. The steeping process is called retting. After a time the stalks are taken out and beaten, and the fibre is extracted. The fibre is cleaned, dried by hanging, and then put into drums ready for the market. The stalks are used for fuel, for thatching, or for fencing betel-leaf plantations. The outturn varies according to circumstances, *e.g.*, the condition of the fields, the quantity of manure used and the care given to cultivation; but for first class lands the average outturn may be taken roughly as 4 to 6 maunds of fibre and 8 to 10 bundles of stalks (*pānkāti*), and for second class lands 3 to 5 maunds and the same quantity of stalks. The Dumjor and Bargachhiā stations on the Howrah-Amtā line are centres of the jute trade, being visited by European and Armenian traders in the season. Jute.

Sugarcane is grown on *sunā* lands, preferably heavy clay soils retaining moisture. The ground is prepared by ploughing and harrowing, and also receives irrigation, if the soil is light and porous. It is next manured with oil-refuse, cow-dung and Sugarcane.

tank-mud. In January cuttings half a foot long are placed, with oil-refuse, in holes arranged in rows a yard apart. In the four months preceding the rains (February to June) the surface is irrigated several times, and after each watering it is hoed. Just before the rains the ground round the roots is cleared, old leaves, etc., being removed, and manure laid at the roots, after which they are carefully earthed over. During the next five months (middle of June to middle of November) the leaves are usually twisted round the stems to prevent insects or jackals from damaging the plants. As soon as the plants are large enough, they are tied together with leaves at the top to prevent the flexible stems falling down. Cutting begins in January, and may continue till April. The chief varieties are Bombay, *shāmsārā* and *deshi*. The cultivation is exhausting to the soil and expensive to the ryots. The crop is therefore alternated with paddy or jute in the following rains and with potatoes or pulses in the following winter, so that the soil has rest for at least a year and a half. The old wooden mill has disappeared and has been replaced by a more effective machine with an iron crusher and pan. A few of the canes are sold in the towns and rural *hāts*; but most are crushed in the iron mill, the juice being converted into *gur* or molasses.

Tobacco and betel-leaf. Tobacco is a minor product, being chiefly found along river banks and on *chars*. Betel-leaf is more largely grown, especially by the Bārui caste, in bamboo enclosures with fences made of jute-stalks. The cuttings are planted in rows in February and watered daily for the first three months. The leaves begin to shoot out in June and July, and continue to do so for a year. Old stems are cut down in April, when the roots send up fresh stems, which begin giving new leaves in June and July. In this way fresh leaves may be got for several years, otherwise the stems die in a year. The trailing plants have to be tied to supports of *dhoinchā* or split bamboo, and the soil manured from time to time with oil-refuse. The betel leaf of Nunti and Bāntul near Uluberiā is famous for its flavour, being exported as far north as Delhi.

FRUITS. The principal fruits of the district are mango, plantain, coconut, jack, papaya, pine-apple and custard-apple (*ātā*). Groves of mango and jack abound, especially in the Howrah subdivision. There are numerous varieties of indigenous mangoes, which though stringy are generally sweet. In orchards owned by the well-to-do classes grafts of Bombay, *fasli* and *lengrā* mangoes are common and yield fine fruit, though it is rather smaller in size than that raised up-country. The jack-fruit usually has a stringy pulp, but the best varieties are sweet and luscious. Pine-apples are regularly cultivated in homestead plots, especially near the Liluāh and Dumjor stations. They are usually large and palatable, while the sub-variety called *rasi*, though smaller, is particularly sweet. Papaya grows almost wild in every homestead, and is a welcome addition to the daily fare, being eaten when unripe as a vegetable, and when ripe as a fruit. Plantains are cultivated on an extensive scale, both unripe and ripe varieties, the chief sub-varieties of the latter being the religiously pure *kāthāli*, the small but delicious *chāmpā*, and the large *martamān* (literally Mārtābān). Coconut and date palms thrive, yielding fruit, coconut oil and date sugar. Limes, tamarind, leechees (*Nephelium litchi*), the Indian blackberry (*jām*), the rose apple (*golāp jām*), the *jāmrul* (*Eugenia javanica*) and guava are found in gardens on the outskirts of the towns.

VEGETABLES. Vegetables are grown extensively round the villagers' homesteads, in private gardens, and along the fertile banks of the numerous *khāls* and streams. Excellent *patals* (*Tricosanthes dioica*) come *viâ* Amtā from the Dāmodar *chars*, and arums (*ol*) from Sāntrāgāchhi and Jagatballabhpur. Amtā also supplies large soft brinjals, fairly big water-melons and good radishes. Several kinds of pot herbs, gourds, beans, yams, cucumbers, potatoes (*deshī* or Nainī Tāl), sweet potatoes and onions are raised for sale; while near the towns cauliflowers, cabbages, peas, beet, and other European vegetables are grown.

MISCELLANEOUS PRODUCTS. Among miscellaneous products may be mentioned mulberries grown in thāna Jagatballabhpur and Pānchlā outpost on about 500 acres; bamboos grown in the compounds of most households; and the *hoglā* reed, which is plentiful on the banks of the marshes and swamps.

EXTENSION OF CULTIVATION. Figures showing changes in the cultivated area for any lengthy period cannot be given, as the agricultural statistics of Howrah were incorporated with those of Hooghly until 1905-06. It appears, however, to be a well-established fact that practically all the land at present cultivable has been brought under the plough and that very little land is left fallow. It would seem, moreover, that the area under rice and jute is steadily increasing. The lands reclaimed by the three drainage schemes (Howrah, Barajol and Rājāpur) have been almost exclusively devoted to winter paddy, while the *sunā* lands that grew autumn rice have been devoted almost entirely to jute. The area under jute varies, however, with the prices obtained for the fibre and with the stock of rice kept in hand, *e.g.*, the scarcity of rice and the high prices of food-grains in 1908 are reported to have caused a reduction in the area under jute and a corresponding increase in the cultivation of rice. Sugarcane cultivation, which increased a little after the introduction of iron roller mills, is declining owing to the competition of imported sugar and molasses, while the cultivation of vegetables and fruits is, on the whole, increasing. At present a large quantity of food-grains has to be imported from other districts; and the cultivated area can only increase materially by reclaiming some of the existing swamps or by protecting part of the country liable to inundation.

IMPROVEMENTS IN PRACTICE. The substitution of jute for autumn rice as a more paying crop commanding a ready sale is becoming general. In the flooded tracts, the losses due to floods are counteracted by sowing pulses along with winter rice, for if the latter is damaged or destroyed, a good crop of the former can be got from the deposit of silt left by the receding water. The value of manure as a fertilizer is understood. It is generally applied in the case of special crops, and is also coming into use for rice on higher lands. The usual manures are decomposed cow-deung and the refuse of oil-seeds; but the scarcity of firewood leads to an increased use of dried cow-dung for fuel among the poorer classes. A certain amount of rotation is practised, *e.g.*, jute or autumn rice is rotated with pulses, sugarcane with jute and pulses, etc.

Several new kinds of ploughs have been tried, but have not yet passed the experimental stage. The improved Sibpur plough is somewhat in favour, as it has the advantage of better work combined with cheapness and simplicity. The use of iron roller mills and pans for converting sugarcane into *gur* has already been alluded to.

The cultivators keep seed for sowing from their old stock, and there is no conscious selection of the best kinds; but there is a general tendency to select the better varieties for planting, *e.g.*, Bombay and *shāmsārā* in the place of *deshī* sugarcane, while Sāntrāgāchhi arums (*ol*) are substituted for the ordinary kind, *muktakeshī* brinjals for the common varieties, up-country mangoes for the indigenous kinds, etc. In urban gardens imported European seeds are largely used.

CATTLE. The breeds of cattle are of the usual kinds found in Lower Bengal. Cows are kept by house-holders and Goālās, who also keep buffaloes; bullocks by Goālās and cultivators of all classes; sheep and goats by Musalmāns and low caste Hindus; pigs by the lowest castes, such as Kāorās and Hāris; ponies by the more wealthy Muhammadans and Hindus. The cows and plough-bullocks are weak and stunted in growth, no sustained efforts having yet been made to improve the breed. Epidemics often break out, and from ignorance and want of prompt treatment many die. The Saturday *hāt* at Uluberiā is the largest cattle market in the district.

Cattle suffer much from want of pasturage. Once every village had its grazing grounds, but now there are practically none, nearly every acre having been appropriated and rented out to cultivators. The ryot consequently has to feed his bullocks with straw, etc., for the greater part of the year; for though the cattle get some grazing in the fields after harvesting, they are kept out of them as soon the crops are sown, and have to be tethered on some more or less barren patches, off which the grass is quickly browsed. Pasturage.

Among the castes engaged in agriculture the Kaibarttas predominate, a thrifty industrious class, who have migrated largely into the southern thānas, probably from the east of Midnapore. The other principal agricultural castes are Pods, originally a fishing caste, who came to the Uluberiā subdivision, probably from the other side of the river Hooghly; Sadgops, a characteristic caste of West Bengal; Chandāls, probably emigrants from Eastern Bengal; Bāruis or hereditary betel-leaf growers; and among the Musalmāns that heterogeneous class, the Sheikhs. From various causes, chiefly economic, recruits have been received from other important classes, such as the weaving classes (Tāntis, Suklis and Jolāhās), the fishing castes (Tiyars and Bāgdis), and other castes, such as Telis, Chhutars and others. At present, owing to the high price of food-grains, there is a tendency for many persons in the rural tracts, who previously had no connection with cultivation, to take up land in order that they may have a stock of rice to fall back upon. Consequently, there is no important class or caste of which a certain proportion does not hold some land. AGRICULTURAL CLASSES.

CHAPTER VI.

CANALS, DRAINAGE AND EMBANKMENTS.

CANALS. THE only locked canal in this district forms part of the Midnapore Canal and comprises two tidal reaches extending from Uluberiā to Bānsberiā, where it crosses the Dāmodar river, and from Kultāpārā to Kāntāpukur, where it joins the Rūpnārāyan. On the opposite site of the Rūpnārāyan the canal is continued from Dainān to Midnapore, crossing the Kāsāi river at Pānskurā and at Mohanpur close by Midnapore. The total length of the canal, including 16¾ miles of canalized distributaries, is 69¾ miles. The tidal reaches were constructed chiefly for the purpose of navigation and were opened for traffic in 1873. Each range has two parallel distributaries, and their water, when available, is used for irrigation, but the supply is variable and cannot be depended on. Before the opening of the Bengal-Nāgpur Railway the canal formed part of the main route from Calcutta to Midnapore, but the traffic, once considerable, has fallen off owing to railway competition.

There is also an improved natural channel, called the Gāighātā and Bakshi *Khāls*, 7½ miles long, which forms a connecting link between the Dāmodar and Rūpnārāyan rivers. It was taken up and improved by Government in 1856-57, and was in charge of the Public Works Department until 1872-73, when it was transferred to the District Board. In 1894 the maintenance and management of the channel were resumed by Government, which makes an annual grant of Rs. 2,500 to the District Board in order to recoup the loss occasioned to that body by the re-transfer. The right of collecting tolls has been leased out for two years (1908-09 and 1909-10) at Rs. 4,500 per annum.

DRAINAGE CHANNELS. The drainage of the large swamps in the district is a far more important question than that of canal irrigation or navigation. Such swamps are found in the depressions between the rivers and their principal branches, one set (the Howrah swamps) lying between the raised banks of the Hooghly and the Saraswatī, another (the Rājāpur swamps) between the Saraswatī and the Kānā Dāmodar, and a third (the Amtā swamps) between the Kānā Dāmodar and the Dāmodar. The first schemes for the drainage of these swamps appear to have been put forward as a result of the epidemic of a virulent type of fever called Burdwān fever, which raged in Hooghly and part of Howrah. The heavy mortality it caused formed the subject of repeated enquiries by civil, medical and engineering officers. One of the latter, Mr. Adley, C.E., who had been appointed by Government to determine whether want of drainage had caused or intensified the prevailing fever, reported in 1869 that defective drainage caused by the silting up of rivers and *khāls* was a main cause of the fever and recommended the reclamation of the Dānkuni, Kātliā and Rājāpur swamps. Government approved a portion of his scheme, viz., that for draining the Dānkuni marsh, which lies just outside the district with its outfall in the Bally *Khāl*, and the work was taken in hand.

Subsequently, in 1873, Colonel Haig, Chief Engineer of Bengal, who had been deputed to make an engineering survey of the locality, recommended that the Dānkuni scheme should be extended to the tidal tracts in this district. He suggested three schemes for the reclamation of the three sets of swamps mentioned above, viz., (1) the Amtā scheme for the drainage of 84 square miles lying in the western drainage basin; (2) the Rājāpur scheme for the drainage of the tidal portion of the central basin comprising the Rājāpur, Pānchlā and Barajol (apparently a corruption of *bara jhil*) swamps; and (3) the Howrah scheme for the drainage of the tract lying between the Bally *Khāl* on the north, the river Hooghly on the east and south, and the Saraswatī on the west. The Howrah scheme was taken up first, being begun in November 1884 and completed in October 1885 at a cost of 5¼ lakhs. The larger Rājāpur scheme was next begun and completed in 1894-95 at a cost of 14½ lakhs. The Amtā scheme is still under consideration, the zamīndārs concerned having been averse to it hitherto, but Drainage Commissioners have recently been appointed. The cost of upkeep in 1907-08 was Rs. 2,672 in the case of the Howrah works, as against Rs. 862 in 1906-07 and Rs. 5,303 in 1905-06, and Rs. 8,635 in the case of the Rājāpur and Barajol works, as against Rs. 9,604 in 1906-07.

The Howrah and Rājāpur (including Barajol) drainage works, which are in charge of the Executive Engineer, Northern Drainage and Embankment Division, were undertaken under the provisions of the Bengal Drainage Act, VI (B.C.) of 1880. That Act repealed Bengal Act V of 1871, which laid down, in regard to the Dānkuni scheme, that a moiety of the proprietors of the lands concerned might assent to the drainage works, whereon the whole proprietary body would be obliged to combine to cause execution of the works, to obtain the necessary advance of money from Government, and to apportion among themselves the liability for the recovery of the advance. The Drainage Act of 1880 empowered the Lieutenant-Governor to carry out similar works for the drainage and reclamation of land throughout Bengal. It provided that each scheme under the Act should be prepared with plans and estimates by the Government engineers and published for general information. The cost of the works was to be assessed, on the lands reclaimed and improved, in proportion to the benefit derived, by Commissioners appointed by the Lieutenant-Governor, of whom the majority were to be proprietors. The recovery of the sums apportioned on the several proprietors was left in the hands of the Collector. The works, when completed, were to be kept up in the same manner as public embankments at the expense of those whose lands were benefited, and in their maintenance the Collector was to be assisted by a committee of proprietors appointed for that purpose. A material alteration from the procedure under Act V of 1871 consisted in allowing the Commissioners an opportunity of watching results for three years after the works were completed before they proceeded to apportion the costs. Thus the liability to repay any portion of the capital was deferred for three years.

The Act was amended in 1902 by the Bengal Drainage Amendment Act, II (B.C.) of 1902, which provides further facilities for the recovery by landholders from their tenants of a proportionate share of the expenses connected with the carrying out of drainage schemes. It also authorizes the recovery of contributions when one co-sharer pays the whole of the expenses for carrying drainage works; and it provides a procedure for amending the list of persons who have been formally declared to be liable to pay the expenses of drainage schemes. The most noticeable results of this last Act are that it has empowered the zamīndārs to file certificates against their tenants and has reduced the rate of interest from 5 per cent. to 4 per cent. The landlords realize the drainage demands from the tenants of the benefited lands either directly as additions to rents and cesses or indirectly by enhancing their rents in view of the estimated benefits to their lands.

Howrah drainage scheme. The tract of country drained by the Howrah drainage scheme is bounded by the river Hooghly on the south, by the towns of

Bally and Howrah on the east, by the river Saraswatī on the west, and by the Bally *Khāl* and the road from Bally to Chandītalā on the north. Its area is about 49½ square miles, of which nearly 18 square miles consist of pure swamp. The lowest part is 7½ feet above mean sea-level and even when tidal water is excluded, the rainfall is enough to fill it to a depth of 4½ feet. The most prominent characteristic of these swamps is that instead of forming a single large basin, like the Dānkuni swamp to the north, they are divided into four catchment basins, each separated from the other by a low ridge.

The works consist of (1) a main channel 8½ miles long, the width of the base varying from 10 feet at the end to 80 feet near the sluice on the river; (2) branch and subsidiary channels with a total length of 10 miles; (3) an outfall sluice near the Botanical Garden, having seven vents of 5 feet each, with self-acting shutters on the river side and drop-gates worked by screws on the land side; (4) another outlet sluice, having one vent (5 feet by 5 feet) with a drop-gate worked by screws, near the Banderbil sluice on the Bally *Khāl*; and (5) an embankment extending for about 2½ miles along the river Hooghly from the Botanical Garden to the mouth of the Māhisdhārā *Khāl*, the object of which is to exclude tidal water from the swamps.

Rājāpur drainage scheme. The Rājāpur scheme drains an area of 269·85 square miles and is divided into two sections, viz., Barajol and Rājāpur. The Barajol section drains an area of 30·5 square miles, of which more than half is swamp. The works consist of (1) a main channel (9,600 feet long); (2) two branch channels, with a combined length of about 9 miles, which run from the villages of Jangalpur and Sātghariā to the river Hooghly; and (3) an outfall sluice, with four vents, 8 feet by 5 feet each.

The Rājāpur section is a large engineering work, affecting the drainage of 239·35 square miles comprised in five basins, viz., the upland basin (140 square miles), Jhanāi basin (32·70 square miles), Pānchlā Jol basin (22·50 square miles), Rājāpur Jol basin (31·90 square miles), and an area of 12·35 square miles draining directly into the Hooghly. The works consist of (1) a main channel, 16 miles long, extending from half a mile north of Rājāpur to Sijberiā a mile above Uluberiā; (2) three branch channels, with a combined length of about 7 miles, three *khāls* with a combined length of 9½ miles serving as branch channels, and four detached channels with a total length of about one mile; (3) a big outfall sluice on the Hooghly river at Sijberiā, having 20 vents, each 8 feet by 5 feet; (4) a protective embankment, about 1½ miles long, from Sijberiā to Chakkāsi *Khāl*, with three irrigation sluices. There are also two bungalows, one at Sijberiā and the other at Rājāpur, three road-bridges and four foot-bridges.

The main channel, starting from the outfall sluice at Sijberiā, follows the course of the Kālsāpā *Khāl* or Kānā Dāmodar (which has been remodelled) for 3½ miles as far as Bāsdeopur. From that place it passes through the low lands of Danchlā and Dhanki to Siddheswar, and thence through the Rājāpur Jol, finally ending about half a mile beyond the Howrah-Amtā road. The first branch channel leaves the main channel in the 12th mile, and going north-west passes under the Howrah-Amtā road, about one mile from Bargachhiā, connecting with the low lands of Santoshpur. The second branch leaves the main channel in the 14th mile, and going north-east passes under the Howrah-Amtā road, and connects at Jhāpardah with the Mātiā *Khāl*, of which a length of 5 miles has been improved to serve as a branch channel. The cost of maintenance is small, averaging Rs. 8,370 only in the five years ending in 1907-08.

It has been estimated that the Rājāpur scheme has reclaimed from its three principal swamps, Rājāpur, Pānchlā and Barajol, 4,122 acres of waste land and has improved no less than 37,972 acres of low land. The western portion of Rājāpur is, however, being affected by floods pouring in from the Amtā, Madāriā and upland basins, largely through breaches in the Kānā Dāmodar and Madāriā *Khāl* left embankments. Crops were damaged by such floods in 1893-94, 1899-1900, 1904-05 and 1905-06. The left embankment of the Madāriā *Khāl* from Amtā to Harishpur is consequently to be raised, and the portion from Penro to Dilakhās is being remodelled.

These schemes are interesting examples of large reclamation works, beyond the means of the cultivators or of individual landlords, which are practicable only for a combination of landed proprietors or capitalists working under the protection of the Drainage Act. Both have amply fulfilled expectations. The Magistrate of Howrah in the Annual Administration Report of 1897-98 remarked:—"All the drainage schemes have proved to be of immense benefit in reclaiming the waste swamps and improving the other lands. They were originally intended for the drainage of the swamps, but they are now advantageously utilized in irrigating the lands, in years of drought and scanty rainfall, with fresh water from the Hooghly river." More recently, in 1905, the Commissioner remarked :—"These schemes have proved very successful in reclaiming the extensive waste swampy lands west of Howrah and improving other lands. The surplus water is drained out by the channels and sluices in years of heavy rainfall; while in years of drought water from the river is let in for cultivation and drinking purposes. The schemes have been of great benefit to the people of the neighbouring tracts, who can reap a good harvest in years of drought as well as in years of heavy rainfall."

The completion of the entire project for the drainage of the district by carrying out the Amtā scheme proposed over 30 years ago appears desirable on many grounds. It would not only add hundreds of acres to the cultivated area and improve thousands of acres of low lands—an important consideration in a district which does not raise enough food for its consumption. It would also drain a water-logged locality in which malarial fever threatens to be endemic, owing to the stagnant water being the breeding ground of the malaria-bearing anopheles mosquito. In its present state, moreover, the waters flooding the Amtā basin not only damage the Amtā crops three or four years out of every five, but also threaten to swamp the western part of the Rājāpur basin.

A large part of the district being very little above mean sea-level is liable to be flooded every year by the principal rivers and their branches Protective embankments have, therefore, long been held to be necessary and during the early years of British administration the main channels of the three chief rivers were embanked, viz., the right bank of the Hooghly, the left and right banks of the Dāmodar, and the left bank of the Rūpnārāyan. The effect of these embankments was that the rivers, depositing silt in their beds, gradually raised them above the level of the adjoining country. Hence, when a river burst through its bank, it flooded a considerable area causing serious damage. This was more especially the case with the Dāmodar, a large river liable to flood with a rapid stream and narrow bed. The embankments along its banks were originally maintained by the Burdwān Rāj, but the damage caused from time to time by the floods pouring through imperfectly repaired breaches forced Government to take them over. In course of time the Government was obliged to abandon the embankment on the right side of the Dāmodar in order to protect the more valuable lands on the left side. This at first caused much hardship to villages on the right side, but gradually the silt-deposit not only raised the land, but enabled splendid crops of *rabi* to be grown, thus compensating for the loss of paddy crops. During the last 20 years, on account EMBANKMENTS.

of a large breach at Beguā in the Burdwān district, a reduced volume of water has been passing along the present channel of the Dāmodar, and the effect of the floods is consequently not felt on the right side. It is now proposed to close the Beguā breach up to ordinary flood-height so as to minimize damage to crops in the Burdwān district and the Arāmbāgh subdivision of the Hooghly district. The result of this change remains to be seen.

Along the right bank of the Hooghly there are zamīndāri embankments from Sānkrāil to Alipore on the mouth of the Dāmodar, except a portion measuring about 1½ miles in length from Chakkāsi *Khāl* to Sijberiā, which is being maintained by Government as a portion of the Rājāpur drainage works. They were badly breached by high floods in 1904-05, causing serious loss of crops in the interior. The zamīndārs concerned having failed to repair them properly, the Government has taken charge of two sections (one at Chakkāsi, 3 miles above Uluberiā, and the other from Uluberiā to Chāmpā *Khāl* on the south) and has put them in proper order, the cost being realized from the zamīndārs under the Embankment Act.

Government now maintains the following embankments :—(1) the Hooghly right embankment from the Botanical Garden to Māhisdhārā *Khāl* and the Chakkāsi embankment from Chakkāsi *Khāl* to Sijberiā ; (2) the Dāmodar left embankment through the whole length of the district and the right embankment from the Beguā breach to the Majā Dāmodar and from the mouth of the Gāighātā *Khāl* to the outfall into the Hooghly ; (3) the Rūpnārāyan left embankment from the mouth of the Bakshi *Khāl* to the outfall in the Hooghly ; (4) the embankment on the south of the Bakshi and Gāighātā *Khāls*, joining the Rūpnārāyan left with the Dāmodar right embankment ; (5) a *takāvi* embankment along the left bank of the Madāriā *Khāl* from Dilakhās to Amtā, about half of which has been raised, while the other half is being remodelled in order to protect the Rājāpur basin.

CHAPTER VII.

NATURAL CALAMITIES.

EARTHQUAKE shocks are felt occasionally, but as a rule do little damage. The severest shock in the memory of the present generation occurred on the 12th June 1897. It damaged many of the masonry buildings in Howrah town and brought down a number of the weakest. There are also records of earthquakes damaging houses in Howrah town in 1737, 1812 and 1857. **EARTHQUAKES.**

Howrah does not lie on the usual track of cyclones coming up from the Bay of Bengal, but occasionally it is visited by them. The earliest of which there appears to be any record occurred in 1737 at the same time as the earthquake mentioned above. An account published in *The Gentleman's Magazine* of 1738 runs as follows:—"On the 30th September last happened a furious hurricane in the Bay of Bengal, attended with a very heavy rain, which raised 15 inches of water in five hours, and a violent earthquake which threw down abundance of houses, and, as the storm reached 60 leagues up the river, it is computed that 20,000 ships, barks, sloops, boats, canoes, etc., have been cast away. A prodigious quantity of cattle of all sorts, a great many tigers and several rhinoceroses were drowned: even a great many caymans were stifled by the furious agitation of the waters, and an innumerable quantity of birds were beat down into the river by the storm. Two English ships of 500 tons were thrown into a village about 200 fathoms from the bed of the river Ganges, broke to pieces, and all the people drowned pell-mell amongst the inhabitants and cattle. Barks of 60 tons were blown two leagues up the land over the tops of high trees. The water rose, in all, 40 feet higher than usual. The English ships which drove ashore and broke to pieces were the *Decker*, *Devonshire* and *Newcastle*, and the *Pelham* is missing. A French ship was drove on shore and bulged; after the wind and water abated they opened the hatches and took out several bales of merchandize, etc., but the man who was in the hold to sling the bales suddenly ceased working, nor by calling him could they get any reply, on which they sent down another but heard nothing of him, which very much added to their fear, so that for some time no one would venture down. At **CYCLONES.**

length, one more hardy than the rest went down and became silent and inactive as the two former to the astonishment of all. They then agreed by lights to look down into the hold, which had a great quantity of water in it, and to their great surprise they saw a huge alligator staring as expecting more prey. It had come in through a hole in the ship's side and it was with difficulty they killed it, when they found the three men in the creature's belly."*

Coming to more recent times there were severe cyclones in October 1832, May 1833, June 1842, October 1864 and November 1869, of which the worst was that of 1864. This cyclone burst on the 5th October and was of unprecedented violence. While the fury of the wind caused widespread destruction to houses and trees, the storm-wave brought up by the gale carried havoc for 8 miles inland. Only after its force was expended by being spread over a wide extent of country, and after it had reached as high up as Achipur within 20 miles of Calcutta, was the wave so far diminished as to be confined mainly within the river banks. In this district nearly 2,000 persons and 20,000 cattle were returned as killed or drowned; the Bishop's College presented, it is said, "a picture of desolation"; and the Botanic Garden was devastated. But by far the greatest harm done by the cyclone was the damage caused to the shipping in the river. On the 5th October there were 195 vessels within the limits of the Calcutta port. They withstood the force of the wind with success, but when to this, at about 1 P.M., was added the storm-wave, the force of which was still not entirely spent, one vessel after another broke from her moorings. As each ship was swept on, she fouled others in her course, and they, carrying others with them, and getting massed in hopeless confusion, were driven on the Sumatra Sand and along the Howrah shore from Sibpur to Ghusuri. There was no bridge, it must be remembered, between Calcutta and Howrah in 1864. Ten vessels were sunk in the river and 145 driven on shore. The P. & O. vessel *Bengal* and the P. & O. mail steamer *Nemesis* were landed high and dry on the bank at Bishop's College, and the *Great Tasmania*, which, with over 2,000 tons register, was the largest sailing ship in the port, went aground on Ghusuri Sands.†

FAMINES.

The district is largely dependent for its food-supply on imports, especially imports of rice, so that it is closely affected

* See also *A Short History of Old Fort William in Bengal*, by C. R. Wilson, *Bengal, Past and Present*, Vol. I, pp. 44, 45.

† C. E. Buckland, *Bengal under the Lieutenant-Governors*, Vol. I, pp. 2983-02. A full and interesting account is also given in *Bengal, Past and Present*, October 1907, pp. 112-122.

by famine or scarcity in the great rice-growing and exporting tracts of India. The people are consequently liable to feel the pinch caused by high prices in famine years, but local famine is unknown. The supply of water from different sources is so ample, that the crops are immune from failure due to drought, and though they often suffer from floods, the people are comparatively so well-off that beyond making small *takāvi* loans no special measures of relief are found necessary. In fact, since the great Bengal famine of 1770, no famine, except possibly a famine in 1788, has visited this district, a fact which is eloquent testimony to its wealth and the facility with which it obtains its supplies.

Famine of 1866.

Relief measures were, it is true, taken in 1866, though there was no famine in the district, because a considerable number of paupers flocked into it from other districts. Assistance was given from local sources till August, when, in consequence of its becoming necessary to stop the influx of paupers into Calcutta from Howrah, public relief had to be given at Uluberiā. That place is situated on the high road from Orissa and Midnapore, where the famine raged and large numbers of poor starving creatures flocked to it trying to reach Calcutta. Many could go no farther, and the scenes of misery were very painful. In July a private gentleman, Mr. Sykes, organized a special fund for Uluberiā, and established a feeding depôt there, of which Government subsequently took charge. A pauper camp was established at Howrah, and a relief centre was formed at Nārit in the Uluberiā subdivision. Pauper hospitals were also established at each of the three relief centres. As regards the mortality, the Famine Commissioners reported:—"Many must have died on the part of the Midnapore and Uluberiā road which lies in the district, but of these no record was kept. Among the paupers, however, who reached the kitchens first established and the relief centres which replaced them, including the whole period from June to the end of December 1866, the number of deaths reported was about 1,235. At the Howrah relief centre, the majority were weavers from Jahānābād and its neighbourhood. At Uluberiā the persons relieved came chiefly from the districts of Cuttack, Balasore and Midnapore. At the Nārit centre, the applicants for relief consisted, for the most part, of persons of the poorest classes in Howrah district."

FLOODS

Though immune from famine, the district is peculiarly subject to floods. Floods occur every year in the three great rivers, and most of the adjoining country has to be protected by embankments.

The most destructive inundations occur when the rivers rise very high owing to excessive rainfall, and being met by high tides are unable to discharge their water quickly. Such floods have occurred in 1787, 1823, 1833, 1844, 1845, 1864, 1885, 1900 and 1905. In October 1823 the banks of the Dāmodar gave way, and the following description has been left:—"Howrah and Sulkeah and all the adjacent country is completely under water. On the main road at Howrah there stand two and three feet of water, and all the space between that and the other side of the Benares road is one expanse of water."* The tide also rose very high, for it was stated—"The tide of Wednesday, the 2nd instant, noticed in our last as having overflowed the platform of the Custom House Jetty, was the highest that has taken place."† Further inland the thāna buildings at Uluberiā and Bāgnān were either completely swept away or destroyed; and it was reported—"The extent of injury that has been sustained is beyond human belief."

In May 1833, a cyclone, accompanied by a storm-wave and followed by floods, devastated Mandalghāt and the southern *parganas*. The Rūpnārāyan and Dāmodar rose eight feet above the ordinary level of the spring tides; almost every embankment was swept away, and the greater part of the country was covered with salt water. In August 1834 the Mandálghāt *pargana* between the rivers Rūpnārāyan and Dāmodar was again under water, and the flood was followed by a somewhat severe drought. The next serious flood was in August 1844, when the Dāmodar burst its banks and *bāndhs* in 170 places, and submerged the whole country between Bally and Dhaniākhāli. Next year, in September 1845, there was a similar state of affairs in Mandalghāt and the south of the district, where not a stalk of paddy was to be seen after the floods for many square miles. This flood was also followed by drought, and not a drop of rain fell between the end of August and the second week in October.‡

Floods of 1885. Coming to more recent times, one of the most disastrous floods on record occurred in August 1885. The rainfall in that month was exceptionally heavy, no less than 27·67 inches being registered at Uluberiā. The rivers were everywhere in high flood, and unfortunately high tides also came up from the Bay of Bengal. The embankments were breached at Meluk

---

* *Selections from the Calcutta Gazette*, Vol. V, pp. 558-9.

† Ditto, p. 560. This great flood is the subject of several Bengali doggerel rhymes.

‡ G. Toynbee, *Sketch of the Administration of the Hooghly District* (1888), pp. 141-43.

on the left bank of the Rūpnārāyan, and at Tholyā on the right bank of the Dāmodar, where the flood rushed through in a stream 100 yards wide and 11 feet deep, inundating the country to a depth of 10 feet. The whole of the tract between the Dāmodar and Rūpnārāyan from the Uluberiā Canal northwards and eastwards as far as the Saraswatī river was inundated: in fact, the only portions that escaped were that south of the canal and the north-east corner round Howrah town. Roughly speaking, the inundation extended over 353 square miles. No lives were lost, as the villages are generally above flood-level and the people are well provided with light boats. The destruction of houses was, however, very great, over 10,000 falling or being rendered uninhabitable. The damage done to the standing crops was still more disastrous, the rice on 294,000 *bighās* being destroyed, besides sugarcane (5,900), jute (8,900), vegetables (7,450) and betel or *pān* (1,224 *bighās*.) Young fruit trees were also much injured, and another important item of damage was the loss of fish, which escaped from the tanks. The betel growers suffered especially, as the grass sheds, in which this plant is cultivated, involve a considerable outlay of capital, all of which was sacrificed. Near Tholyā, the place where the Dāmodar embankment was breached, much land was rendered sterile by a deposit of sand. The total damage, so far as it could be estimated in money, was returned by the District Officer at 30 lakhs of rupees. It was not found necessary, however, to establish relief works or to make remissions of revenue. It is noteworthy that the district was able to tide over such a calamity without any assistance from Government and little from private charity.

Floods of 1900.

The most serious floods during the present century have been those of 1900, 1904, and 1905. In 1900 there was heavy and incessant rain from the 19th to the 24th September, there being an abnormal fall of 24·18 inches at Howrah in 48 hours (20th and 21st September). All the low-lying tracts were submerged; a large number of cattle were drowned and hundreds of houses destroyed; while the crop on an area of 150 square miles, containing all the best rice lands, was totally destroyed. No distress requiring Government relief came to notice, such temporary assistance as was required being rendered by local funds and private subscriptions. These floods caused much inconvenience and discomfort in Howrah city. On the 20th September the water stood 3 feet above the Grand Trunk Road and the neighbouring streets in the city, the gasworks were badly flooded, and no gas could be supplied for upwards of three weeks.

Floods of 1904.

There were again floods in August 1904 owing to the rise of the Hooghly, which breached the embankment on the right bank of the river south of Uluberiā. The area affected included 41 villages in thāna Uluberiā with 8,000 acres under rice, which was practically all destroyed. The damage to house property, however, was insignificant; no lives were lost, nor were any cattle drowned. Seven villages north of the canal in the Bāuriā outpost also suffered, but the damage was less than in the south of the thāna and the crops were only partially destroyed. These floods were attributed to the breaches in the embankment along the Hooghly, which had been neglected for some years by the zamīndārs responsible for its maintenance and repair.

Floods of 1905.

In 1905 a considerable area was submerged owing to heavy rainfall at the end of July. The fall on the 27th and 28th in the Rājāpur basin, which has a catchment area of 227 square miles, was 17·47 inches, and water also poured in from the Amtā basin on the west with an area of 112 square miles, as well as from the Madāriā and upland basins on the north with an area of 76 square miles. The basin was consequently under water, and the crops on the lower lands were lost, as the channel could not drain off the accumulated mass of water in less than 26 days. The Hooghly river also rose high, and, breaching the zamīndāri embankment on the right side, seriously damaged the crops beyond Uluberiā.

CHAPTER VIII.

RENTS, WAGES AND PRICES.

THE cultivators of Howrah nearly all pay cash rents, and very rarely pay rents in kind, *i.e.*, make over to the landlord a certain proportion of the produce of their fields as rental. Such rents are confined almost exclusively to the *nij-jot* lands of the landlords and to lands recently brought under cultivation by reclamation from swamp. Occasionally also they are paid for land sublet by a ryot to another cultivator. Under this system, the cultivator tills the land at his own cost, reaps the crop in the presence of the landlord's agent and carries it to the threshing floor, where the paddy and straw are divided in equal shares. The system of produce rents met with elsewhere, under which a fixed quantity of paddy is made over to the landlord, whatever may be the actual outturn, is almost unknown in this district. When orchards and fishing rights are leased out, the rent is frequently paid partly in cash and partly in kind, *i.e.*, the lessee pays his rental by making over to the lessor a certain quantity of fruit or fish. **RENTS.** Produce rents.

Reliable statistics showing the rates of rent prevalent are not available, as settlement operations have not yet been extended to the district. It is known that the rates are high and that they are gradually becoming higher owing to the increase in the agricultural population and the growing competition for land. The following table shows the difference in the average annual rents paid per *bighā* for various classes of lands in the Howrah subdivision between 1873 and 1903 :— Cash rents.

	1873.		1903.
	Rs.	A.	Rs.
1. High land bearing autumn rice with a second crop.	12	0	16
2. Low land bearing winter rice (1st quality) ...	9	0	13
Do. (2nd quality) ...	7	8	
3. Jute land	7	8	22

The increase in the rent of lands growing special crops is remarkable, especially in the case of jute land, where it amounts to 300 per cent. Sugarcane lands are assessed to a rent of about

Rs. 26 a *bighā*; and for low lands reclaimed by means of drainage channels, and producing a crop of coarse winter paddy, the rate of rent is Rs. 3 to Rs. 5 per *bighā*, a rate higher than that for ordinary lands in many other districts. Rents in the Uluberiā subdivision range somewhat lower than in the Howrah subdivision.

WAGES. Wages both for skilled and unskilled labour are fairly high. The wages in mills and other factories are higher than those paid outside, and the ever-increasing demand for skilled labour causes a steady rise. In 1908, the lowest wages per mensem paid in factories were as follows, the variations depending on the class of labour required, *e.g.*, whether for dockyards, iron works or engineering workshops:—blacksmiths, Rs. 12 to Rs. 20; fitters, Rs. 10 to Rs. 27; carpenters, Rs. 12 to Rs. 17; engine drivers, Rs. 14-8 to Rs. 20; boilermen, Rs. 14 to Rs. 16; masons and bricklayers, Rs. 12 to Rs. 15. In jute and cotton mills, the lowest wages were:—weavers, Rs. 12 to Rs. 14; spinners, Rs. 10-8 to Rs. 13; dyers, Rs. 9 to Rs. 11. For unskilled labour, the lowest rate was:—coolies and porters, Rs. 7 to Rs. 9 for a man and Rs. 6 for a woman; *darwāns* and messengers, Rs. 8 to Rs. 10; *jamādār darwāns*, Rs. 13 to Rs. 18.

During the 15 years 1893 to 1908, daily wages have risen in the town very considerably, viz., for a common mason from 4 annas to 8 annas; for a common carpenter from 8 annas to 10 annas; for a common blacksmith from 6 annas to 10 annas; and for a common cooly from 4 annas to 5 and 5½ annas. The exceptional rise in the wages of masons is due to the large increase in the number of buildings creating a special demand for these artisans. It is not easy to get local servants, and consequently domestic work is usually done by immigrants from Bānkurā and Midnapore or from Orissa and up-country districts. Servants are generally paid in the towns at the rate of Rs. 4 per mensem for a male, and Rs. 3 for a female, besides food and clothing; if paid in cash only (*tolā*), the monthly wages are Rs. 8 for a male and Rs. 5 to Rs. 6 for a maid servant. The salary of a cook is higher, viz., Rs. 7 to Rs. 8 besides food and clothing. In the rural tracts menial servants are paid either in cash, at a somewhat lower rate than in the towns, or hold service lands, in which case their masters only give them their food. The village artisans used to be paid in kind at harvest time, but this custom is dying out. Watchmen are paid by ryots in kind, after harvesting, for assisting in watching the crops, and usually hold some land from the landlord in return for their services in respect of *tāgādā*, *i.e.*, calling on ryots to pay their rents.

It is a general practice for landlords and well-to-do husbandmen, *i.e.*, ryots holding five acres or more, to engage farm servants to assist in the various agricultural operations. These farm-hands, if employed permanently, are called *krishāns* (*i.e.*, cultivators from *krisha*, to cultivate) and are paid monthly. If employed temporarily, they are known as *majurs* (*i.e.*, labourers, from *majuri*, daily wage) and are paid daily. They generally hold no land or only a small quantity, and belong to the lowest classes, such as Kaibarttas, Bāgdis, Bauris, Pods and low class Musalmāns. Able-bodied *krishāns* get a monthly wage of Rs. 10 to Rs. 12, or Rs. 3 to Rs. 5 with food and clothing. The *majurs* are paid daily at the rate of 4 to 5 annas, besides a light midday meal of parched rice and tobacco, or one pice extra in lieu thereof. So many of these adult labourers now find employment in factories and other industrial works in the towns, that during harvest time complaints are frequently made of shortage of labour.

PRICES.

A marked feature in the recent economic history of the district is the steady rise in the price of food-grains. Common rice, the staple crop of the district, was sold at Howrah in March 1893 at 11 seers per rupee, and in March 1908 at 7¼ seers, a rise of over 50 per cent. in 15 years. In 1860 and 1870 the rates were reported at 36 and 31 seers respectively per rupee. Similarly the price of gram, the cheapest of the pulses, rose from 16 seers in March 1893 to 9 seers in the corresponding month of 1908, or by nearly 100 per cent.; and that of another pulse, *arhar*, from 11¾ seers in 1903 to 8 seers in 1908, or by nearly 50 per cent. within five years. The price of other articles of food has also been steadily rising. Milk, for instance, now sells at 5 seers per rupee as compared with 7 seers 20 years ago, and in the same period, the price of common fish has risen from 4 to 6 annas, and of carp from 5 to 7 or 8 annas per seer. *Ghi* (clarified butter), mustard oil and potatoes, which are used by all but the poorest classes, are also very much dearer, as may be gathered from the marginal statement

	1893.			1906 (January).		
	Rs.	A.	P.	Rs.	A.	P.
Ghi	30	0	0	35	0	0
Mustard oil	13	14	0	17	8	0
Potatoes	2	8	0	3	4	3

showing the wholesale prices per maund in the adjoining market of Calcutta. Nor is the rise confined to articles of food. It is also noticeable in the case of coal, kerosene oil, tobacco, one of the few luxuries of the ryot, and grey shirtings or cloths. In the case of bricks and bamboos, again the wholesale prices in Calcutta rose from Rs. 9 (per thousand) and Rs. 12 (per hundred) in 1893 to Rs. 12-9 and Rs. 20 to Rs. 25 respectively in January 1906.

Salt, sugar and tea are notable exceptions. Salt was sold at Howrah in 1893 at 10½ seers per rupee, and in March 1908 at 20 seers per rupee. This large decrease is due partly to the fall in the price of imported salt, but chiefly to the reduction of duty from Rs. 2-8 to Re. 1 per maund. The price of tea has fallen a little, and that of sugar and molasses considerably, owing to large imports from Java and Mauritius.

MATERIAL CONDITION OF THE PEOPLE. In the rural tracts the zamīndārs are mostly absentees living in Calcutta or other towns. Their estates are usually let out in *patni tāluks*, *i.e.*, the lessees are permitted, on payment of a large sum as a premium (*salāmi*), to hold the tenure at an annual rent fixed in perpetuity, the rental often largely exceeding the Government revenue. These *patnidārs* in their turn have in many instances sublet on nearly similar conditions. The result is a system of subinfeudation, which has many disadvantages. The landlords are converted into mere rent-receivers and with a few honorable exceptions take little or no personal interest in the land and its cultivators. Agricultural improvements are rarely executed; and existing works, like embankments, are more or less in bad repair. There are also a number of petty revenue-free-holders scattered throughout the district, who have mostly leased out all their lands, except the homestead, to ryots with or without *salāmi*, and are in much the same position as the proprietors of larger estates. Both classes are practically annuitants living on small fixed incomes, often harassed by family disputes and involved in debt.

Professional classes. Those engaged in professional pursuits, such as teachers, members of the legal profession, doctors, compounders, and engineers, are comparatively few in number in spite of the proximity of Calcutta. The dearth of qualified medical men is particularly felt in rural areas. Members of the priestly class have usually a few acres of *brahmottar* land, *i.e.*, revenue-free lands granted to Brāhmans; and they eke out their income from it by the gifts and offerings with which Hindus remunerate the services they render at times of festivals, either in the temples or in private households, and at domestic ceremonies, such as marriages in families of the higher castes. The value and number of such gifts and offerings are decreasing, and the poorest of the priests are now obliged to serve as cooks, peons and collecting *sarkārs*.

Trading classes. The trading classes as a body are thriving owing to the larger demand for necessaries of life and luxuries among the general population, and also to the development of communications, which has made it easier and cheaper to bring goods from Calcutta and Howrah. Grocers and petty shopkeepers are numerous in the mofussil, and add to their profits by judicious usury, advancing paddy or money to the ryots in the slack season and being repaid after harvest with 25 per cent. interest. They also make a profit of 2 to 4 annas in the rupee from paddy-husking. They advance paddy to the ryots, whose women-folk husk it, and then the husked rice is sold in the market by the ryot, who repays the *mahājan*. To this practice is due the large number of paddy-huskers, almost exclusively women, shown in the census returns. The Mārwāris have cloth shops in some of the important villages; Kābulis hawk about cloths and other miscellaneous goods; and near the towns up-country men have set up grocers' shops. The number of the latter is relatively small in the mofussil, where the bulk of the trade is in the hands of local men.

Of late years the condition of the cultivators has improved owing both to the rise in the price of rice and jute, the staple crops of the district, and of such subsidiary crops as pulses, sugarcane and vegetables, and also to the increase in the cultivated area caused by the drainage schemes. On the other hand, the cost of production has also increased because of the higher price they have to pay for bullocks, straw and grass, the higher wages obtained by labourers, and in many instances the enhanced rents imposed by landlords; while the new lands brought under cultivation, being mostly less fertile, give a smaller yield. Nevertheless, their profits have so largely increased, that the cultivators are much better off than they were 30 years ago or than the ryots of many other districts in the Province, such as those of Bihār and Orissa. Cultivators.

The bulk of the tenants are Kaibarttas, "who are," as Mr. Ritchie remarked 20 years ago, "beyond comparison, the best cultivators and the most industrious and thrifty class in this district." They usually keep a fair quantity of their produce at home, and the women help by paddy husking. They catch fish almost for nothing in the pools, *khāls* and rice-fields; and they supplement their daily food, or add to their savings, by getting vegetables and pot herbs from the fields or homestead nurseries, and by growing fruit like plantains, mangoes and pine-apples in their orchards. They can afford a number of silver ornaments and brass utensils, their houses are substantially built, and two meals a day are general. As a class, they are but little indebted to the *mahājans*, while their poorer brethren can get loans from the more well-to-do at a lower rate of interest than the *mahājan* will allow. In slack seasons they can earn good wages by working in the towns and factories. No relief operations have been necessary since 1866, when most of the persons relieved were paupers from other districts; and emigration to other districts is uncommon. These facts go to prove that the cultivators have generally something to fall back upon in times of distress and find sufficient employment in their own district or in Calcutta. On the other hand, there is a reverse to this somewhat bright picture in the sickness which prevails in certain thânas during the greater part of the year and the loss it necessarily entails.

Artisans. Among artisans, those whose handicrafts have had to face foreign competition, such as cotton-weavers, are going down in the world. A few of them have had recourse to cotton or jute mills, but the majority have taken to cultivation; and as new-comers they have had to be content with the poorer lands of the village. The *Swadeshī* movement, started in 1905, has however, led to an increased demand for cloths made locally in hand-looms, and the prospects of the cotton-weavers have consequently improved. They are now selling cloths as fast as they can make them; and with the introduction in several villages of improved Serampore looms, which ensure a better outturn, the weavers are generally able to earn enough to maintain their families.

Village potters, carpenters and blacksmiths are said to be little or no better off than they were half a century ago. Money wages have replaced the old system of payment in kind, and have risen in amount, but it is open to question whether they have increased proportionately to the rise in prices. On the other hand, with an increased population and a larger area under cultivation, more orders are received, and the services of the blacksmith or carpenter are more frequently required for work other than agricultural work. In slack seasons, moreover, they can migrate to the towns and secure good wages.

Labourers. The same changes have affected the ordinary agricultural labourer. Payments in kind have practically ceased, and he now receives his wages in cash. The field of labour has widened, and he has not only the chance of working in the cultivation of rice, the area of which has extended, of jute and sugarcane, but also in building and thatching houses, in fishing and boating. There are no signs that this class is increasing unduly, for though a number of weavers joined their ranks on the decline of weaving, this movement is dying out; while a large number are now employed in the numerous factories and other urban industries and thus prevent the supply exceeding the demand for field labour.

In the mills and factories most of the employés earn much higher wages than they could get at home. Many of them spend money freely on drink and women; but most live frugally, and send their savings home through their friends or by money orders. The number of the latter is very noticeable, no less than 34½ lakhs being sent out of the district in 1907-08. Some deposit money in the Savings Banks, but many more give out petty loans or set up betel-shops or groceries.

Less than one per cent. of the population are beggars or their dependents. This class includes religious mendicant, *fakīrs*, Vaishnavas and *sanyāsīs*, but consists more largely of old women, cripples, blind-persons and lepers. They suffer from the high price of food and the consequent gradual shrinking of the flow of private charity. **Beggars.**

CHAPTER IX.

OCCUPATIONS, MANUFACTURES AND TRADE.

OCCUPATIONS. THE statistics showing the occupations of the people obtained at the census of 1901 furnish ample proof of the industrial activity of the district. No less than 26 per cent. of the population are supported by various industries, this being the highest proportion in the Province. On the other hand, the percentage dependent on agriculture is the lowest in Bengal, viz., 42·3 per cent., the adjoining Hooghly district following *longo intervallo* with 52·8 per cent. Those supported by trade and professional pursuits represent 2·3 and 3·7 per cent. respectively of the population—proportions exceeded only in Hooghly, where conditions are similar, and, as regards the professional classes, in Purī, where there is an unusually large number of temple servants and pilgrim-recruiters.

Those classed as actual workers in agriculture numbered 98,012, including 2,362 rent-receivers, 82,556 rent-payers, 3,262 betel-leaf growers and 8,213 farm labourers. Among the commercial classes the actual workers numbered only 7,157, including 2,551 petty shopkeepers and their servants. The actual workers in the learned and artistic professions numbered 10,505, including 3,697 priests, 989 teachers, 1,657 writers, and 1,617 medical practitioners and midwives. In the numerous industries which flourish in the district the actual workers aggregated 101,535, including 17,215 rice-pounders, of whom no less than 16,956 were females, 3,011 operatives in cotton mills, 1,694 cotton weavers using hand-looms, and 17,733 operatives in jute mills. Among actual workers in other occupations may be mentioned railway employés (6,011), herdsmen (1,904), washermen (2,710), boatmen (4,612), general labourers (43,060), prostitutes (2,172) and beggars (3,797). The proportion of dependents varied considerably, being 27 per cent. among the agricultural population, 46 per cent. among the industrial, 37 per cent. among the commercial, and 33 per cent. among the professional classes. The difference is mainly due to the fact that a large number of those engaged in commerce and manufacture are immigrants who leave their families at home.

The industries of Howrah may be broadly divided into two classes, viz., (1) large industries in which machinery or steam power is used, and (2) hand industries or village handicrafts. The latter are of little economic importance, merely supplying local wants. The case is far otherwise with the large industries, for the Howrah side of the Hooghly is lined with factories employing over 70,000 hands. These include cotton mills, jute mills, jute presses, flour mills, engineering works and foundries, railway workshops, rope works, dockyards, etc., of which an account is given in the next chapter. MANUFACTURES.

In the rural tracts hand industries or village handicrafts are nearly all directly associated with the simple requirements of an agricultural life. The potter makes the villagers' earthenware utensils and the brazier their brass vessels; the carpenter fashions wooden or bamboo posts and rafters for their houses and makes their simple furniture; the weavers turn out coarse cotton cloths and the silversmiths crude silver ornaments; while the smith makes or repairs ploughshares, *dāos*, sickles and other iron utensils required for domestic or agricultural use. These artisans have little capital and few instruments, and generally work single-handed or with the help of their families. Little is made for export, but fishing is a fairly important industry. Hand industries.

Weaving was once an important industry in this district. As early as 1580, Bator was a local trade centre subsidiary to the great market of Sātgāon, which, according to Cesare Federici, who visited it in that year, was a place where merchants sold "cloth of Bombast of diverse sortes."* In 1758 the East India Company is said to have issued orders that weavers were to be encouraged to form settlements on this side of the Hooghly, so as to meet the demand for cloth for its trade.† The trade in hand-made cotton fabrics flourished in the 18th century, large exports being sent to England, but from 1800 onwards the heavy duties levied on Indian cotton cloths in England and subsequently the large imports of Lancashire machine-made piece-goods dealt a fatal blow to the industry. The latter were far cheaper, the lowest price of an ordinary hand-made *dhuti* or *sāri* being not less than Re. 1-8 to Rs. 2-8, and of a *chādar* from Re. 1 to Re. 1-8, whereas the imported machine-made *dhuti* or *sāri* cost 10 annas to Re. 1 and a *chādar* 8 annas to 12 annas. The cheaper cloths were naturally preferred, and with the decline in the demand for the produce of their looms, the weavers gradually took to other Weaving.

* Richard Hakluyt, *The Principal Navigations, etc.*, reprint, Vol. V, p. 411.
† *Howrah, Past and Present*, p. 19.

occupations in the villages, chiefly to cultivation, while in the towns a number found employment in the cotton mills started in Ghusuri and elsewhere.

The decline of the industry may be gathered from the statistics compiled during the census. Weaving is the hereditary occupation of two Hindu castes, Tāntis and Jugis, and of the Musalmān Jolāhās, though formerly it also gave employment to a few members of other castes, Kaibarttas, Pods, and a small number of other Musalmāns, especially in carding. The census of 1901 showed the number of males among the weaving classes as Jugis 2,065, Tāntis 7,790 and Jolāhās 4,570, in all 14,425; but the number of actual cotton weavers, both male and female, was only 1,694, as compared with 2,261 in 1891. The chief centres of cotton weaving were in thāna Dumjor, in thāna Jagatballabhpur, west of Kānā Nadī, and in thānas Amtā and Bāgnān. The village Nabosān in thāna Jagatballabhpur was particularly well-known for the fine cloth it produced. Since 1906 the *Swadesī* movement has helped to resuscitate hand-loom weaving. The weavers are now using the Serampore looms, with which a man can finish $2\frac{1}{2}$ to 3 yards per day as against $1\frac{1}{2}$ yard with the ordinary loom. The increased outturn obtained thereby is enabling the weavers to meet the growing demand for country-made cloths more fully, and to make larger profits.

The chief articles made for export are *dhutis* and *chādars*, plain or with coloured borders, *sārīs* for females, and *gāmchhās* or napkins, all of somewhat coarse yarn. Finer cloths are woven in thāna Dumjor, but in very small quantities. The chief centre of export is the *hāt* at Rāmkristapur in Howrah town, but cloths are also taken direct to Calcutta. No statistics are available as to the quantity exported. The general impression is that the number and value of exported cloths have increased considerably in the last two years.

Chikan work.

A few Muhammadan ladies in thānas Dumjor and Jagatballabhpur employ their spare time in *chikan* work (derived from the Persian *chikin*, meaning art embroidery), *i.e.*, embroidering handkerchiefs and fine muslin cloths, which are bought up by Calcutta dealers for export.

Silk spinning.

Silk rearing is a local industry which can be traced to the middle of the 18th century, when the cultivation of domesticated silkworms for the silk trade of the East India Company was carried on in parts of the district.* This cultivation was kept up in the palmy days of the Company's silk trade (1790 to 1835),

* *Some Account of Silk in India*, Geoghegan, I. page 2.

and, even after the withdrawal of the Company from the trade, until 1875. Since then it has been rapidly dying out and only a vestige of it now remains, most of those who engaged in it having taken to agriculture. According to Mr. N. G. Mukherji's *Monograph on the Silk Fabrics of Bengal* (1903) it is carried on by about 600 persons, who also follow other agricultural pursuits. The cocoons reared are mulberry silk cocoons, the mulberry tree being grown chiefly along the Dāmodar and Kānā Nadī. The rearers and spinners are scattered through thāna Jagatballabhpur and the Sānkrāil outpost in the Sadar subdivision and through all the thānas of Uluberiā; but it is only in the Jagatballabhpur thāna that cocoon-rearing and silk spinning are carried on to any considerable extent.* The work is carried on mostly by Kaibarttas, Bāgdis and low class Musalmāns. The Kaibarttas are known as Tutiā Kaibarttas (from *tut*, a mulberry), and a group of them is found at Jugeswar in thāna Jagatballabhpur (outpost Pānchlā). Silk is sold to the dealers, from whom the mulberry cultivators receive small advances. The silk produced in Jagatballabhpur thāna is largely exported to Phurphurā in thāna Krishnanagar in the Serampore subdivision, and that produced in other thānas to the silk filatures in Ghātāl subdivision of Midnapore and to Calcutta. It is estimated that about 500 *bighās* grow mulberry, and the value of the annual produce is roughly estimated at about Rs. 12,500.

Pottery making is a more important industry, the census of 1901 returning 1,650 persons as actual workers. During the dry months of the year, Kumhārs or village potters make earthenware vessels in the primitive manner handed down to them by past generations, and sell them in the local *hāts*. The earth in parts of the Sadar subdivision is believed to provide the best material, and the vessels made there are preferred, as likely to stand the fire better and to last longer, and are exported to Calcutta, Howrah and other towns. Among such vessels the cooking-vessels of Pātihāl in Jagatballabhpur thāna and the large jars of Sānkrāil have a local repute, and among painted earthen articles, the toys of Chandīpur, the masks, brackets, imitations of fruit, and pots made at Dumjor and Uluberiā are noticeable, yellow being the favourite colour used. Pottery.

Formerly a number of Musalmāns in thānas Amtā and Bāgnān found employment in the manufacture of brown country paper, but this trade is now dying owing to the competition of European and Indian machine-made products. This class of Minor industries.

---

* N. G. Mukherji, *Silk Fabrics of Bengal* (1903), pp. 4, 5.

Muhammadans (called *Kāghazi*) is still found at Mainān. Other minor industries are the manufacture of hookahs and cane work. The hookahs are made from the shells of local coconuts, which are carved and exported to Calcutta. Larger shells are imported from Ceylon and Singapore, and carved in thāna Dumjor, where they are sold for export at Begri Hāt. In Howrah town and its suburbs a number of Dom families turn out excellent cane-work, *e.g.*, baskets, chairs, cradles and fancy articles, which are said to be in no way inferior to the Chinese work of Bentinck Street, Calcutta. They find a ready sale in Calcutta, Howrah and elsewhere.

Fisheries. In a riparian district like Howrah fishing is naturally an important industry. Fish is eaten by almost all classes except the rigid Vaishnavas and widows belonging to the higher castes; and it is the main luxury the poor allow themselves in addition to rice. The industry gives employment to some 10,000 actual workers, the chief castes engaged being Jaliyā Kaibarttas, Tiyars, Bāgdis and Pods. Fishing takes place in the three rivers, their network of branches and *khāls,* in the numerous swamps, tanks and ponds, and towards the end of rains in the flooded rice-fields.

The fish commonly brought to market are (1) estuarine fish, such as *hilsā* (Clupea ilisha), *bhetki* (Lates calcarifer), *tapsi* or mango-fish (Polynemus paradiseus), *bele* (Eliotris and Gobiodes), *pānkāl* (Mastacembelus unicolor), *bhāngan* (Mugil tade), *kharānti* (Pagrus spinifer); (2) fresh-water fish found in running water or tanks, including representatives of the carp family, *e.g.*, *rui* (Labeo rohita), *kātlā* (Catla Buchanani), *mirgel* (Cirrhina mrigal), *bātā* (Labeo bata), *chital* (Notopterus chitala), *saral punti* (Barbus sarana), *vāchā* (Eutropiichthys vacha), *pābdā* (Callichrous pabda), *tengrā* (Macrones tengara), and *ār* (M. aor); (3) fresh-water fish found in stagnant muddy water, such as *koi* (Anabas scandens) *māgur* (Clarius magur), *singi* (Saccobranchus fossilis), *sol* (Ophiocephalus striatus), *letā* (O. gachua); and (4) small fish found in *jhils* and rice fields, such as *mauralā* (Aspidoparea morar), *punti* (Barbus punti), *khalse* (Trichogaster chuna), *chelā* (Chela phulo). Besides these several species of estuarine crustacea are caught, viz., shrimps, prawns and crabs.*

Fishing apparatus. In the rivers, especially the Hooghly, fish are caught with nets worked from boats. In the upper reaches the boats used are generally *dingis*, managed by two to five men and 25 feet by 4 feet in size, with a capacity of 10 to 15 maunds. Lower down,

* Most of the information here given is derived from Mr. K. G. Gupta's *Report on Fisheries in Bengal*, 1908.

near Uluberiā, bigger boats are used of 100 to 500 maunds burthen. The largest of these visit Saugor regularly and are indeed the only fishing boats that venture out to sea. The nets commonly used are drag nets (*ber* or *bara jāl*), running to 150 feet or more in length. They are provided with floats and weights, and are dragged close to the bank. During the rains the fishermen substitute a labyrinth net (called *konī jāl*), *i.e.*, a drift net with a capacious purse and two net side walls, to one of which is attached a guiding net. The purse and side walls are kept in position by bamboo poles. Gill nets are used for catching *hilsā*, and purse nets (*suti jāl*) where the current is strong. The latter are shaped like a long funnel, the narrow end of which is secured by a string. The net is kept stretched by the current, and from time to time the fisherman comes round in his boat and clears out, through the narrow end, all the fish imprisoned in it.

In the shallower water of creeks and branch channels cast nets (*kheplā jāl*) are commonly used from dug-outs. The latter, which are merely the trunks of mango, palmyra or *sāl* trees scooped out, have a capacity of 3 to 10 maunds and are usually managed by one or two men. The cast net is either of cotton or hemp with small meshes, and has iron weights at the end. It is whirled over the head and then cast, when it falls to the bottom in a circle. In the rice fields and in sluggish channels dammed up with weirs, fixed engines are preferred. The apparatus commonly used is *ghunī*, a split bamboo trap with a double screen. In flowing streams dammed from bank to bank, a *tatur jāl*, *i.e.*, an enclosure of net or split bamboos, is placed in a passage left open in midstream. A screen or guide from this enclosure floats downstream and is kept in position by the current and by floats and weights. Fish in their upward journey creep along the screen to the enclosure, and then try to jump over it, and thus are caught in the nets hanging over its top. In muddy sloughs the *koi* fish is caught in the meshes of gill nets or by baited hooks. In tanks and ponds larger fish are usually caught by cast nets, and smaller fish by bamboo *ghunīs* set up near the bank in shallow waters.

Fish is generally brought dead to the market, except *koi*, *māgur*, etc., which are brought alive, as they can live for a long time on a little water. Small fish and shrimps are dried in the sun for 3 or 4 days and then go by the name of *suntki*. Fish are not salted or smoked in this district, and ice is not used for preserving.

The fish most in request are *hilsā* and mango-fish among the estuarine fish, and carp among fresh-water fish. *Hilsā* or Indian *Hilsā* and mango-fish.

shad comes up the Hooghly from the sea in enormous shoals. It begins its upward journey with the freshets and moves up the river till about the close of the rains, depositing spawn. During the spawning season, when the fish is rich and of good flavour, the river is crowded with fishing boats, and big hauls are made. Rājganj and Uluberiā are the chief centres of the trade, the fish being conveyed thence by boats to Calcutta and Howrah, and also partly by steamer from Rājganj and partly by the Bengal-Nāgpur Railway from Uluberiā. Uluberiā is also a centre of the trade in mango-fish, the river from that place to Diamond Harbour being its favourite haunt. It is caught with or without roe in great numbers from April to June and is exported to Calcutta in boats and partly by rail.

Carp. *Hilsā* and mango-fish are especially popular among Europeans; but among Indians carps take the first place, the *rui* (Sanskrit *rohita*) being considered the king of fresh-water fish. They abound in the rivers and bigger channels, and on account of the good prices they command, are eagerly sought after by the fishermen. They are also reared in private tanks and ponds. There is a general belief that they do not spawn in confined waters, and the eggs and spawn are therefore collected in the Hooghly from above Howrah and in the Dāmodar near Amtā, and hatched in shallow ponds. The fry thus reared, as well as fry taken direct from the rivers, are sold alive to tank-owners at Rs. 5 to Rs. 10 per 1,000. This business is most active towards the end of the rains, *i.e.*, from September to November. The small fry stocking the tanks are allowed to grow, usually for a year, after which they are taken out for private consumption or for sale. The *kātlā* is said to grow most rapidly, going up in weight to 2 or 3 seers in the second season, when they are worth about a rupee each in the Howrah markets.

TRADE. The great centre of trade is Howrah town, which for commercial purposes practically forms part of Calcutta. Bally, Dumjor, Mahiāri with Andul, Uluberiā and Amtā are important subsidiary markets. The trade of Howrah town is increasing yearly, but that of Bally, Uluberiā and Amtā has declined considerably. The opening of the Bengal-Nāgpur Railway has increased exports from Uluberiā, but has affected local daily sales. Similarly, Amtā, a place once noted for its trade in salt and coal, which were brought by the Dāmodar, has practically lost it now. It has still an export trade, however, in rice and straw, and an import trade in kerosene oil and piece-goods. In the jute season, Dumjor and Bargāchhiā have a considerable trade in raw jute, but the sales in Andul are declining.

Besides the daily markets, the various *hāts* or periodical markets have a brisk trade. Of these the Tuesday *hāt* at Rāmkristapur in Howrah town is the most important, being indeed the largest mart for hand-woven cloths in Western and Central Bengal. Numerous varieties and large quantities of these cloths are brought here from Howrah, Hooghly, Nadiā, Jessore, Midnapore and the 24-Parganas, and find a ready sale, chiefly among Calcutta dealers. In the Uluberiā *hāt*, too, a large number of cows and plough cattle are sold. In Dumjor thāna, Mahiāri is a centre of the rice trade, while in Begri Hāt coconuts and hookahs form a speciality. Traders and hucksters also do a brisk business during the various religious festivals, when fairs are held at Nārnā, Mākardah, Amtā and elsewhere. *Hāts.*

CHAPTER X.

FACTORY INDUSTRIES.

DEVELOPMENT OF LARGE INDUSTRIES.

"THERE is," wrote Mr. J. C. Marshman, C.S.I., in 1845, "little to notice in the villages of Seebpore, Howrah and Sulkea, the Southwark of Calcutta. The establishment of the Docks and a few manufactures, and of the Company's Salt Ware-houses, gives an air of life and activity to the place, but the number of European residents, though not inconsiderable, is by no means proportioned to the vast population and wealth of Calcutta, of which it constitutes a suburb. Southwark enjoyed greater distinction, as compared with the magnitude of London three or four centuries ago, than Howrah does in this age of expansion and improvement, when viewed in connection with the commercial importance of Calcutta. But London had a bridge, and Calcutta has none . . . Above Howrah is the village of Ghoosory, without anything to attract attention, but two or three manufactories and a little Hindu shrine on the banks of the river. The reach of the river from the point of Ghoosory to the village of Bali is singularly uninteresting, and offers no ancient associations or modern improvements to attract attention. While the opposite bank of the river, comprising Cossipore and Baranagore, presents a lively scene of manufacturing and engineering industry, and is gradually becoming studded with elegant villas, the right bank does not contain a single European or civilized residence. It has a wild and almost jungly appearance, which is diversified only by stacks of timber and brick or tile kilns quite unworthy of the approach to a great metropolis."*

During the time which has since elapsed, Howrah has become a busy centre of industrial life. The riparian strip along the Hooghly is now studded with tall chimneys, and even a casual observer cannot mistake the signs of manufacturing activity afforded by the mills and factories which line its bank from Bally to Uluberiā. In fact, besides a number of minor concerns, such as pug mills, oil and flour mills, soda-water manufactories, etc., worked by hand or by small engines, there are, according to the returns for 1908, no less than 56 factories in the district

* *Notes on the Right Bank of the Hooghly*, Calcutta Review, Vol. IV, 1845.

registered under the Indian Factories Act (XV of 1881 amended by Act XI of 1891); and in 1908 these factories employed 69,790 operatives, or 8 per cent. of the total population. The bulk of the factories are situated in Howrah town, only twelve being outside it, viz., one at Liluāh and the rest to the south between Mānikpur and Uluberiā. All are worked by steam, except the paint works at Goābandi (Sānkrāil), which are worked by an oil engine. Electricity is being slowly introduced. It forms a part of the motive power in the Howrah Iron Works of Messrs. Burn and Co., and is being used to drive fans, etc., in several other factories.

The first large industries worked by European capital and with European methods appear to have been started, towards the close of the 18th century, to meet the requirements of the ships visiting Calcutta, and consisted chiefly of dockyards and roperies. The deep stream then flowed along the northern part of the town, crossing to the Calcutta side below the present Armenian Ghāt, and on the right bank of the Hooghly from Ghusuri to Howrah extended a series of docks and rope works. These continued to be the principal industries during the first half of the 19th century, and in 1823 we find Bishop Heber remarking:—"Westward flows the Hooghly, covered with large ships and craft of all kinds, and offering on its farther bank the prospect of another considerable suburb, that of Howrah chiefly inhabited by shipbuilders, but with some pretty villas interspersed."* In 1845 the prosperity of the town of Howrah still depended chiefly on its dockyards and shipbuilding establishments; but extensive sugar factories had been erected on the south bank of the Bally *Khāl*, which, according to the contemporary writer above quoted, "give it a pleasing air of manufacturing activity. Indeed, no place for twenty miles above Calcutta exhibits so much bustle and animation." Soon after this the selection of Howrah for the terminus of the East Indian Railway, and the construction of the bridge over the Hooghly, gave an impetus to the industrial development of the riparian tract. Iron foundries and engineering works were erected, and they were followed by cotton mills, jute mills, and jute presses. More recently brick manufacture by means of pug mills has been spreading fast along the river bank.

DOCK-YARDS.

The following sketch of the history of the dockyards in Howrah is condensed from *Howrah, Past and Present* (published in 1872) by the late Mr. Chandra Nāth Banarji, Deputy Magistrate, Howrah. Docks are known to have been established at

* Bishop Heber's Journal (1828) Vol. I. p. 26.

Howrah as early as 1796, when a Mr. Bacon opened a dockyard in Sālkhiā, a frigate named the *Orpheus* being the first vessel hauled in for repairs. In 1800 James Mackenzie constructed another dock at Golābāri and next year opened a branch dock close by. These docks were formerly known as Mackenzie's Old Dock and New Dock. The "Patent Slip" was founded at Golābāri about 1810 by Mr. Beauchamp, and after working for 39 years, was sold to Tārak Nāth Parāmānik, who converted it into a dock in 1850, and called it the Caledonia Dock, under which name it still exists. George Walker also set up a dock in 1815 at Golābāri, which subsequently received the name of the Commercial Dock; while James Mackenzie established another ship-building yard in Sālkhiā in 1824. "In 1823 the opening out of the Strand Road in Calcutta, by the exertions of the Lottery Committee, caused the breaking up of the docks, which had been established in Clive Street. Consequently the ship-builders came over to Howrah, and by degrees set up docks there." The first of those so set up were known as the Lower, Upper and Middle Docks. The Lower Dock was first established by Blackmore, and the Upper and Middle Docks were opened two years later by Matthew Smith. They eventually became the property of a Joint Stock Company under the name of the Calcutta Docking Company. In 1826 there were eight shipwrights in Howrah with yards along the river-side between Sibpur and Ghusuri.

The building of docks appears to have received a fresh impetus about the year 1840. Ambrose and Co. set up a yard for building ships in 1840 in Sālkhiā, and at the same place Thomas Reeves built a dock, which went by his name. He retired in 1858, selling his property to the Peninsular and Oriental Steam Navigation Company. Hardly had the sale been effected, when MacNicol and Brown took a contract for working the dock, which was then named the Union Dock. The contract expired in 1869, when the Calcutta Docking Company stepped in. A man named Reid, in conjunction with Jay Gopāl Mallik, built the Hooghly dockyard in Sālkhiā in 1842, and carried on business under the name of Reid and Co.; while Bremner set up a dock in 1844 immediately above the Howrah Ghāt, but had to close it in a few years owing to the formation of a *char* in front of it. The Albion Dock in 1847 was established by Cochar, Roberts, Pītāmbar Mukharji and Gladstone in partnership; and the Ganges Steam Navigation Company built a mud dock in 1848 in Sālkhiā. The East India Dock was built at Sālkhiā in 1849 by Ramkinu Sarkār, Jay Nārāyan Sattra and Kālī Kumār Kundu, but owing to disputes among the partners had to be closed in 1865. "The plot of land on which the dock was situated was originally (in 1790) occupied by Gilmore & Co., for building ships. In 1836 Gilmore & Co., however, gave up ship-building, and from that date, till Kundu & Co. took up the land. it was a mere waste."

The above account may be supplemented from other sources. In the *Calcutta Gazette*, under date 25th April 1790, the news is given that a large vessel "drifted up the river opposite to Mr. White's shipwright at Sulkeah."* In the same year, under date 25th July, a notice appeared to the effect that "George Foreman & Co., have the pleasure of informing their employers and the public that their new dock at Sulkea will be ready to receive ships by the end of August. The dock is large enough to take in any ship of less than 42½ feet beam, and the sill and the blocks are so low, that there will be more than 13½ feet over them in the lowest springs in the year, and 20 or 21 feet in the highest."† Between 1811 and 1828, 27 vessels, with an aggregate tonnage of 9,322 tons, are said to have been built at Fort Gloster. A Government steamer, the *Burhampooter*, was launched from Howrah in 1827, and the *Forbes*, the first Calcutta steam tug, in 1828.‡ The *Falcon* was launched from the New Howrah Dock in 1829. This was a private steamer intended to serve as a tug for the port shipping, and as a practical test was sent next year to China towing an opium trader.§ Mr. Marshman in his *Notes on the Right Bank of the Hooghly* (1845) also refers, in mentioning the dockyards, to "the establishment created by Mr. Reeves, the ship-builder, a man of great enterprise, who has recently enlarged it so as to accommodate our magnificent steamers, the largest vessels which have ever come up to Calcutta."

In 1872 there were eight large docks along the river between Howrah and Ghusuri, besides small mud docks, but the number has since fallen off, the returns for 1908 shewing only four dockyards at work. Details of these docks are given in the following table :—

Name.	Locality.	No. of Operatives.
Port Commissioners' Dock	Howrah ...	559
British India Dock	Sālkhiā ...	670
Hooghly Docking Works	Golābāri ...	200
Caledonia Docks	Ditto ...	105

* *Selections*, Vol. III, pp. 226, 535.

† *Calcutta in the Olden Time*, Calcutta Review, Vol. XVIII, 1852, p. 282.

‡ Calcutta Review, Vol. XXV, p. 282.

§ W. H. Carey, *The Good Old Days of Honorable John Company*, Vol. II, pp. 21, 22, 116.

A large amount of dock work is also done in the foundries of Burn & Co., Ld., of John King & Co., Ld. at Telkalghāt, of Jessop & Co., Ld., at Howrah Bridge Road, and of Turner Morrison & Co. at the Shālimār works.

ROPERIES. The roperies of Howrah are probably even older than the dockyards. The map of Calcutta and its environs prepared from a survey made in 1792 and 1793 by A. Upjohn shows on the north and south of "Salkia Point" two lanes named "Rope Walk" evidently because there were roperies on them. Mr. Banarji also states that the earliest industrial concern at Ghusuri was "the rope walk and screw house supposed to have been established about a century ago by the Stalkarts."* Again, in the *Calcutta Gazette*, it is announced, under date 13th August 1801, that the *Dart* "had only a coir cable of 14 inch on the ground, manufactured at the Rope Walk of Messrs. Clarke and Co. at Gusseree, and rode two days with a nine inch stream cable, made at the same Rope Walk, of Ceylon coir."† The present Ghusuri Rope Works (if the same as those mentioned above) must be the oldest of the Howrah factories; while the Shālimār Rope Works, at Sibpur, are probably the same as those referred to as follows by Mr. C. N. Banarji. "Ahmuty & Co. rented this place (Shālimār) from the Ranee (Surnomayi of Murshidābād) and founded a ropery which is carried on still."‡ These two rope works employed 434 and 174 hands respectively in 1908, while the Ganges Rope Works at Rāmkristapur employed 205 hands.

IRON AND ENGINEERING WORKS. Iron works, which now form one of the most important industries of Howrah, can be traced to the beginning of the 19th century. The Albion Mills were erected before 1811 by William Jones, also known as Guru Jones, who came to India in 1800 as a mechanic but by 1810 had become a manufacturer for the East India Company. A portion of the land he acquired was bought by Matilāl Sīl, and leased to Apcar & Co., who set up engineering works there, when their original yard in Telkalghāt was destroyed by fire in 1849. These works are now known as the Albion Foundry. Bābu Kishorīlāl Mukharji also started iron works in Sibpur, which were removed a few years ago to Sālkhiā, where they are still working under the name of the Sibpur Iron Works. A number of other foundries were started about the middle of the 19th century in Howrah city,

* *Howrah, Past and Present*, p. 84.

† *Selections*, III, p. 288.

‡ *Howrah*, p. 80. It is advertised in Thacker's *Directory* as "established 1815."

and more especially in Telkalghāt. Mr. C. N. Banarji has given the following account of a curious relic of those early days. "The visitor to Howrah, if he goes towards our Strand Road, will observe a building in the shape of a tower, and, if he enquires, he will learn that it belongs to Burn & Co. of Calcutta, a firm of long standing. The tower was constructed in imitation of the tower of Babel of old by Mr. Gray, who opened a branch of Burn & Co., at Telkalghāt in 1846. If our enquirer steps inside the premises, he will see a number of different faces on the first building to the left. This, he will learn, was also built by Mr. Gray as the nucleus of the large engineering yard now in existence. Mr. Gray called this establishment the "Babel Foundry," from the fact of his employés speaking so many different languages." The following table shows the different iron-works, foundries and engineering works, with the average daily number of operatives employed in 1908:—

Name.	Locality.	No. of operatives.
1. Howrah Iron Works	Howrah ...	3,968
2. Victoria Engine Works	" ...	709
3. Howrah Foundry	" ...	660
4. British India Engineering Department ...	Sālkhiā ...	1,216
5. Sibpur Iron Works	" ...	110
6. Albion Foundry	Sibpur ...	110
7. Shālimār Workshop	" ...	400
8. Civil Engineering College	" ...	368
9. Ganges Engineering Works ...	" ...	252

Of these works the Howrah Iron Works of Messrs. Burn & Co., Ld., call for special mention. They have the advantage of a considerable length of river front for shipbuilding and for taking in and despatching goods, and are also well connected with the railway. The works may for convenience be divided into four sections, viz., (*a*) the foundry, turning, fitting and engine-shops; (*b*) the bridge and girder-shop; (*c*) the wagon-building yards; (*d*) the shipbuilding department. Besides these, there are also large store godowns for the storage not only of materials for construction, but also of goods which are sold by the Company as dealers. The shipbuilding department is necessarily on the river-front; the bridge-shop runs at right angles to the river-front right away back from the river to the public road on the Howrah side. It is a very large shop, 1,200 feet in length, and is fitted up in the most modern fashion for systematically turning out large quantities of work. It has overhead electric cranes, multiple electrically-driven drills and hydraulic and pneumatic rivetters. The wagon yards run parallel to the bridge-shop on the one side, and on the other side are the turning shops, fitting shops, foundry, etc. The whole works are conveniently fed by a system of rails running from the river-front.

Messrs. Jessop & Co.'s works are essentially bridge and roof works. There is one long bridge-shop which comes up to the river-front at one end and is supplied with electric overhead cranes, multiple drills, hydraulic rivetters, etc. There is also a foundry which used to belong to Ahmuty & Co., this section of the Company's work having been lately transferred from Calcutta.*

RAILWAY WORKSHOPS.

Both the East Indian and Bengal-Nāgpur Railways have their own engineering workshops, the former at Howrah and the latter at Shālimār, and also separate workshops for the repair and construction of rolling stock. The table below shows the different railway workshops and the average daily number of operatives employed in 1908:—

Name.	Locality.	No. of operatives.
E. I. R. Carriage and Wagon Department ...	Liluāh ...	5,097
E. I. R. Engineering Works	Howrah ...	319
Shālimār Loco. Engineering Workshop ...	Sibpur ...	205
Loco. and Carriage Workshop	Howrah ...	190

COTTON MILLS.

Cotton-spinning and the weaving of cloth in Howrah date back to the early days of British administration. As early as 1796 a Mr. Samuel Clark wrote from Ghusuri that he had been employed by the East India Company "for the past two years in receiving, packing and screwing *paut* and *sun* for England." Again, in July 1797 Mr. James Frieshard wrote to the Judge and Magistrate to ask him to excuse the attendance of "Cali Persad Lahory, who has charge of our cotton screws at Sulkeah, where we have just received 4,000 maunds from the Board of Trade with orders to begin upon it on Tuesday."† In 1817 Mr. Brightman and Mr. Hogue had cotton screws on the Hooghly, and about the same time, in 1817 or in 1822, the Bāuriā Cotton Mills started work, these being, it is said,

* E. R. Watson, *Monograph on Iron and Steel Work in Bengal*, 1907.

† G. Toynbee, *Sketch of the Administration of the Hooghly District* (1888) p. 92.

the oldest cotton mills in India. After Howrah was made the terminus of the railway, several other mills were erected, chiefly at Ghusuri and Sālkhiā, and we find mention made of cotton screws belonging to Mr. Robinson and a Parsi in Ghusuri, to Colvin Cowie & Co. and Rushton Brothers in Rāmkristapur, to Collin Fielman & Co. in Sibpur and at Sāntrāgāchhi. The following table shows the cotton mills at work in 1908 and the average daily number of employés; the Bhārat Abhyaday Cotton Mills were till recently known as the Ramdayāl Cotton Mills:—

Name.	Locality.	No. of operatives.
Bāuriā Cotton Mills (Old)	Bāuriā .	873
Bāuriā Cotton Mills (New)	,, ...	686
Ghusuri Cotton Mills	Ghusuri ...	2,495
Victoria Cotton Mills	,, ..	523
Bhārat Abhyaday Cotton Mills	,,	520
New Ring Mills	Phuleswar ...	628
Sālkhiā Cotton Ginning Factory ...	Sālkhiā ...	95

The export of jute to Europe, in loose fibres or in pressed bales, and its manufacture into yarns, bags and cloths have given rise to an industry of immense economic importance in this district. In fact, the jute mills are predominant among the industrial concerns conducted on European lines. The industry may be said to have been in its infancy 50 years ago, when a few jute presses were started to supply the export trade. Among these we find a jute press at Cullen Place, while Mr. Robinson, already referred to as the proprietor of a cotton mill, also owned jute and gunny screws. Later, other jute screws were set up by Mr. Hyde, and after him by Anstruther & Co. at the junction of Dobson's Lane with Rosemary Lane, by Collin Fielman & Co. in Sibpur and by Cowie & Co. near the old salt *golās* at Sibpur. JUTE MILLS AND PRESSES.

In the seventies a number of jute mills, organized on a large scale, were started, viz., the Fort Gloster Mills at Uluberiā being opened in 1873, the Howrah and Sibpur Mills in 1879 and the Ganges Mills at Sibpur in 1875. Still more mills began work in the nineties, the Central Mills at Ghusuri being started in 1890, the National Mills at Rājganj in 1896, and the adjoining Delta Mills at Mānikpur in 1899. In 1907 the Lawrence Mills were opened at Chakkāsi near Uluberiā, and a branch of the Baranagar Jute Mill at Bally on the site of the old Bally Paper Mills. A considerable number of jute presses have also sprung up, of which seven are large enough to be worked by steam.

The following table gives the salient statistics for the jute mil and presses now at work, from which it will be seen that the employ a labour force of over 46,000 men *

NAME.	Locality.	No. of operatives (1908).	No. of looms.	No. of spindles.	Year in which opened.	Value of first year's outturn.	Value of outturn in 1907.
Jute Mills.						Rs.	Rs.
1. Fort Gloster (New).	Uluberiā ..	4,260	900	18,856	1873	8,47,842 (1876)	94,41,968
2. Ditto (Old).	Ditto ...	2,829					
3. Ganges ...	Sibpur ...	3,762	568	11,946	1875	£119,786	£ 395,618
4. Sibpur (Old)	Do.	3,733	940	20,240	1874	22,50,000	(Not available).
5. Do. (New)	Do.	2,307					
6. Central ..	Ghusuri ...	3,650	560	10,568	1890	7,22,840	38,56,313
7. Howrah ...	Rāmkristapur ..	7,956	1,300	27,300	1874	22,50,000	96,00,000
8. National ...	Sānkrāil (Rājganj)	4,025	601	12,000	1896	10,21,663	46,61,713
9. Delta	Ditto (Mānikpur)	3,484	595	12,000	1899	6,83,843	42,65,438
10. Belvedere .	Ditto ..	3,160	...	...	...	.	...
11. New Bally ...	Bally	2,812	...	...	...	...	...
12. Lawrence ...	Bāuriā ...	2,355	400	8,400	1907	(Not available).	
Jute Presses.							
1. Imperial ...	Ghusuri .	102	...	...	...	...	...
2. Ghusuri ...	Ditto ...	55	...	...	..	...	..
3. Nasmyth ...	Ditto ...	550	...	.	...	...	...
4. Sālkhiā ...	Sālkhiā ...	380	...	...	...	...	...
5. Empress of India.	Ditto .	380	...	...	...	..	...
6. West Patent ...	Ditto ...	250	.	..	...	...	...
7. Howrah Hydraulic.	Howrah ...	431	...	..	..	..	..

FLOUR MILLS.

Flour mills appear to have been started in Howrah more than half a century ago. A part of William Jones' landin Sibpur was taken up by Ahmuty & Co., who erected on it a rum factory, biscuit bakery and flour mill. Aerated bread was made for a short time, but had to be given up on account of the heavy expenses incurred. This flour mill has survived to the present day. About the same time Jessop & Co. started the Phœnix Steam Flour Mills near the *kachhari* at Howrah, but

* The details given in the last five columns have been supplied by the courtesy of the Indian Jute Mills Association.

when the land was acquired for the East Indian Railway in 1849, the mills were removed to Sibpur. In 1859 Mr. W. L. Atkinson started another mill with a bakery at Sibpur, which was also sold to Ahmuty & Co. in 1866. At present there are four flour mills, viz., the Bengal Mill at Sibpur and the Howrah, Monarch and Fort William Mills at Rāmkristapur. These mills employed 571 persons daily on the average in 1908.

OIL MILLS.

Oil mills were also started in the first half of the 19th century. In 1830 Jessop & Co. opened a mustard oil mill by the river-side to the south of the *kachhari*, and from this mill the river-side got the name Telkalghāt, *i.e.*, the oil mill *ghāt*. Oil mills were also started in Sāntrāgāchhi, but were not successful. At present there is one large oil mill, the Howrah Oil Mill at Rāmkristapur, which is worked by steam and employed 59 hands daily in 1908, besides three smaller mills at Sālkhiā.

OTHER FACTORIES.

Among other factories the following may be mentioned: (1) the Salt Crushing Mills of Messrs. Balmer Lawrie & Co. at Sālkhiā; (2) the Sylhet Lime Works of Messrs. Kilburn & Co. on the river bank at Mānikpur; (3) the Bally Khāl Bone Mills at Bally; (4) the Paint Works at Goābandi (Goberiā Pānchpārā), Sānkrāil; (5) the Caledonian Steam Printing Works at Sālkhiā employing 415 hands daily in 1908. There are also large timber yards with saw mills in Sibpur and Sālkhiā; Messrs. Turner Morrison & Co. have established paint works at Shālimār; and *surki* mills are found in various parts of the town.

SUGAR FACTORIES AND DISTILLERIES.

Sugar factories and distilleries were set up in Howrah before the close of the 18th century. The original *kachhari* buildings at Howrah are said to have been built in 1767 for a rum distillery, but after a few years passed into the hands of Mr. Levett, after whom the premises were called "Levett's house and garden." In 1785 they were sold to the Military Orphan Society and converted into an orphanage and school.* An advertisement in the *Calcutta Gazette*, under date 10th June 1784, offered for sale "all the stock-in-trade and effects belonging to the estate of the late Tom Fatt Chinese at his distillery at Sulky" as well as the distillery itself.† In the forties of the 19th century we find mention of a large sugar-house and rum distillery on the site of the cotton mills in Ghusuri, south of which were another small rum distillery, owned by a German firm, Putz & Co., and another sugar mill and rum factory belonging to Mr. Robertson, besides the sugar factory built on William Jones' land by Scott & Co., which was

* *Howrah, Past and Present.*

† *Selections from Calcutta Gazette,* Vol. I, p. 45.

subsequently converted into a rum factory by Ahmuty & Co. The Albion Factory of Ahmuty & Co. has continued to the present day. For some years past the industry has not been flourishing, owing to foreign competition.

Rice trade. The rice trade has long been of importance in Howrah. Indeed, it was carried on to such an extent by one Sambhu Chandra Pāl, that the *ghāt* leading to his godowns was called Chelapati Ghāt, *i.e.*, the rice-quarter *ghāt*. The trade has now shifted to the Rāmkristapur *char*, lately reclaimed by the Port Commissioners. Rows of godowns lie along the river bank, stored with the rice of Western Bengal; while a number of rice-cleaning machines are at work in the season, producing clean white rice for export or for consumption in Calcutta. These machines are worked partly by steam, partly by hand, and are all managed by Indians. In this way, an industry has been developed during the twentieth century giving employment, in boating, cleaning, storing, carting, etc., to about two thousand hands.

Brick manufacture. The enormous demand for bricks in the metropolis and neighbouring towns has led to a large manufacture of bricks along the Bally *Khāl* and the river bank from Bally to Bāuriā. The apparatus used consists chiefly of Bull's patent pugmills and moulding machines worked partly by steam and partly by bullocks. In the working season, *i.e.*, November to May, a large number of coolies are employed, estimated at from three to five thousand daily. Barrackpore in thāna Bally is a centre of the tile making industry.

Supply of labour. A special enquiry regarding the adequacy of the supply of labour for mills, factories, etc., was carried out by Mr. B. Foley, I.C.S., in 1905. The enquiry extended to other districts, but its results are specially applicable to Howrah. They are given at length in Mr. Foley's *Report on Labour in Bengal* (1906), but may be briefly summarized as follows. It was found that, in spite of the large increase in the number of looms and operatives, and in spite of the absence of any recruiting agency, the jute mills obtained sufficient labour except for three months during the hot weather. The shortage was mostly felt by those mills which are dependent on up-country labour only, men from Bihār and the United Provinces insisting on going away between March 15th and June 15th. In the jute presses, however, no deficiency of labour was experienced. There the season is generally from July to March, the busiest time being between August and December, and there is practically no work during April, May and June. This industry, therefore, exactly suits the up-country men, who form the bulk of the hands, since they come down and work for nine months of the year and go home in the hot weather. As regards the other classes of factories Mr. Foley wrote:—"Cotton mills are in much the same position with regard to labour as jute mills, except that the deficiency in the hot weather months is not so marked. In the paper mills, potteries and iron works no shortage of labour is experienced; in small miscellaneous works there is either no shortage, or it is due to special causes; in engineering works there is no lack of unskilled labour. Lastly, railways have abundance of labour for construction works, but require more skilled workmen in their workshops."

As regards the *personnel* of the operatives, it is stated that twenty years ago all the hands in jute mills were Bengalis, but they have gradually been replaced by Hindustānis from the United Provinces and Bihār. In the jute presses most of the employés are also men from up-country, but the reverse is the case in the cotton mills. The work is cleaner, the machines run slower, and less physical exertion is called for than in jute mills. For these reasons, apparently, cotton would seem to be more popular with the Bengali and Oriyā than with the up-country man. As regards engineering works, iron works and railway workshops, where skilled labour is required, complaints are general both of the insufficiency of the number and the inefficiency of the work of the local artizans The enormous industrial expansion of Calcutta and its neighbourhood has created a demand for this kind of labour which the supply has failed to meet. This is especially the case with carpenters, and it is found necessary to employ a considerable number of Chinamen and Punjābī carpenters at high wages.

CONDITIONS OF FACTORY LIFE.

The general conclusion is that the vast majority of the factory operatives are immigrants, the nature of whose work has been well described in *The Report of the Indian Factory Labour Commission, 1908*—a description which is particularly applicable to the Howrah factories. "The habits of the Indian factory operatives are determined by the fact that he is primarily an agriculturist, or a labourer on the land. In almost all cases his hereditary occupation is agriculture; his home is in the village from which he comes, not in the city in which he labours; his wife and family ordinarily continue to live in that village; he regularly remits a portion of his wages there; and he returns there periodically to look after his affairs and to obtain rest after the strain of factory life. There is as yet practically no factory population, such as exists in European countries, consisting of a large number of operatives trained from their youth to one particular class of work, and dependent upon employment at that work for their livelihood. It follows that the Indian operative is, in general, independent of factory work to the extent that he does not rely exclusively upon factory employment in order to obtain a livelihood; at most seasons he can command a wage sufficient to keep him, probably on a somewhat lower scale of comfort, by accepting work on the land; and there are also numerous other avenues of employment, more remunerative than agricultural labour, which are open to every worker in any large industrial centre. If the operative is not merely a landless labourer, he will in general be bound by strong ties to the land and to the village from which he originally came; he can at any time abandon factory life in order to revert to agriculture; and the claims of the village, where he has a definite and accepted position, are in practice, as experience has shewn, sufficiently powerful to recall him from city life for a period which extends, on the average, to at least a month in each year. The Bombay operative, resident in the Konkan, probably returns to his village for one month each year; and the jute weaver of Bengal, working longer hours and earning higher wages, is not content with less than two or three months. Whenever factory life becomes irksome, the operative can return to his village; there is probably always work of some kind for him there if he wishes it; and in most cases he is secured against want by the joint-family system.

"The position of the operative has been greatly strengthened by the fact that the supply of factory labour undoubtedly is, and has been, inadequate; and there is, and has been, the keenest competition among employers to secure a full labour supply. These two main causes—the independence of the Indian labourer, owing to the fact that he possesses other and congenial means of earning a livelihood, and the deficient labour supply—govern the whole situation. . . . We have been impressed with the fact that employers are generally disposed to concede promptly all reasonable demands made by their workers; and, even where the demands made are unreasonable, to treat them as proposals which it is desirable to accede to, if possible. Great nervousness is frequently displayed by employers of labour as to the effect even of trivial changes on the workers; numerous expedients are adopted to conciliate them, and the attitude of the employers throughout appears to be based upon the knowledge that the operatives are in fact the masters of the situation.

"While the operatives fully understand the machinery of local strikes, and have repeatedly forced employers to comply with their demands in isolated cases, they are as yet unable to combine over any large area with the object of securing a common end by concerted action. One of the main difficulties experienced at present, when unrest appears among the workers, is in ascertaining the causes of that unrest. Frequently no definite demands are formulated, no grievances are stated, no indication is given as to the cause of the discontent; the operatives simply leave work in a body, or more commonly they drop off one by one without explanation, and accept employment under more congenial conditions in other factories."

It should be added, however, that there is reason to believe that in the last few years, where strikes have assumed any proportions, they have mostly been engineered by outsiders. Also, in this district the mill authorities are already forming the nucleus of a permanent labour force by building commodious settlements near the mill premises, ten of the factories having provided quarters for their operatives. Most of the mill hands in the other factories in and round Howrah live in the *bastis* of that town.

CHAPTER XI.

MEANS OF COMMUNICATION.

EARLY MEANS OF COMMUNICATION.

DURING the period preceding British rule roads in the modern sense of the word appear to have been unknown in the district. The earliest existing European map showing roads in Bengal, viz., that of Valentijn (published in 1726, but based on data gathered by Matheus Broucke, the Dutch Governor of Chinsura from 1658 to 1664) shows not a single road in this part of the delta. Nor is this to be wondered at, for, the country being intersected by rivers, creeks, and channels, the waterways then as now furnished a natural and easy means of transit. The river Hooghly formed the great highway of commerce. It was used by boats and small ships, and had on its banks several important *hāts* or markets, to which grain, cloth and other merchandise were brought by coolies or pack-bullocks from the neighbouring villages and by small boats from the interior. Here there is a network of channels, among which the Sarasswatī, the Kānā, the Dāmodar and the Rūpnārāyan served as tributaries to the Hooghly, while the smaller creeks were their sub-tributaries. In the rains, moreover, when the low lands are turned into wide sheets of water, the villagers moved from place to place in tiny skiffs (*sāltis*). On the cessation of the rains there was access from one village to another along the footpaths formed by the passage of men and cattle over the low ridges bounding the fields. Vehicular traffic was a luxury rather than a necessity. Horses were used chiefly by Muhammadans and up-country men. Ladies were borne in closed doolies, while men of position travelled in *sukhāsans*,* *i.e.*, long litters carried by Goālās, Bāgdis or Bāuris. The cultivators and others rarely left the neighbourhood of their villages, except to go to the nearest marts; and long

* *Ain-i-Akbari*, Garrett, II, 122. "This is a crescent-shaped litter covered with camlet or scarlet cloth and the like, the two sides of which have fastenings of various metals, and a pole supporting it is attached by means of iron hooks. It is conveniently adapted for sitting in, lying at full length, or sleeping during travel. As a protection against sun and rain they provide a commodious covering, which is removable at pleasure." *cf.* Thevenot, III, page 54, and Thomas Bowrey, pp. 86-7, where a rough sketch is given.

journeys were even rarer, being confined almost entirely to visits to the holy Ganges on festival days.

Several roads can be traced in the early days of British administration. Rennell's Atlas, Plate VII (A.D. 1779) shows Sālkhiā as a centre from which four roads radiated. One road ran along the river bank to Bally, Serampore and further north; a second passed *viâ* Aubinagar, Chanditalā and Dhaniākhāli to Burdwān; a third went due west to Mākardah and Rājāpur, and thence north-west to Rājbalhāt and Bārkurā; the fourth connected Sālkhiā with Tanna fort, and turned west to Sānkrāil and Amtā, where it bifurcated, one branch going to Ghātāl and Khīrpāi, and the other south-west to Midnapore. Besides these four, a road is shewn running from Uluberiā *viâ* Bāgnān and terminating at Mānkur on the Amtā-Midnapore road. A sixth road from the north joined Dhaniākhāli with Amtā and Bāgnān, and crossing the river Rūpnārāyan ended at Tamluk. No roads are found south of the Uluberiā-Bāgnān road, and all those shewn in the Atlas were apparently unmetalled fair-weather roads. EARLY ROADS.

By the middle of the nineteenth century a great change had been effected. There were four roads known as Imperial roads, *i.e.*, roads borne on the books of the Public Works Department and repaired by that Department, and a number of others, called local roads, under the control of the local officers. Of the Imperial roads the oldest was the Old Benāres Road, called Ahalyā Bāi's Road, because it was constructed at her cost about 1780 A.D., or the New Military Road, as it was the chief route for troops proceeding to Benāres and other stations in the Upper Provinces. Starting from Bāndā Ghāt in Sālkhiā the Benāres Road was a narrow *cutcha-pucka* road extending within the limits of this district as far as the Chariāl *Khāl*, which it crossed by a bridge of six arches. The road was flooded almost every year by the Dāmodar in Hooghly district, and by 1840 the troops had ceased to use it. The other two were the Grand Trunk Road, having a length of a little more than six miles in the Howrah district, and a branch from Sālkhiā to Bally *Khāl*, both metalled throughout. The Grand Trunk Road, which starting from Sibpur joined the main branch at Ghireti near Chandernagore, was begun in 1804, and completed during the administration of Lord William Bentinck. In addition to these roads, the Public Works Department maintained the wide but then unmetalled Orissa Trunk Road from Uluberiā to the bank of the Rūpnārāyan; this section of the road was begun in 1825 and completed by 1829.

Besides Imperial and Municipal roads there were six local roads, viz., (1) from Howrah to Jagatballabhpur (16 miles),

(2) from Jagatballabhpur to Amtā (9 miles), (3) from Sibpur to Mahiāri (8 miles), (4) from Mahiāri to Dumjor (4 miles), (5) from Dumjor to Jagdīspur (6 miles), and (6) from Sālkhiā to Chandītalā (10 miles). All these roads were unmetalled but bridged.

MODERN ROADS. At present the district is well provided with means of communication, being traversed by railways, roads, rivers and canals. The roads are maintained by three authorities, the Public Works Department, the District Board and the Municipalities.

Provincial roads. Three important roads are kept up by the Public Works Department, (1) the Grand Trunk Road from Sibpur to Bally (6 miles), passing through the two Municipalities of Howrah and Bally; (2) the Howrah Foreshore Road running parallel to the right bank of the Hooghly from Elliot Bridge to the Royal Botanic Garden (1 mile); (3) the Orissa Trunk Road from Uluberiā to the left bank of the Rūpnārāyan river (20 miles). All these roads are metalled throughout. The Grand Trunk Road still continues to be the most thronged with traffic; but the opening of the Bengal-Nāgpur Railway has diverted it from the Orissa Trunk Road, whose former glory as a noble highway now survives only in a number of splendid banyan trees.

District roads. All other roads outside municipal areas are kept up by the District Board. In 1907-08, this body had under its charge 40·8 miles of metalled roads, 110·6 miles of unmetalled roads, and 400 miles of village tracks. The more important roads are metalled, at least in some portions, and the metalled surface, which is generally of stone, occupies 8 feet out of a width of 20 feet, or 7½ feet where the width is less. The more important metalled roads are (1) the Old Benāres Road, from Howrah to Jagdīspur, 5 miles 3 furlongs; (2) Howrah to Jagatballabhpur, 15 miles 6 furlongs, of which the first 8 miles are metalled; (3) Dumjor to Bāuriā station, 13 miles 7 furlongs, of which the last mile only is metalled; (4) Dumjor to Jagdīspur, 4 miles 4 furlongs; (5) Dumjor to Mahiāri, 3 miles, of which the first half is metalled; (6) Mahiāri to Mākardah, 1 mile 7 furlongs; (7) Mahiāri to Sāntrāgāchhi, 4 miles 4 furlongs, of which the last mile only is metalled; (8) Mahiāri to Kundu Road, 5 miles 4 furlongs; (9) Andul to Ekabbarpur, 8 miles, of which the first two miles are metalled; (10) Andul to Rājganj, 2 miles.

There are also a few short lengths of metalled road, viz., (1) Thāna Makwā to Goberiā, 1 mile 2 furlongs; (2) Mākardah to Begri, 2 miles 4 furlongs; (3) Uluberiā town to the railway station, 1 furlong; (4) Liluāh station to the Old Benāres Road, 1 mile 1 furlong. Besides these roads twenty unmetalled second class roads are kept up by the District Board, all more or less bridged.

South of the Orissa Trunk Road the land is too low to permit the maintenance of any roads. Here the embankments along the Dāmodar, Hooghly and Rūpnārāyan form raised thoroughfares during the rains. The western parts of thāna Amtā and the north-western part of thāna Bāgnān are also too much cut up by creeks and channels to allow any but fair-weather pathways to be made. Consequently, the roads are few in number, and none are metalled.

Municipal roads. The Howrah Municipality maintains an extensive network of roads and lanes, all more or less macadamized. In 1907 it kept up 59·5 miles of metalled and 4 miles of unmetalled roads, while in the Bally Municipality there were 18 miles of metalled and 10 miles of unmetalled roads.

Staging bungalows. The District Board maintains three inspection bungalows at Dumjor, Jagatballabhpur and Syāmpur. The Public Works Department keeps up one dâk bungalow at Uluberiā; three embankment bungalows at Amtā and Mahishrekhā on the Dāmodar and at Sasāti on the Rūpnārāyan; and two drainage bungalows at Rājāpur and Sijberiā. The staging bungalow at Mahisrekhā, the old subdivisional headquarters, is a particularly good building for a staging bungalow, being built on a high plinth and having 4 rooms.

Bridges. On account of the large number of rivers and waterways, both Municipal and District Board roads have to be provided with many bridges, and in Howrah town several bridges have been built over the East Indian Railway and the Bengal-Nāgpur Railway lines, the finest being the Buckland Bridge leading to Howrah station, which is more than a quarter mile long.

Howrah Bridge. By far the most important bridge, however, is the Howrah Bridge over the river Hooghly, which connects Howrah with Calcutta. This is a floating bridge, the middle section of which is movable so as to allow of the passage of vessels up and down the river. It is 1,528 feet between abutments and has a roadway for carriages, 48 feet in width, with footpaths, 7 feet wide, on either side. The construction of a bridge over the Hooghly at or near Calcutta was mooted over half a century ago, a committee being appointed to consider the project in 1855-56; but the idea was given up in 1859-60. The question was revived in 1868, and it was eventually decided that Government should construct the bridge and that its management should be handed over to a Trust. In 1871 an Act was passed empowering the Lieutenant-Governor to have the bridge constructed with

Government capital, to make and maintain ways and approaches, to authorize the levy of tolls and to appoint Port Commissioners to carry out the purposes of the Act. A contract was entered into with Sir Bradford Leslie for its construction, and the work was forthwith commenced in England, the different portions of the bridge being sent out and put together in Calcutta. The work of construction was completed in 1874; and the bridge having been opened to traffic in October of that year, was made over to the Port Commissioners for management under Act IX of 1871, the cost, 22 lakhs of rupees with interest at Rs. 4½ per cent., being made the first charge to be repaid in thirty instalments.

The total net revenue of the bridge since it was opened in 1874 amounts to Rs. 34,11,440. The main item in the receipts consists of a small toll on railway traffic at the rate of Re. 1 per 100 maunds of goods, which is paid by the East Indian Railway. The income from this toll has been growing steadily, rising from Rs. 1,46,695 in 1899-1900 to Rs. 2,16,360 in 1907-08. In that year the total receipts amounted to Rs. 2,40,593 and the expenditure to Rs. 2,21,111. Of the latter Rs. 62,503 were spent on establishment and Rs. 90,847 on repairs, while Rs. 13,000 were paid as a contribution to the Calcutta Port Trust on account of management.

Before 1906, the bridge was opened for the passage of vessels only in the daytime, but since June of that year it has been opened at night for all vessels except ocean steamers, which have to pass through by day. The number of openings was thus raised to 24, while the average number of day openings was reduced from 13 to 4 in a month, with much less inconvenience to general traffic. In 1907-08, 130 sea-going vessels, 2,033 flats and inland steamers, 715 launches and steam-tugs, 133 Port Commissioners' vessels, and 9 Government steamers with flats passed through the bridge—in all 3,020.

WATER-WAYS. Rivers. The chief navigable waterways are the Hooghly, Dāmodar and Rūpnārāyan. The Hooghly and the Rūpnārāyan are navigable at all seasons of the year throughout their course in and along the district. The Dāmodar ceases to be navigable after the rains, except in the lowest section from the mouth of the Gāighātā *Khāl* to its own outfall in the Hooghly; and during the winter it is navigable up to Amtā during spring tides only. Small boats also ply in the rains and winter months along the numerous creeks intersecting the district.

Creeks. Of these creeks the chief are:—(1) the Bally *Khāl* extending from the Dānkuni marsh west of Serampore to the Hooghly.

It is 10 miles long, 30 feet broad and 12 feet deep, and forms the main channel of the Dānkuni drainage works. (2) The Sānkrāil *Khāl* (the old Saraswatī) 8 miles long, 15 feet broad and 9 feet deep. (3) The Kālsāpā *Khāl* (the old Kānā Nadī) so called because it extends from the Hooghly near Kālsāpā, which is 6 miles long, 30 feet broad and 8 feet deep. Its lowest section now forms a channel of the Rājāpur drainage works. (4) The Mithākundu *Khāl*, which connects the Dāmodar with the Hooghly and falls into the latter at Mithākundu below Uluberiā. It is 6 miles long, 50 feet broad and 18 feet deep. (5) The Pukuriā *Khāl* joining the Dāmodar with the Hooghly, 3 miles long, 60 feet broad and 18 feet deep. (6) The Bānspāti *Khāl* from Amtā to Uluberiā, about 15 miles long and 30 feet broad. (7) The Madāriā *Khāl*, extending from beyond the district and falling into the Dāmodar above Amtā. It is an old branch of the Dāmodar with a length of about 10 miles in the district and a breadth of 30 feet. (8) The Gāighātā and Bakshi *Khāl*, a natural channel slightly improved, about 12 miles long. It connects the Dāmodar with the Rūpnārāyan by a tortuous passage which is closed during part of the year. Tolls are levied on boats using this channel according to a scale fixed by Government. The right of levying tolls is now leased out annually.

The only canal in the district is the Uluberiā High Level Canal which has two sections. Its first reach starts from Uluberiā and joins the Dāmodar below Persandpur, two miles below the Bengal-Nāgpur Railway bridge over that river. It is 8 miles in length; its width at top is 92 feet and at bottom 36 feet; and its depth is 9 feet. West of Uluberiā the Orissa Trunk Road runs along its northern bank for 5 miles. The second reach extends from the other side of the Dāmodar to the left bank of the Rūpnārāyan several miles below the railway bridge. This reach is 4 miles long; its width at top is 120 feet and at the bottom 36 feet; and its depth is 14 feet. The traffic on the canal has almost disappeared owing to the opening of the Bengal-Nāgpur Railway. Canals.

The District Board maintain eleven public ferries, all except one being in the Uluberiā subdivision. They are:—(*a*) On the Dāmodar (1) Mahishrekhā ferry, thāna Bāgnān, with two subsidiary ferries, Khādinan and Bānsberiā; (2) Boāliā ferry, thāna Bāgnān; (3) Garchumuk ferry, thāna Syāmpur; (4) Syāmpur ferry, thāna Syāmpur. (*b*) On the river Rūpnārāyan (5) Bakshi ferry on the Bakshi *Khāl* outfall, thāna Amtā; (6) Gopiganj ferry, thana Amtā, with two subsidiary ferries at Pānsuli Ferries.

and Dudkurma; (7) Mānkur, thāna Bāgnān; (8) Sasāti, thāna Syāmpur; (9) Jhumjhumi, thāna Syāmpur, just opposite Tamluk. (c) Two ferries on creeks, viz., (10) Sijberiā ferry on the old Kānā Nadī (present Kālsāpā *Khāl*), thāna Uluberiā; and (11) Sānkrāil ferry on the Old Saraswatī (modern Sānkrāil *Khāl*), Sānkrāil outpost.

On the Hooghly river public ferries are maintained by the Port Commissioners within the limits of their jurisdiction and by the District Board of the 24-Parganas outside those limits. The Port Trust has its northern boundary pillar in Ghusuri a little above the Central Jute Mills; while the southern boundary pillar was lately moved from Pānchpārā above Rājganj to Bāuriā, just north of the Lawrence Jute Mills. When the Howrah bridge is open, railway passengers are ferried across from Armenian Ghāt to the railway pontoon and back by two of the bridge steamers. The Port Commissioners have also started since 1907 two sets of steamer services, one above the bridge and the other below it. Below the bridge three steamers ply regularly between Chāndpāl Ghāt and the Kidderpore Docks on the Calcutta side, and Telkalghāt, Rāmkristapur, Sibpur and Shālimār on the Howrah side. Above the bridge two steamers ply regularly between Barabazar Ghāt and Ahiritolā Ghāt on the Calcutta side and Sālkhiā Bāndā Ghāt on the Howrah side. The services, which run only in the daytime, are popular with the public, the fares being extremely small, viz., an anna to a quarter anna.

STEAMER SERVICES.

Four other steamer services ply daily on week days between Calcutta and places in this district, three below the bridge and one above it, viz., (1) Calcutta (Chāndpāl Ghāt) to Rājganj, Sānkrail outpost; (2) Calcutta (Chāndpāl Ghāt) to Uluberiā; (3) Calcutta (Armenian Ghāt) to Ghātāl in Midnapore, *viâ* Uluberiā; (4) Calcutta (Ahiritolā Ghāt) to Kālnā *viâ* Bally. The first is under Indian management; the others belong to Messrs. Hoare Miller & Co.

BOATS.

A large amount of traffic is conveyed by small native boats, such as *pānsis* rowed by Hindu boatmen and *dingis*, rowed by Muhammadan boatmen, who hail mostly from Noākhāli or Chittagong. They are registered and licensed, and usually ply from early morning to nine o'clock at night. The fare is small, one or two pice per head; or if the whole boat is hired, two to three annas per trip. From Belur, Bally and other places office clerks and others come to Calcutta in slightly larger boats, called *kuthir-pānsi*. From Bally to Barabazar Ghāt the usual charge is one to three annas per head, or eight annas to one rupee for the entire boat.

For conveying goods various other kinds of boats are used. Fishing boats in any number may be seen on the Hooghly throughout the year, and are especially numerous during the *hilsā* fishing season. Heavy boats, with high raised sides and long oars, are built at Sālkhiā and Sibpur for carrying general goods, straw or salt. They also move up and down the Rūpnārāyan and the Dāmodar during the rains, bringing down rice and other agricultural produce and carrying up kerosene oil, etc. In the interior, during the rains and winter months, *sāltis* or small flat-bottomed canoes are very common as they can go over flooded paddy fields and along shallow creeks. They are usually rowed by one man and often carry goods to the nearest mart.

RAILWAYS. The district is traversed by two broad (5 feet 6 inches) gauge railways, the East Indian Railway and the Bengal-Nāgpur Railway, and by two light railways (2 feet gauge), the Howrah-Amtā and Howrah-Shiākhālā Railways.

East Indian Railway. The East Indian Railway has only a very short length in this district, viz., 6 miles to Bally and 2 miles to Shālimār; but as Howrah is its terminus, the growth and prosperity of the town, and indirectly of the whole district, is intimately connected with the line. Survey was begun in 1845, and construction in 1851; and the first section from Howrah to Hooghly was opened in 1854. In 1855 the line was opened as far as Rānīganj and in 1862 up to Benāres. It is unnecessary to refer to the further development of the railway, such as its extension to Delhi and elsewhere, the shortening of the route by the Chord line and in 1907 by the Grand Chord line, the opening of branch lines, the acquisition of collieries, and the expansion of traffic.

During recent years numerous improvements have been made on the line within this district. The Howrah station was remodelled and improved first after the opening of the Hooghly bridge, and later on the formation of a joint station with the Bengal-Nāgpur Railway. The old station buildings have been made over to the latter; and the East Indian Railway has now a large imposing building with six long platforms for trains. Outside, a long row of godowns has been erected for the enormous goods traffic, especially in coal, wheat, rice, and oil-seeds, which comes to Howrah. Quarters have also been built at Howrah and its suburb Bāmangāchhi for the European staff. A small branch line has been run along the Hooghly to Shālimār so as to establish connection with the Kidderpore Docks. A large area has been acquired at Liluāh, to which the carriage and wagon building shops have been removed, and a shunting yard for goods wagons has been laid out at the same place. Lastly, for the convenience of suburban passengers there is a succession of trains running from Howrah to Uttarpārā, in addition to ordinary mail and passenger trains.

Bengal-Nāgpur Railway. The other great line, the Bengal-Nāgpur Railway, was extended to Howrah in 1900, thus connecting the district with the Central Provinces and Bombay on the west, and with Orissa and Madras on the south. It enters the district by a fine bridge over the Rūpnārāyan, goes east up to Uluberiā, running for several miles parallel to the Grand Trunk Road and the High Level Canal, and then north-east along the Hooghly river to Howrah. A short branch, 3 miles long, from Sāntrāgāchhi to Shālimār station carries the heavy traffic intended for export overseas direct to the Kidderpore Docks, the train crossing the Hooghly in large ferry steamers. As far as this district is concerned, the line has developed the goods traffic from the Uluberiā subdivision and has given increased facilities for passenger traffic from that part to Howrah and Calcutta.

Light Railways. The light railways had their origin in an agreement, dated 12th June 1889 between the District Board of Howrah and Messrs. Walsh, Lovett & Co., which was subsequently renewed with Messrs. Martin & Co., and sanctioned by Government notification in the *Calcutta Gazette* of March 27th, 1895. The capital of the Howrah-Shiākhālā line is six lakhs; while the capital of the Howrah-Amtā line was raised from nine lakhs to sixteen lakhs by the issue of additional shares for four lakhs and of debentures for three lakhs. Under the contract all profits in excess of four per cent. on the capital are distributed in equal shares between the companies and the District Boards of Howrah and Hooghly—in the case of the Howrah-Amtā line with the Howrah Board and of the Howrah-Shiākhālā line with the Hooghly Board. The Boards on their part have made over their roads for the use of the railways and guarantee an interest of 4 per cent.

The Howrah-Amtā line was opened up to Dumjor in 1897, and to Amtā in 1898. An extension from Bargachhiā (Bargechhe) junction to Antpur was opened in 1904, and a further extension to Chāmpādāngā in 1908. This extension, however, lies almost exclusively in the Serampore subdivision. Both the Howrah-Amtā and Howrah-Shiākhālā lines start from Telkalghāt on the Hooghly river, and skirting the Court *maidān* pass through the crowded Panchānantalā road to Kadamtalā station. Here they separate, the Howrah-Shiākhālā line running north-west along the Benāres road to the border of the district, and thence to Shiākhālā in the Serampore subdivision. The Howrah-Amtā line runs west, chiefly along the side of the Jagatballabhpur road, and then goes south-west to Amtā, a length of nearly 29 miles. Both lines, and especially the Howrah-Amtā line, have proved profitable concerns, and a remarkable expansion has taken place in goods and passenger traffic. The gross earnings of the Howrah-Amtā line increased from Rs. 2,56,418 in 1900 to Rs. 3,28,722 in 1905; and in 1905-06 and the two succeeding years the Howrah Board received as its share Rs. 39,563, Rs. 38,680 and Rs. 39,696 respectively.

Electric tramway. The Calcutta Tramways Co. has now extended its operations to Howrah. In pursuance of a license granted, under notification No. 9, dated 26th November 1907, the Company has established a central power station at the corner of the Dobson and Golābāri Roads, and is laying down tram lines (4 feet 8½ inches gauge) along four routes. The southern section was opened for traffic on 10th June 1908. Beginning from the Howrah bridge the line in this section runs over the railway overbridge and across the Court *maidān* to Kāorāpārāghāt road, Sibpur, for a distance of nearly two miles. Both the northern routes start from the bridge and terminate at the southern end of Ghusuri road, one passing by Howrah road and Golābāri road, the other by the Grand Trunk Road and Haraganj road. The fourth route connects the Ghusuri road with Kāorāpārāghāt road, Sibpur, passing over the crowded Haraganj and Grand Trunk Roads.

The main conditions of the license are (1) that the Company shall finish the work within two years from the date of the license, (2) that a continuous current at a pressure of 550 volts shall be transmitted from the central generating station by means of underground cables to over-head trolly-wires from which the cars will derive the necessary electric power and (3) that the Municipality or the Local Government shall have the option of purchasing the undertaking at 25 times the difference between the average gross annual receipts and the working expenses either on 1st January 1931 or at the end of every subsequent period of seven years thereafter.

POSTAL STATISTICS. The returns for 1907-08 show that there are 70 post offices and 189 miles of postal communication. The number of postal articles delivered in the same year, including letters, post cards, packets, newspapers and parcels, was 5,431,000. The value of money orders issued was Rs. 3,451,000 and of those paid Rs. 17,86,000; while the number of Savings Bank deposits was 17,200, the amount deposited being Rs. 8,49,000. Postal telegraph offices have been opened at Howrah, Ross Road, Sālkhiā, Sānkrāil, Andul Mauri, Sibpur, Sibpur Botanic Garden, Uluberiā and Liluāh.

CHAPTER XII.

GENERAL ADMINISTRATION.

ADMINISTRATIVE CHARGES AND STAFF.

THE administration of the Howrah district is in some respects peculiar for the chief local executive officer, the Magistrate, is not a Collector, as in other districts, but a Deputy Collector. When first appointed in 1843, the Magistrate was engaged only in criminal work; but gradually he was made responsible, successively, for salt, excise, stamps, land acquisition, income-tax, accounts and the treasury, and more recently, for certificates, collections from *khās mahāls*, the work of the Drainage Department, touring and inspection. The Collector of Hooghly, however, still controls the administration of land revenue, including the collection of the land revenue demand, and of road and public works cesses, for estates lying wholly or partly in this district. In other words, Howrah forms part of Hooghly for land revenue and cess purposes.

There are two subdivisions, Howrah and Uluberiā, each under a Subdivisional Officer. The sanctioned staff at Howrah consists of two Deputy Collectors exercising first class magisterial powers and of one Deputy Collector with second or third class powers; two Sub-Deputy Collectors are also usually stationed there. At Uluberiā the Subdivisional Officer is generally assisted by a Sub-Deputy Collector. The embankments and drainage works are in charge of the Executive Engineer, Northern Drainage and Embankment Division, under the Superintending Engineer, South-Western Circle, both of whom have their offices in Calcutta. Howrah is also the headquarters of the Superintendent, Government Railway Police.

REVENUE.

The land revenue and cess accounts are included in those of Hooghly, and it is only of recent years that those for revenue from other sources have been separated. Among the latter the main sources of income are excise and income-tax (outside the towns of Howrah and Bally), and stamps, which aggregated Rs. 4,06,000 in 1900-01. In 1907-08 the collections amounted (in round figures) to Rs. 5,17,000, of which Rs. 2,68,000 were realized from stamps, Rs. 2,19,000 from excise, and Rs. 30,000 from income-tax.

Land revenue.

The total number of estates borne on the revenue roll of Hooghly (including Howrah) in 1907-08 was 4,309 with a current demand of Rs. 13,70,923. Of the total number 871 estates with an annual demand of about 5½ lakhs lie wholly or for the greater part in this district. One of these, Mandalghāt, the major portion of which is included in the Howrah and Uluberiā subdivisions, has a demand of about 2¼ lakhs. The Government estates consist merely of a few derelict *chaukīdāri chākrān* lands or Public Works Department surplus plots.

Stamps. The receipts from judicial and non-judicial stamps increased from Rs. 1,38,000 in 1896-97 to Rs. 2,40,000 in 1901-02 and rose still further to Rs. 2,68,000 in 1907-08. The gradual expansion of commercial business in the town of Howrah and in the district generally, the growing familiarity of the people with the provisions of the law, their tendency to have recourse to courts of law, the enhanced duty on perpetual leases, and the growing demand for stamps in other miscellaneous transactions account for the increase in revenue. Nearly four-fifths (Rs. 2,14,000) of the receipts in 1907-08 were due to the sale of judicial stamps and in particular of court-fee stamps, while Rs. 54,000 were obtained from the sale of non-judicial stamps, nearly the whole of this sum being due to the demand for impressed stamps.

Excise. The receipts from excise rose from Rs. 1,37,000 in 1896-97, to Rs. 1,46,000 in 1901-02, and further increased in 1907-08 to Rs. 2,19,000, a total lower than that for any other district in the Burdwān Division except Bānkurā. The net excise revenue was Rs. 3,165 per 10,000 of the population (or a little above 5 annas per head), as compared with the Provincial average of Rs. 3,206 per 10,000. These figures exclude the towns of Howrah and Bally, which are grouped with Calcutta and its suburbs for the purposes of excise administration.

The greater portion of the excise revenue is derived from the sale of country spirit, the receipts from which amounted in 1907-08 to Rs. 82,000 or nearly two-fifths of the total excise revenue. The manufacture and sale of country spirit were carried on under both the outstill system and the central distillery system until 1907, when the contract supply system was introduced, *i.e.*, the local manufacture of country spirit has been prohibited, and a contract for the wholesale supply of spirit has been given out to a firm of distillers. The contractors are forbidden to hold any retail licenses for its sale, but are allowed the use of distillery and warehouse buildings for the storage of liquor. The right of retail vend is disposed of by separate shops, each of which is put up to auction; and the retail vendors are forbidden to sell liquor except at the prescribed strengths, for which maximum prices are fixed. According to the returns for 1907-08, there are 33 shops for the retail sale of country spirit, *i.e.*, one retail shop for every 15½ square miles and for 20,432 persons; and the average consumption of the liquor in that year is 14 proof gallons per 1,000 of the population. The consumption of the fermented liquor known as *tāri* is not so great, its sale realizing only Rs. 42,000. The receipts from both *tāri* and country spirit represent an expenditure of Rs. 1,920 per 10,000 of the population, a figure higher than in any other district of the Burdwān Division except Burdwān and Hooghly.

The receipts from opium and hemp drugs account for practically all the remainder of the excise revenue. The greater portion is derived from the duty and license fees on opium, which brought in Rs. 54,000 in 1907-08, representing an expenditure of Rs. 798 for 10,000 of the population, a figure higher than in any other district of the Division except Hooghly. The use of *gānja*, *i.e.*, the dried flowering tops of the cultivated female hemp plant (*Cannabis Indica*) and the resinous exudation on it, appears to be greater than in any district in the Division except Hooghly, the duty and license fees realizing Rs. 32,000 in 1907-08 or Rs. 530 per 10,000 of the population.

Income-tax.

In 1901-02 the income-tax yielded Rs. 27,000 paid by 1,435 assessees, of whom 1,047 paying Rs. 11,000 had incomes of Rs. 500 to Rs. 1,000. At that time the minimum income assessable was Rs. 500, but this was raised in 1903 to Rs. 1,000, thereby giving relief to a number of petty traders, money lenders and clerks; and the number of assessees consequently fell in 1903-04 to 546 and the collections to Rs. 24,000. In 1907-08 the tax yielded Rs. 30,000 paid by 639 assessees. These figures do not include the assessments of Howrah and Bally towns, which are amalgamated with Calcutta for income-tax purposes.

Registration.

There are six offices for the registration of assurances under Act III of 1877. The average number of documents registered annually during the quinquennium ending in 1904 was 21,149, as compared with 20,827 in the five years ending in 1899. The marginal statement shows the number of documents registered

Office.	Documents registered.	Receipts.	Expenditure.
		Rs.	Rs.
Howrah ...	4,884	13,780	6,075
Ditto joint (Dumjor).	3,117	3,221	1,640
Amtā ...	3,870	4,047	2,837
Jagatballabhpur.	2,799	3,120	1,711
Syāmpur ...	3,197	3,251	1,819
Uluberiā ...	4,158	4,368	2,224
Total ..	22,025	31,787	16,306

and the receipts and expenditure at each office in 1907. The number of registrations in that year was less than in any other district in the Division.

The administration of criminal and civil justice is under the District and Sessions Judge of Hooghly. There are seven subordinate Civil Courts, four Munsifs being stationed at Howrah and two more at Amtā and Uluberiā, besides an additional Munsif for Uluberiā and Serampore, who holds his court at Uluberiā. The Small Cause Court Judge of Hooghly and Serampore also holds his court at Howrah for about a week every month; but suits above Rs. 1,000 in value are tried by the Sub-Judge at Hooghly. Criminal justice is administered by the District and Sessions Judge of Hooghly, the District Magistrate, and the Deputy and Sub-Deputy Magistrates stationed at Howrah and Uluberiā. Besides these stipendiary Magistrates, there are benches of Honorary Magistrates at Howrah, Uluberiā, Amtā and Bally. Sessions cases are at present tried at Howrah, not by the Sessions Judge of Hooghly, but by an Additional Sessions Judge. ADMINISTRATION OF JUSTICE.

Howrah, with its large labour force and fluctuating population, is a convenient centre for criminals, and is frequented by professional criminals from up-country. Of recent years steps have been taken to break up the gangs that make the town and its neighbourhood their headquarters. Among such gangs may be mentioned one consisting of Pāsis from the United Provinces, who specialized in burglary and theft, and a band of Banpars from Patna and Monghyr, who settled down in Sālkhiā and worked as river pirates on the Hooghly, sinking boats and broaching cargoes The latter were a dangerous set of criminals, who set out with arms (*lāthis* and *dāos*) to attack and loot unprotected cargo boats and passengers, and did not hesitate to resort to violence. They displayed a considerable amount of ingenuity and adopted up-to-date devices, *e.g.*, by disguising themselves as policemen and using boats like those of the Port Police. Similar ingenuity was displayed by a gang of carters, recently convicted, which used systematically to commit breach of trust in respect of goods entrusted to them to carry. Their *modus operandi*, though simple, was nevertheless effective and clever. Under the rules of the Licensing Department all carts plying for hire carry a number, stamped on a block of wood and affixed to a part of the permanent woodwork of the cart; and it is the practice of firms engaging these carts to register them in their books by these numbers for purposes of subsequent identification, if necessary. The practice of this gang was to steal the block belonging to Crime.

another cart, fix it on one of their own, and then to obtain a load of goods which they would proceed to misappropriate, immediately disposing of the contents to receivers, who were also in the business. If, on receiving information of the non-arrival of their goods, the firm engaging the cart laid a complaint at the police station, this would only lead to the arrest and harassment of the unfortunate carter whose block had been stolen and made use of. Sometimes, moreover, the latter, particularly if he had injudiciously omitted to report the loss of his licensing block, would find himself involved in criminal proceedings; and there were found to be cases on record in which innocent carters had thus been convicted and imprisoned.

POLICE.

For police purposes the district is divided into 11 thānas with 7 outposts as shown in the margin. The Howrah, Golābāri and Sibpur police stations are included in Howrah town. The regular police force consisted in 1907 of the District Superintendent, 7 Inspectors, 40 Sub-Inspectors, one Sergeant, 74 Head-Constables and 817 constables, a total force of 941 men, representing one policeman to every half square mile and to every 904 of the population. The rural force for the watch and ward of villages in the interior is composed of 1,517 *chaukīdārs* and 128 *dafadārs*, of whom 1,506 are *chaukīdārs* under Act VI of 1879, while 11 are *phānridārs* or *phānri-piādās*, *i.e.*, *chaukīdārs* holding service lands.

Subdivision.	Thānas.	Outposts.
Howrah ...	Bally.	
	Dumjor ...	Sānkrāil.
	Golābāri.	
	Howrah ...	Sāntrāgāchhi. Pānchlā.
	Jagatballabhpur.	
	Liluāh.	
	Sibpur.	
Uluberiā ...	Amtā ...	Bāuriā. Bhatorā. Singti.
	Bāgnān.	
	Syāmpur ...	Mandalghāt.
	Uluberiā.	

JAILS.

There is a district jail at Howrah with accommodation for 88 prisoners, viz., barracks without separate sleeping accommodation for 16 male convicts, 8 female convicts, and 44 under-trial prisoners; cells for 4 European prisoners, 8 male and 2 female convicts; and a hospital with 6 beds. This was formerly a sub-jail, but has recently (in 1906-07) been raised to the status of a third class jail. There is also a subsidiary jail at Uluberiā, which has accommodation for 12 prisoners.

CHAPTER XIII.

LOCAL SELF-GOVERNMENT.

DISTRICT BOARD.

IN rural areas, the administration of public roads, ferries, pounds, dispensaries, primary education and sanitation is vested in the District Board, which has delegated some of its powers to Local Boards and Union Committees. The Howrah District Board consists of 13 members, of whom six are elected by the Local Boards, three are nominated by Government, and four are *ex-officio* members. The returns for 1907-08 show that seven of the members are pleaders or *mukhtārs*, five are Government servants, and one represents landed interests. The chief receipts are the local rate (road cess), which is collected by the Collector of Hooghly, receipts from pounds and ferries, profits from the Howrah-Amtā Light Railway, and contributions made by the Local Government for roads and education. The receipts from the local rate increased from Rs. 41,485 in 1888-89 to Rs. 48,950 in 1907-08; those of pounds and ferries were practically stationary, amounting to Rs. 3,821 and Rs. 6,402, respectively, in the year last named; while the share of profits in the Howrah-Amtā line (opened in 1897-98) increased to Rs. 39,696.

Exclusive of the opening balance, the total receipts in 1907-08 amounted to Rs. 1,35,046 or more than double the total receipts in 1888-89 (Rs. 62,323), while the average incidence of taxation per head was 1 anna 2 pies. The total disbursements in the same year were Rs. 1,59,100, the chief items being Rs. 1,13,545 expended on public works, Rs. 24,117 on education, and Rs. 6,537 on medical relief and sanitation. The District Board maintained in that year 40·8 miles of metalled roads and 110·6 miles of unmetalled roads, besides 400 miles of village tracks, the average cost of repairing which were Rs. 471, Rs. 110 and Rs. 22 per mile respectively. The pounds, which are usually leased out, numbered 59, while several public ferries were kept up on the rivers Rūpnārāyan and Dāmodar. The income obtained from the ferries on the Hooghly is handed over to the District Board of the 24-Parganas. The District Board maintains the Zilā school of Howrah jointly with the Howrah Municipality, and also maintains one Middle school and gives grants-in-aid to one High school, 21 Middle schools, 63 Upper Primary and 516 Lower Primary schools. Two dispensaries are maintained and four others are aided, at a total cost in 1907-08 of Rs. 4,803 or 4·7 per cent. of the ordinary income of the Board. A contribution is also made to the Howrah Veterinary Dispensary.

LOCAL BOARDS. Two Local Boards have been established, one for each subdivision. The Sadar or Howrah Local Board has nine members, of whom five are nominated and four are elected; while the Uluberiā Local Board has 15 members, of whom five are nominated and ten are elected. They do little work beyond managing pounds and ferries and looking after the village roads.

UNION COMMITTEES. In July 1895, Union Committees were formed in thānas Dumjor and Jagatballabhpur in the Howrah subdivision and in Amtā and Bāgnān in the Uluberiā subdivision; while Uluberiā was constituted an Union Committee in September 1907. The marginal table shows the area and population of each Union as constituted in 1907-08; but in 1908 the area of the Dumjor Union was increased by the inclusion of the villages of Pārbatīpur and Daffarpur. They are each managed by a committee of nine members, and the average income of each is a little over Rs. 500 per annum, the contributions from the District Board varying in 1907-08 from Rs. 400 to Rs. 410; the remainder of the receipts consists almost entirely of the amounts raised by local taxation under Section 118 of the Act.

Name of Union.	Area in square miles.	Population.
Amtā ...	11·0	22,726
Bāgnān ...	9·5	12,456
Dumjor ...	8·5	23,770
Jagatballabhpur ...	10·5	13,634
Uluberiā ...	2·2	5,395

As regards the latest Union, Uluberiā, it may be explained that the town was constituted a municipality on 1st April 1903 with nine members. A small municipality with a population of a little over 5,000, it had in 1906-07 a total income of Rs. 3,910, mainly derived from a tax on persons. It was abolished in April 1907, and an Union Committee appointed in September of the same year.

MUNICIPALITIES. Bally. At present the only municipalities in the district are Bally and Howrah. The former was created in 1883 by the separation of the northern portion of the Howrah Municipality. The area within municipal limits is 2·92 square miles with a population of 18,662, of whom 3,197 or 17·1 per cent. are tax-payers. It is administered by 21 Commissioners, of whom 14 are elected and 7 are nominated. The total receipts amounted in 1907-08 to

Rs. 33,770 (as against Rs. 16,207 in 1892-93), of which the major portion was obtained from a tax on holdings, assessed at the rate of 7½ per cent. on their annual valuation, which yielded Rs. 20,090, and from latrine rates (Rs. 8,516). The incidence of taxation was Re. 1-11-2 per head of the population; and the total expenditure in the same year was Rs. 29,803. The town is ill-drained and its supply of drinking water is bad. It is also studded with shallow tanks, of which no less than 885 have been counted; and it consequently suffers from epidemics of fever. The railway settlement at Liluāh forms part of the municipality, and has been formed into a semi-independent Ward Committee. A scheme for constructing water-works for the supply of water to riparian municipalities on the west bank of the Hooghly from Bally to Baidyabāti has been prepared.

Howrah is, next to Calcutta, the largest municipality in the Province, and its administration is of special importance because of its metropolitan character and its close association with Calcutta. The terminus of two of the largest railway systems of India, and the home of many important industries, the administration of Howrah is, on a smaller scale, almost as difficult and arduous a task as that of its larger neighbour, Calcutta. Its Municipal Commissioners are the trustees of a current income falling little short of eight lakhs of rupees, nearly four times greater than that of any other individual mofussil municipality. The water-works are the largest in the Province outside Calcutta; its drainage system is the most extensive; it is the possessor of a conservancy tramway; electric tram lines have been introduced and are to be still further extended with the ultimate objective of linking the tramway system with that of Calcutta. Briefly, the scale of its administration differs widely from that of an ordinary mofussil municipality; and the lines on which its municipal problems have to be dealt with resemble closely those followed in the metropolis. Howrah.

The area included in municipal limits is 8½ square miles with a population in 1901 of 157,594; and the difficulties of administration are increased by the fact that a large proportion of the inhabitants consists of up-country immigrants who come to work on the railways or in the numerous mills and factories. They live in overcrowded *bastis* and impose a heavy burden on drainage and conservancy. A further difficulty is presented by the numerous shallow tanks and pools—some eighteen hundred have been counted—which are rarely cleansed and form breeding grounds for malaria-bearing mosquitoes. The steps taken ot improve this state of affairs, and the arrangements made for the drainage, conservancy and water-supply of this great city, have already been mentioned in Chapter IV.

For some years past it has been found most difficult to meet the rapidly increasing demand for improved roads, sanitation, lighting and water-supply in a growing city with a nearly stationary income; and a revaluation, carried out in face of considerable opposition, has recently been effected. It was found that many rate-payers had either escaped taxation altogether or had been under-assessed; and the result of the revision of assessment, which took effect from the 1st April 1907, was to give a net increase of Rs. 2,21,814 in the taxation, representing an increase of 58·4 per cent. in the case of railways, of 56·6 per cent. in the case of private houses, of 20 per cent. in the case of mills and factories, and of 21·9 per cent. in the case of the Port Commissioners and public holdings. The growth in the resources at the disposal of the Municipal Commissioners produced by this revision will, it is hoped, lead to a higher standard of road maintenance and conservancy, the extension of the lighting and water-supply, the creation of new markets and public conveniences, and the completion of the drainage of the town.

The revaluation showed that a great extension of business premises had taken place, that the population had increased by 16 per cent., and that there had been in the last few years a remarkable rise in the value of land, rents being in some parts double what they were ten years ago. There is little doubt that this expansion will continue. Communications in Howrah itself, between Calcutta and Howrah, and between Howrah and the surrounding country, are being rapidly improved. A service of ferry steamers has been started, tram cars have commenced to run (from June 1908) over a portion of the proposed routes, and the introduction of the system of opening the Hooghly Bridge chiefly at night has furnished further facilities for uninterrupted communication with Calcutta. These improvements are expected to make Howrah more accessible to workers in Calcutta, to stimulate the expansion of wholesale trading on the south foreshore, and to throw open for residential purposes the rural area in the south and west of the municipality. Further, improved services of trains on the East Indian, Bengal-Nāgpur and Howrah-Amtā Railways have made Howrah more accessible and convenient as a business centre, while the construction of an overbridge on the East Indian Railway on the northern boundary of the municipality will, when complete, facilitate traffic between Howrah and the market gardens to the north. Finally, the scheme for the improvement of Calcutta, recently sanctioned by the Secretary of State, is bound to affect Howrah; and when it is brought into operation it may be expected that the town, and especially its southern and western portions, will expand enormously.

As regards the details of administration, the municipal area is divided into 10 wards and there are 30 Commissioners, of whom 20 are elected, and ten are nominated, including four *ex-officio* members. There are 19,611 rate-payers or only 12·44 per cent. of the population—a low percentage which shows that Howrah is a town of the poor, a "cooly town" as it has been called. About two-thirds of the rate-payers are registered, and the elections excite a fair amount of interest. At the last elections (in 1906-07) four of the wards were uncontested, but in the other six the percentage of voters voting varied from 32·5 per cent. in Ward II to 74·6 per cent. in Ward X.

The chief sources of income are (1) a tax on holdings, assessed at the rate of 7½ per cent. on their annual valuation, (2) a water-rate levied at the rate of 5 and 6 per cent., (3) a lighting rate at the rate of 3 per cent., and (4) latrine rates. The incidence of taxation is high; in fact, it is the highest in any mofussil municipality except Darjeeling, being Rs. 4-9-9 per head of the population in 1907-08. In that year the total income amounted to Rs. 7,97,177 (or inclusive of loans and deposits, Rs. 11,02,494) as against Rs. 2,94,813 in 1892-93, showing that the net income has been more than doubled in the last 15 years. The chief receipts were Rs. 2,46,502 from the tax on holdings, Rs. 1,85,599 from the water-rate, Rs. 1,99,392 from latrine rates, Rs. 76,189 from the lighting rate, and Rs. 54,738 from municipal property. The total expenditure in the same year amounted to Rs. 8,68,888, (excluding Rs. 1,83,022 expended from loan funds), or inclusive of repayment of loans, deposits, etc., Rs. 10,51,910. Altogether Rs. 26,84,000 had been taken as loans from Government, and the outstanding loans at the end of the year amounted to more than 20 lakhs (Rs. 20,09,364).

CHAPTER XIV.

EDUCATION.

INDIGENOUS SYSTEMS.

Pāthshālās and maktabs.

UNDER native rule elementary instruction was given in *pāthshālās* and *maktabs*, nearly every important village with a number of higher class Hindu families having its *pāthshālā*, and where Muhammadans congregated, its *maktab*. In the Hindu *pāthshālā* the teacher (*guru mahāsaya*) was a poor Kāyasth or less often a Brāhman, who was usually paid in kind, or was given a contribution in cowries by each boy's family, and also got a small share of grain at harvest time. The school was held in his hut, and often in fine weather under some tree in the village. Here the boys were taught reading, writing and mental arithmetic. They practised writing with ink on palm or plantain leaves, or with chalk on the floor, and after they had learnt the Bengali alphabet, some small collections of verses were committed to memory. Particular attention was paid to mental arithmetic and mensuration, the boys learning by heart the verses of one Bhrigurām Dās, better known as the *Subhankarī*, which contain formulas for calculating arithmetical figures, interest, land measurements, etc. Boys were sent to the *pāthshālā* in their fifth year and stayed there three to six years. In *maktabs*, the teacher (*ākhungi*) taught arithmetic and the rudiments of Persian or Urdu, the boys writing not only on leaves but also on country paper. The bulk of the pupils finished their education in these elementary schools, and then followed their hereditary occupations. Many of the Kāyasths went on to the landlords' *kachharis* and learnt zamīndāri accounts, thus qualifying for employment as writers or *gumāshtas* (agents). A few read at home the vernacular versions of the epics or Purānas, while Brāhmans studied the rudiments of Sanskrit under some *pandit* in the neighbourhood, and thus qualified themselves for the priesthood.

Tols.

The more ambitious of the Brāhmans, however, were not so easily satisfied and studied at one or other of the educational centres in Bengal containing *tols* or Sanskrit colleges. The most famous of these were at Nadiā and in its neighbourhood; but there were smaller circles at Bally in this district, Bānsberiā and Khānākul in the Hooghly district, Bhātpārā in the 24-Parganas,

Bhāngāmodā in Burdwān, etc. The students resided in the house of some learned *pandits* and were treated as members of the family, doing domestic work, and if they had means, contributing to the cost of the household. Every pupil learnt grammar in the first instance for some years, and then read some easy literary works. After this he selected some special subject for study, usually higher literature, *Nyāya* or logic, and *Smriti* or law. The whole period of learning lasted usually from eight to sixteen years. After finishing the course, many went on a tour to complete their studies, visiting Mithilā (Darbhangā) to learn *Darshana* or philosophy and law, and Benāres for grammar, rhetoric and the Vedas. On returning home, many of them set up small *tols* in their own houses

Well-to-do Musalmāns sent promising boys to *madrasas*, which were established at nearly all the headquarters of the local Governors. These institutions date back to the beginning of Muhammadan rule in Bengal, for we find that Muhammad-i-Bakhtiyār Khiljī and his Amīrs set up *madrasas* at Lakhnauti, and in 1313 A. D. Zafar Khān built one at Tribenī. They were usually attached to some mosque and were often liberally endowed. The students had lodging and boarding free, though contributions were frequently made by those whose parents were better-off. The pupils were taught the Korān and Persian classics by Maulvis, while special instruction was also given in the *Hadis* or Musalmān law and in Arabic literature. **Madrasas.**

No special arrangements appear to have been made for female education. Hindu girls of a tender age often attended *pāthshālās*, but few were permitted to go there after seven or eight years of age. The Muhammadans were stricter and apparently did not permit them to go to any *maktab*, but many of the more affluent allowed their girls to be taught at home. Among the Kāyasths and Brāhmans, a few managed to learn Bengali or Sanskrit at home. The Vaishnavas were more liberal-minded, allowing girls and even elderly ladies to read and write; indeed, there were several poetesses among them. **Female education.**

In the early days of British rule, several schools for Indian boys were started by missionaries. First we find that in 1786 the Revd. David Brown, the then Superintendent of the Bengal Military Orphanage, started a boarding school for young Hindus in Howrah. Mr. Brown himself paid Rs. 1,800 for the site and building; but the school collapsed on his removal from Howrah in 1788.* The Serampore Baptist missionaries next opened bazar **PROGRESS OF MODERN EDUCATION. English schools.**

* H. B. Hyde, *Parochial Annals of Bengal*, pp. 251-2.

schools in Howrah and Sālkhiā in 1793, and in 1820 set up a regular English school for Indian boys. The first Government aided English school was opened in 1845, on the application of nearly two hundred Hindu parents. Nearly Rs. 4,000 were subscribed locally for the building, and Government granted a site of 2½ *bighās* to the east of the Salt Office on the *maidān*. The school was managed by a local committee, with the Magistrate as president, and began to send up students for the Entrance Examination in 1858, the year after the foundation of the University. The first English school under Indian management appears to have been started at Sālkhiā in 1855 through the public spirit of a *mukhtār*. It received a monthly grant of Rs. 87 from Government in 1857, and began to send up students for the Entrance Examination in 1859. Other schools were started shortly afterwards in various parts of the town and also in the interior, English schools, aided or unaided, being established at Andul, Bāgnān, Mugkalyān and Amtā before 1870-71.

Vernacular schools.

Missionaries were also the first to start vernacular schools. In 1818 the Christian Knowledge Society began to open a number of vernacular schools, which were grouped into circles, one such circle being located in Howrah district. In 1824 the Howrah circle had six schools extending from Sibpur to Bally, and in 1827 an additional school was opened at Bāntrā in Howrah town. It is not known when the Government opened its own vernacular schools; but in 1856-57 six such institutions were reported as in existence. The first vernacular school under Indian management was established in Sāntrāgāchhi in 1857 with the aid of a Government grant.

Special schools for Europeans.

Schools for European and Eurasian children were opened in the early years of British administration. The earliest that can be traced was the Bengal Military Orphan Asylum, intended for the education of the orphans of soldiers. This school was managed by a committee and received from Government an allowance of Rs. 3 (subsequently raised to Rs. 5) for each orphan. Originally located at Dakshineswar in the 24-Parganas, it was transferred in 1785 to Levett's house at Howrah, a site now occupied by the Courts. It contained 500 children, and its first Superintendent was the Revd. David Brown, who when an undergraduate at Cambridge was offered the appointment on condition that within two months he took Holy Orders and married. He fulfilled both conditions and took over charge in 1786; but his services were dispensed with in 1788, because he gave up too much time to his work as Garrison Chaplain and to preaching at the Mission Church. In 1790 the wards of the upper school were removed to Barwell's old house at Alipore, and in 1815 those of the lower school to Bārāsāt in consequence of an outbreak of opthalmia. From an advertisement in the *Calcutta Gazette* of 1807 we find that "the girls were taught, among other accomplishments, embroidery or chicundoz work," and orders for needle-work were asked for by the Secretary.*

Other attempts to found schools were made, chiefly by missionaries, but were unsuccessful. A boarding school for European and Eurasian boys was opened in 1821 by Mr. Statham, the first Baptist missionary resident at Howrah, and a free school in 1842 by another Baptist missionary, the Revd. T. Morgan; but both had to be closed, the first after six, and the second after sixteen years. Several other schools started by ladies in 1860 and 1861 also failed. At length, with the help of grants from the Government and the East Indian Railway Company, of private subscriptions, and a sum of Rs. 15,000 realised from a fancy fair, St. Thomas' School was opened in 1864. This school is located in a fine building on the Grand Trunk Road opposite the *maidān*.

Missionaries also took the lead in regard to collegiate education. Bishop's College, which was intended to serve as a Missionary College, was opened at Sibpur in 1824 owing mainly to the zeal of Bishop Middleton for the missionary cause. Government gave it 62 *bighās* of land, but other expenses were met chiefly by the Missionary Societies. The buildings are now occupied by the Civil Engineering College. This College was first started in 1856 under the control of the Public Works Department, when it was located in Writers' Buildings, Calcutta. In 1864 it was transferred to the charge of the Education Department and moved to the Presidency College. In 1880 the institution was made independent and removed to Sibpur. It is now the centre of technical education in Bengal, with six affiliated schools in Eastern Bengal and five in Bengal; and the course of teaching, formerly confined to mechanical engineering, has been extended by means of special classes in electrical and mining engineering and industrial chemistry. Colleges.

The educational activity of the Serampore missionaries also displayed itself in female education. They appear to have been the first to open a school for Indian girls at Howrah (in 1820), and in 1839 the Misses Hampton had a similar school. The first native girls' school under Indian management was established at Sāntrāgāchhi in 1863 with a small grant-in-aid from Government. Girls' English schools.

* H. B. Hyde, *Parochial Annals of Bengal*, pp. 246-52; *Selections*, Vol. IV, p. 429.

It was followed shortly after by other girls' schools at Sibpur and Sālkhiā, and a little later at Bally. By 1870-71 the well-known Hitakārī Sabhā of Uttarpārā began its course of examinations for girls.

PRESENT STATE OF EDUCATION.

The statistics obtained at the census of 1901 show that at the present day Howrah is the most advanced district in Bengal from an educational point of view. No less than 98,001 or 11·5 per cent. of the population were returned as literate, *i.e.*, able to read and write some language, while 17,903 could read and write in English. Among males 21·2 per cent. were literate —the highest proportion for any district in the Province—and among females 1·2 per cent., a proportion exceeded in only three other districts, viz., Hooghly, the 24-Parganas and Darjeeling, where conditions are exceptional owing to the number of European residents and visitors. As regards knowledge of English, Howrah was *facile princeps*, 38·9 males and 2 females in every thousand being returned as literate in that language. It is somewhat surprising that outside the municipalities the highest percentage of those able to read and write is returned for Syāmpur thāna, where Brāhmans and Kāyasths are proportionately few and the principal caste consists of Kaibarttas, who are not known to have any predilection for letters.

The advance made in recent years is apparent from the fact that in 1891 only 17·9 per cent. of the male population were returned as literate, while only 7 per mille of the female population could read and write. Similar evidence of progress is afforded by the returns prepared by the Education Department. The number of public educational institutions rose from 859 in 1892-93 to 894 in 1907-08, and of pupils from 33,200 to 39,535, while the percentage of boys to the male population of school-going age advanced from 56·8 per cent. to 59·4 per cent. The number of Musalmān pupils in schools of all classes increased from 3,674 to 5,333, of whom 5·7 per cent. were in secondary schools, 79·6 in primary schools and 13·6 per cent. in *maktabs*. The inspecting staff in 1907-08 consists of three Deputy Inspectors, six Sub-Inspectors, two Assistant Sub-Inspectors and five Inspecting Pandits.

Collegiate education.

The only college in the district is the Civil Engineering College at Sibpur, which on the 31st March 1908 had 349 students on the rolls. It is divided into two departments, the Engineer Department and the Apprentice Department. The former is intended for the training of engineers for the Public Works Department and other Government bodies; the latter for training men to fill subordinate ranks of the Public Works

Department and to carry out similar duties under public or private bodies. In 1907 the number of students being trained in these two Departments was 94 and 233 respectively.

In the Engineer Department prominence is given to practical work in the workshops and science laboratories. The qualification for admission is the Intermediate Examination of the Calcutta University or its equivalent; and the course, which is for four years, leads to the Calcutta University degree of Bachelor of Engineering in Civil Engineering.

In the Apprentice Department there are three courses of instruction, viz., (1) the sub-overseer course for two years, (2) the overseer course for another 2 years, and (3) a course of practical workshop training extending over about 16 months. An examination is held at the end of the sub-overseer course, and the successful candidate receives a certificate showing that he possesses the qualifications required for a sub-overseer in the Public Works Department. Having passed the sub-overseer examination, the student proceeds to the overseer course, which is offered in two branches, viz., (1) general engineering, leading to an overseer certificate, and (2) mining, leading to the Government of India diploma in the principles of mining. The practical workshop training is for the general branch only and leads to the certificate of foreman mechanic or upper subordinate.

A third branch of work consists of industrial classes in the various workshops, viz., carpenters, blacksmiths, fitters, turners, pattern-making and founding in iron and brass. For the first year the student attends the carpentry shop; in the second, the smith-shop; in the third, the pattern-making and foundry shop; in the fourth year, the fitting shop. The fifth year is devoted to all-round practical training.

Among recent developments may be mentioned the establishment in 1896 of a special course for electrical training and of mining classes in 1905. A student who has passed the sub-overseer standard may join the classes for a specialized course of two years, six weeks of each year being spent in a mining district, in the study of mining survey, and in practical training. A scheme has also been inaugurated for providing instruction in mining for assistants and others employed in the Bengal colliery districts, and a special Mining Advisory Board has been attached to the college. Since November 1906 there has been a regular course of instruction at colliery centres, viz., Sanctoria and Charanpur in the Rānīganj coal-field and Jherriā and Sijuā in the Jherriā field. A further development of some interest has been the establishment of a class for training motor-driver mechanics, the course of instruction including both maintenance and driving.

It has recently been decided to remove the college to Rānchī, on account of the general unhealthiness and unsuitability of the site.

Secondary schools. There are no less than 59 secondary schools in the district, including 26 High English schools, 27 Middle English schools and 6 Middle Vernacular schools. Considering the size of the district, the number is unusually large, representing approximately one secondary school for every eight square miles. Of the High English schools, eight are situated in Howrah, one in Bally and 17 in the mofussil. Seven (five in Howrah and two in the Uluberiā subdivision) are unaided; 18 receive grants-in-aid from public funds; and one, the Howrah Zilā school, is maintained jointly by the District Board and the Municipality. The number of pupils attending these schools increased from 3,601 in 1892-93 to 5,162 in 1907-08, when the total expenditure was Rs. 90,395, of which Rs. 7,580 or 8·3 per cent. were derived from public funds and the rest from fees, endowments and subscriptions. The following table gives the salient statistics for the High schools in 1907-08.

Maintained by District Board and Municipality.

School.	Number of pupils.
Howrah Zilā school	479

Aided.

School.	Number of pupils.	School.	Number of pupils.
Amtā	132	Jhinkrā	115
Andul	198	Māju (R. N. Bose's) ...	217
Bāgnān	151	Mugkalyān	211
Bally (Rivers Thompson) ...	372	Nārit (Nyāyaratna Institution)	122
Baluti	101	Pānitrās	117
Howrah Bible	64	Pānpur	134
Jagatballabhpur ...	123	Rāspur	156
Jaypur (Fakirdās Institution)	156	Sasāti (Nahala Abināsh) ...	94
Jhāpardah (Duke Institution)	117	Sālkhiā (A. S. School) ...	253

Unaided.

School.	Number of pupils.	School.	Number of pupils.
Bāntrā	306	Gārhbhabānīpur ...	149
Bāntrā (Belileo's Institution)	250	Sālkhiā (Hindu) ...	170
Howrah (Ripon Collegiate) ...	369	Sibpur	322
Uluberiā	284		

Of the Middle English schools, one is managed by the District Board, 21 are aided and 5 are unaided. They had 1,945 boys on the rolls in 1907-08, as against 1,728 in 1892-93, when there were 23 such schools. Of the Middle Vernacular schools, five are aided and one is unaided, and the attendance in 1907-08 was 629 pupils as against 1,002 (in 11 schools) in 1892-93. The total cost in 1907-08 of Middle English schools was Rs. 22,858 and of Middle Vernacular schools Rs. 5,425—in all Rs. 28,283, of which Rs. 5,885 or 20·9 per cent. were paid from public funds.

Primary schools. Primary education is given in two classes of schools, Upper and Lower Primary schools. In 1907-08 there were 68 Upper Primary schools for boys and 634 Lower Primary schools, with an attendance of 30,230 boys and 802 girls. The total expenditure in that year was Rs. 78,726, of which 21 per cent. (Rs. 16,637) was derived from public funds, while 71·6 per cent. was realised from fees. Including the pupils attending Primary schools for girls, the total number taught in Primary schools was 33,313 as against 26,284 in 1892-93, representing an increase of 26·8 per cent. in fifteen years, although the number of schools remained practically stationary, being 772 as against 773 in 1892-93.

Girls' schools. In 1907-08 there were 71 girls' schools, of which one (the Bāniban School) was a Middle English school, while 11 were Upper Primary and 59 Lower Primary schools. The total number of pupils attending these schools, including a few young boys, was 2,317. Excluding the boys, and adding the girls reading in boys' schools, the total number of girls under instruction in 1907-08 was 3,186. Sixty-seven girls' schools received aid, and four Lower Primary schools were unaided. The total cost amounted to Rs. 11,342, of which Rs. 2,418 were paid from Provincial revenues, Rs. 2,159 by the District Board, Rs. 1,135 from Municipal funds and Rs. 5,630 from private sources. No fees were charged in any girl's schools except in the Bāniban Middle English school and the Mission schools, but only Rs. 641 were thus realised. The Mission schools generally prepare candidates for the Calcutta Standard Examination; but the other schools send up pupils for the examinations conducted by the Uttarpārā Hitakārī Sabhā.

Special schools. At the Carriage and Wagon Workshops of the East Indian Railway at Liluāh there is a technical school for apprentices. With this exception, there is no separate technical or industrial school in the district, but the District Board and Howrah Municipality make contributions for the grant of scholarships tenable at the artisan class of the Sibpur Engineering College.

There are 19 *tols* and 28 *maktabs* with 866 pupils. Of these, eight *tols* receive small grants-in-aid, seven from the Howrah and two from the Bally Municipality, while 18 *maktabs* are aided, *viz.*, 16 from the special Government allotment and two from the Howrah Municipality. There are also 14 unaided indigenous schools, including *tols*, *maktabs* and Korān schools, with 376 pupils.

Eleven night schools, *i.e.*, Primary schools attended by adult labourers and cultivators in the evening after their day's work, are in existence, and had 189 pupils on the rolls in 1907-08. For training *gurus* or Primary school teachers, four schools were started in 1907-08, two in each subdivision, at which 45 teachers were instructed. Three students' hostels are maintained, all of which are self-supporting.

European education. There are four European schools in the district with 287 pupils on the rolls on 31st March 1908, viz., St. Aloysius' School (71 pupils), St. Agnes' School (77), St. Thomas' School (45), and St. Elizabeth's School (94).

MISCELLANEOUS. Fifteen public libraries are reported, all kept up by local subscriptions except one at Bally and another at Belur, which receive small grants from the Bally Municipality. There are also several reading rooms in the town and in the interior. The library of the Howrah Institute, which is managed by a committee of European gentlemen, is said to be a useful institution, while the Public Libraries at Howrah and Bally and the Friends' Union Club at Sibpur are growing in importance. The other libraries call for no special notice, containing mainly novels. Some are maintained from a percentage on the sale of sweep-stake tickets. Two weekly papers, the *Howrah Hitaishi* published in Bengali, and *Truth* published in English, are issued to a limited public. There are a number of printing presses in Howrah town, of which the most important are the Caledonia Steam Printing Press, the Municipal Press and the East Indian Railway Press. The oldest press in the district was probably the Encyclopoedia Press at Bishop's College, which can be traced back to 1852. At this press religious books and missionary reports were printed, among others the *Satyārnaba* of the Revd. K. M. Banerjee. Among social and political institutions may be mentioned the Rate-payers' Association at Howrah, a branch of the Indian Association at Uluberiā, the Sādhāranī Sabhā at Bally, and a branch of the Calcutta Anusilan Samiti at Phuleswar in the Uluberiā subdivision.

CHAPTER XV.

GAZETTEER.

Amtā.—A village in the north-east of the Uluberiā subdivision, situated on the left bank of the Dāmodar river, 30 miles from Howrah by rail and 26 miles by road. It is connected with the latter place by the Howrah-Amtá Railway, of which it is the terminus. Amtā is the headquarters of an Union Committee, and may be regarded for practical purposes as consisting of a group of villages about a mile and a half long north to south and a mile broad. It contains a Munsif's court, a court of Honorary Magistrates, a sub-registry office, police station, post office, charitable dispensary, a High English school founded by the late Bābu Pītāmbar Chakravarti, with a public library attached, and a Public Works Department bungalow. Several of its roads are brick-paved. It is protected from the Dāmodar floods by a high Government embankment, and from floods in the upland basins by a *takāvi* embankment built along the left bank of the Madāriā *Khāl*. It is fairly free from the malaria that prevails in the north and north-west of the thāna.

Amtā has long been an important centre of trade. Formerly it contained many salt and coal depôts, being an entrepôt for salt brought from Midnapore and coal brought from the Rānīganj coal-field. The Dāmodar then formed a broad highway of commerce, bearing hundreds of cargo boats; a memorial of this time still exists in the name *bandar*, *i.e.*, port, given to a part of the river bank. The railways have killed the river-borne trade in salt and coal; but, on the other hand, the trade in paddy and straw, carried partly by boats and partly by rail, has flourished, and there are also large exports to Howrah of jute, vegetables and fish. Brown country paper used to be manufactured here, but this industry has been crushed by the pressure of competition.

Among Hindus the place is best known for a temple dedicated to Melāi Chandī, a goddess mentioned in *Chandī*, a poem written by Kavikankan 300 years ago. Tradition says that her shrine was originally at Jayantī, a place on the other side of the river, about a mile from its present site. It marked one of the fifty-two *tīrthas* sanctified by receiving portions of the dismembered body of Satī (Durgā), being the spot on which her knee-joint fell. Her worshippers had to cross the river to reach the shrine, and this caused no little inconvenience, especially when the country was flooded in the rains. An ancestor of the present *sebāits*, therefore, prayed that the goddess would take pity on her votaries and come to Amtā. The goddess appeared to him in a dream and granted his prayer; and next day her image was found at the foot of a tree near the site of the present High school. A temple was next built by a merchant, whose salt boats had sunk in the river near Amtā. He vowed that, if the boats were restored, he would erect a temple over the image. They were raised miraculously with the cargo undamaged, and the grateful merchant built the present temple. It has a Bengali inscription in two lines on the outside at a height of about ten feet above the plinth. Owing to frequent coats of whitewash, it is somewhat illegible, but is said to ascribe the building of the temple to a Karmakār in the year 1056 of the Bengali era, *i.e.*, 260 years ago. The temple has a marble floor and a roof of the usual Bengali type. The image is in stone, 3½ feet high, with a vermilion-painted face. In the ame enclosure stands another temple of Siva with a roof of the Bengali style of architecture, which was built at the expense of the late Bābu Madanmohan Datta of Hātkholā, Calcutta. The temple has a valuable endowment (*debottar*) of about a thousand *bighās* of land, a part of which is occupied by a bazar, the largest in the district outside Howrah.

There are several important villages with High English schools in the jurisdiction of Amtā thāna, such as Rāspur, Jaypur, Pānpur, Jhinkrā, and Nārit, the home of the late Pandit Mahesh Chandra Nyāyaratna. Other places which may be mentioned are Panduā, with the ruins of a fort on the Kānā Nadī, which was the home of the well-known poet Bhārat Chandra Rāi, whose ability won for him the title of Gunākar, *i.e.*, the mine of talents (1712-1760 A.D.); Amrāgorī with a charitable dispensary chiefly maintained from an endowment given by the late Bābu Iswar Chandra Hāzrā; Rāutrā, the home of Bābu Jīban Krishna Rāi, said to be the richest Kaibartta in the subdivision; and Bhātorā on the Rūpnārāyan river with a police beat-house.

Andul.—A village in the Howrah subdivision, situated on the right bank of the old Saraswatī river, 4 miles west by road of Howrah town. It is connected with Andul station on the Bengal-Nāgpur Railway by a road a mile and a half long. Speaking generally, Andul may be taken as including Mahiāri (Mauri) and several other villages, and thus covers an area of about a square mile and a half. Andul itself has a High English school and a considerable daily bazar, while a post office is situated at Mahiāri, where an important *hāt* is held, the chief articles sold being paddy, coconuts, etc. At the latter place there is a high brick tower with five stories, about 165 feet in height, the top of which can be reached by a long series of steps inside. This tower is one of several erected in the early days of British rule for semaphore signalling before the introduction of the electric telegraph. Another neighbouring village, Argoriā, was once noted for its fine cotton *dhutis*.

Andul is of local importance owing to its being the head-quarters of well-to-do families, such as the Malliks and Mitras of Andul and the Kundu-Chaudhris of Mahiāri. The founder of the Mallik family was Gaur Charan Mallik, who settled at Andul when the district was under Muhammadan rule. His grandson Kāsī Nāth, is said to have been appointed *Dīwān* of Cuttack in the time of Lord Cornwallis and secured lands in that district. He next became head *mukhtār* of Mahārājā Tejchandra of Burdwān, and his services were rewarded by a grant of the bulk of Nawābpur *Mahāl* in Howrah. His son, Jagannāth Prasād, left three sons, Jogendra Nāth, Nagendra Nāth and Khagendra Nāth, besides two daughters. Jogendra Nāth built a large house with grounds attached known as the *Golāb-bāg* or rose garden, which may still be seen at Andul. He also opened a vernacular school in 1848, which was subsequently raised to the status of a High English school and still exists. He was a good scholar, and several small compositions of his in Sanskrit are known. He died childless in 1884, and his two brothers left no sons. The property being heavily mortgaged was then sold and bought by Mati Lāl Sīl.

The founder of the Mitra zamīndāri was Dīwān Rām Chandra Rāi, who, according to the family chronicles, served under Lord Clive. At the instance of Clive, it is said, the Emperor Shāh Alam conferred on his son Rām Lochan the title of Rājā with a command of 4,000 troops in 1765. The latter started a local era called *Andulābda*, beginning in 1771 A.D., for observance in his estates. Rām Lochan's grandson, Rājnārāyan Rāi, was a liberal patron of Indian music; and in 1836 Lord Auckland recognized his title of Rājā, and bestowed on him a dress of honour with a jewelled sword and dagger. His son Bijay Keshab Rāi died childless, but gave permission to both his widows to adopt. Both adopted boys, and litigation followed, the Privy Council ultimately holding the adoptions illegal. The property, heavily burdened with the cost of litigation, was inherited by the daughter's son, the late Bābu Kshetra Krishna Mitra, who died in 1907 leaving two sons, Upendra Nāth and Nagendra Nāth. Their house, adorned with high columns, is one of the sights of Andul.*

The third family, the Kundu-Chaudhris of Mahiāri, were originally traders and money-lenders who gradually attained the dignity of zamīndārs. Tekauri Datta, who was the first to settle at Mahiāri, acquired the estate of *pargana* Muzaffarpur; and his descendants, Bābu Kedār Nāth Kundu, Bābu Hīrāman Kundu and others, still combine money-lending with zamīndāri.†

Bāgnān.—Village and headquarters of a thāna in the Uluberiā subdivision, situated 12 miles from Uluberiā and a quarter of a mile from the Bengal-Nāgpur Railway station of the same name. It is situated on the Orissa Trunk Road, and contains a High English school and post office. Two miles to the east, on the other side of the Dāmodar, is Mahishrekhā, which was for twenty years the headquarters of the subdivision, until it was removed to Uluberiā in 1883-84. Traces of its former importance are found in a ferry, a post office and a large Public Works Department bungalow. Excellent snipe shooting can be had here. Other noticeable villages are Pānitrās and Mugkalyān with High English schools, and Agunshe, the home of the late Mr. Justice Dwārkā Nāth Mitra.

Bally (Bāli).—A town in the Howrah subdivision, situated on the right bank of the Hooghly. It forms a continuation of Howrah City northwards up to the Bally *Khāl*, and in 1901 it had a population of 18,662, as compared with 13,715 in 1872. Many of the inhabitants are immigrants, as may be gathered from the fact that the increase since 1872 occurred almost exclusively among the male population, and that more than 60 per cent. were born outside the district. The majority of the inhabitants are Hindus, the Muhammadans representing only 13 per cent.

The name is evidently derived from the accumulations of sand (*bāli*) deposited by the river. It is an old place, mentioned in *Chandi*, a poem composed by Kavikankan 300 years ago, and in Bengali poems of the 17th and 18th centuries; it also appears in Rennell's Atlas (Plates VII and XIX). It was a stronghold of Brahmanism, having several *tols* and being inhabited by many Rārhī Brāhmans. The almanacs issued by its Achāryas or astrologers were much in vogue before the days of printing. Tradition relates that some of its Brāhmans stood

---

* *A Brief History of the Andul Rāj*, 1900.

† Much of the above information has been kindly supplied by Bābu Nibāran Chandra Ghatak, Deputy Magistrate, Howrah.

round the scaffold on which Nand Kumār was hanged in 1775, and, to quote from Macaulay's essay on Warren Hastings, horrified at the execution of their fellow Brāhman "fled with loud wailings towards the Hooghly and plunged into its holy waters, as if to purify themselves from the guilt of having looked on such a crime." They then, so the story runs, returned to Bally and took a vow never to set foot in the city which had been polluted by the hanging of a Brāhman. It is said that this oath was religiously observed for many years, but, according to an article written in 1848, "the necessities of trade and other causes have long since rendered their resolution nugatory." In the beginning of the nineteenth century the place became a den of thieves, robbers and dacoits, whose depredations continued until they were checked by the Dacoity Department in the middle of that century.

Bally formed a part of the Howrah Municipality until 1882-83, when Bally, Belur, Barrackpore and a part of Ghusuri were formed into a distinct municipality under the name of Bally with an area of about 2 square miles. The chief industrial concern is the Bally Mill on the creek close to the railway station. Originally (in 1839) a sugar factory, it passed through various hands until purchased by the Borneo Company, which converted it into a paper mill, long known as the Bally Paper Mill. In 1906 the paper works were sold to Messrs. Heilger & Co., the site being utilized for a branch mill of the Baranagar Jute Mill Company. On the other side of the railway line a bone mill has been recently started; and at Belur on the river bank is a masonry building with a compound occupied by the Rāmkrishna Mission. Here an annual *melā* is held on the anniversary of the death of Rāmkrishna Paramhansa. Among other institutions may be mentioned a police station, a post office, a High English school and a charitable dispensary.

Bator.—One of the quarters of Howrah city, which is mentioned in early works long before Howrah itself. A reference to it appears as early as 1495 in a Bengali poem by one Bipradās. The hero of the poem, Chānd Saudāgar, was rowed in his boat down the Bhāgīrathī, keeping Ariādaha on the east and Ghusuri on the west, after which he arrived at Bator, where he worshipped its presiding goddess Betāi Chandī. Bator was apparently, therefore, situated along the reach of the river, extending from Shālimār Point to the Sibpur Engineering College; and the deep stream probably ran close to the bank. Later it became an entrepôt of European trade up to which sea-going vessels sailed, while from it boats and smaller sloops went further up the Hooghly, returning with cargoes. From the account left by Cesare Federici, who visited Bator in 1575, it appears that a large temporary mart (the modern *hāt*) was held here during the winter months, many thatched huts being built for the time and a brisk trade carried on. His account will be found in Chapter II, and need not therefore be reproduced here.

Bator was subsequently abandoned by the European traders. The Portugese removed their trade to Hooghly town; the Dutch to Baranagar and Chinsura; the French to Chandernagore; the English at first to Hooghly and then to Calcutta. Hence Bator, which was shewn as an important place in the maps of De Barros (1552-1613) and Blaev (1645-50), disappears from the maps of the second half of the seventeenth century downwards except Rennell's. Its abandonment as a haven may have been due partly to a change in the course of the river, the deep stream flowing on the east side instead of the west. The village, however, survived, and was one of those for the inclusion of which in their zamīndāri the English administration of Fort William made an application to the Emperor Farrukhsiyar in May 1714.* It now appears under the name Bhatore in the latest survey maps.

Bāuriā.—A village, situated 4½ miles above Uluberiā, and 12 miles by road and 15 miles by rail from Howrah. It is an old place, being found in Rennell's Atlas (Plate XIX), while adjoining it on the north was Fort Gloster with some powder mills (Plates VII and XIX). It contains an independent police outpost and a post office; but it is best known for its mills, the Fort Gloster Jute Mills, Bāuriā Cotton Mills, and Lawrence Jute Mills. The first two are connected with the railway station by a siding. The new boundary pillar of the Port Commissioners is located just above the Lawrence Jute Mills. The Bāuriā Cotton Mills are said to be the oldest in India, having started work in 1817 or 1822.

Bhot-bāgān.—A part of Ghusuri, in Howrah city, situated a little to the north of Sālkhiā. The name means the Tibetan garden and is due to the fact that it contains an old Tibetan temple or monastery, called the Bhot-Mandir or Bhot-Math. The building has an interesting history, having been established by Warren Hastings at the request of the Tāshi Lāmā of Tibet. In 1772 the Bhutanese invaded Cooch Behār, where they captured and carried off the Rājā. A punitive force sent by the British defeated the Bhutanese, at the request of whose Chief the Tāshi Lāmā

---

* C. R. Wilson, *Early Annals of the English in Bengal*, Vol. II, p. 172.

interceded and sent an envoy to Warren Hastings. Quick to grasp this opportunity of opening up trade with Tibet, Warren Hastings in 1774 despatched a mission under Mr. Bogle to negotiate with the Tāshi Lāmā, whom he believed to be the chief pontiff of that priest-ridden country. At Tāshilumpo, Bogle, a man of considerable tact, had a friendly reception. The Tāshi Lāmā, on his part, asked that he might be given a place on the banks of the Ganges—a river sacred to Buddhists as well as Hindus—to which he might send his people to pray. Bogle returned in 1775, and Warren Hastings at once granted a site for the Tibetan temple, and had it built under the supervision of Bogle. When it was complete, the Tāshi Lāmā sent down Tibetan images and sacred books, to be enshrined in it, and assigned the land and temple to a Saivite *sannyāsi* named Puran Gir Gosāin.

Puran Gir, who had a reputation for piety and integrity, was in the confidence of both the Tibetans and the British. He was the envoy of the Tāshi Lāmā, when he interceded for the Bhutanese in 1773, bringing talents of gold and silver, gold dust and musk. He accompanied Bogle on his mission next year, and when the Tāshi Lāmā went to the court of the Emperor of China, Puran Gir Gosāin went with him. From Pekin he returned to Calcutta with the news that the Lāmā had died of small-pox while at the Chinese Court in 1781. He next accompanied the Turner Mission to the new Tashi Lāmā in 1783; and in 1785 Warren Hastings made him his accredited agent to the latter. After his return in 1785, he settled as *Mahant* or abbot at the Bhot-bāgān monastery, which was regularly used by Tibetan traders visiting Calcutta, for whom he built rest-houses. The fame of the monastery treasures brought about his death, for in 1795 it was attacked by a band of dacoits, whom Puran Gir gallantly resisted until he was pierced through by a spear. Four of the dacoits were caught and hanged on a gallows set up in the monastery. The next *Mahant* was Daljit Gir, and his successors were Kalit Gir, Bilās Gir and Umrāo Gir. The present *Mahant*, Trilokh Chandra Gir, was elected in 1905 by the other *Dasnāmi Mahants* of Bengal, of whom the most influential was the *Mahant* of Tārakeswar in the Hooghly district.

The temple itself is quaint rather than beautiful, consisting of a two-storied building, in which the absence of arches is noticeable. Both Hindu and Lamaistic or Tibeto-Buddhistic gods are worshipped; and there is a Tibetan Dungten, cubiform in shape, like a Hindu *samādhi mandir* or tomb, and surmounted by Siva's phallus, which is kept in a small low-roofed room having a Bengali inscription on its door-top.

"The Bhot-bāgān *math* now remains a solitary monument of the genius and of a special policy of the first Governor-General of India, of the piety of Tāshi Lāmā as exhibited in Bengal, of the work of Puran Gir, and of the Tibeto-Bengal trade, which flourished centuries ago and was restored, though in a stifled form, a hundred years ago."*

Botanic Garden, Sibpur.—The Royal Botanic Garden is situated in Sibpur, on the bank of the Hooghly, just outside the limits of Howrah city. It was established in 1787 for the collection of plants indigenous to the country and for the introduction and acclimatization of plants from foreign parts. Its establishment was directly due to Colonel Robert Kyd, Military Secretary to Government, who urged upon the acting Governor-General, Sir John Macpherson, the utility of such an institution for the growth of teak for ship building, the cultivation of spices, the introduction or development of cotton, tobacco, and other products of economic and commercial importance. The proposal having been accepted by the Court of Directors, a large piece of land was set aside for the garden immediately below Colonel Kyd's private garden at Shālimār. Colonel Kyd, who was an ardent horticulturist and had a large collection of exotic plants, chiefly from the Straits, was appointed the first Superintendent of the Garden. On his death in 1793, Government decided to put the garden under the charge of a special officer who should have no other duty, and selected Dr. William Roxburgh, the "father of Indian botany," who was then the Company's Botanist in Madras. Roxburgh having retired on account of ill health in 1813 was succeeded by Dr. Francis Buchanan, who on succeeding to his mother's property took the name of Buchanan-Hamilton, by which he is generally known. He was not only an accomplished botanist and zoologist, but was also the first writer of gazetteers for Bengal districts, his work, after many years and with much mutilation, being published by Montgomery Martin under the title of *History, Topography and Statistics of Eastern India.* He was succeeded in 1817 by Dr. Nathaniel Wallich, Surgeon to the Danish Settlement at Serampore, an able and energetic botanist, who had already carried out a botanical survey of a large portion of India. During the lengthened absence of Dr. Wallich in Europe, his place at the garden was filled by Dr. W. Griffith, and on Wallich's retirement in 1846 Dr. Hugh Falconer was appointed.

---

* Gaurdās Bysack, *Buddhistic Monastery at Bhot-bāgān*, Proc. A. S. B., March 1890.

It was during the incumbency of the latter that Sir Joseph Hooker visited the garden, which he describes as 'classic ground to the naturalist.' He found it on his first visit in 1848 in a neglected state. "There had," he wrote, "been a great want of judgment in the alterations made since Dr. Wallich's time, when the gardens were celebrated as the most beautiful gardens in the East, and were the great object of attraction to strangers and townspeople. I found instead an unsightly wilderness, without shade (the first requirement of every tropical garden) or other beauties than some isolated grand trees, which had survived the indiscriminate destruction of the useful and ornamental which had attended the well-meant but ill-judged attempt to render a garden a botanical class-book." Great improvements had, however, been effected by the time of his second visit in 1850. "The destruction of most of the palms, and of all the noble tropical features of the gardens, during Dr. Griffith's incumbency, had necessitated the replanting of the greater part of the grounds, the obliteration of old walks, and the construction of new: it was also necessary to fill up tanks whose waters, by injudicious cuttings, were destroying some of the most valuable parts of the land, to drain many acres, and to raise embankments to prevent the encroachments of the Hooghly. The avenue of Cycas trees (*Cycas circinalis*), once the admiration of all visitors, and which for beauty and singularity was unmatched in any tropical garden, had been swept away by the same unsparing hand which had destroyed the teak, mahogany, clove, nutmeg, and cinnamon groves. In 1848, when I first visited the establishment, nothing was to be seen of its former beauty and grandeur but a few noble trees or graceful palms rearing their heads over a low ragged jungle, or spreading their broad leaves or naked limbs over the forlorn hope of a botanical garden, that consisted of open clay beds, disposed in concentric circles, and baking into brick under the fervid heat of a Bengal sun.

"The rapidity of growth is so great in this climate, that within eight months from the commencement of the improvements, a great change had already taken place. The grounds bore a park-like appearance; broad shady walks had replaced the narrow winding paths that ran in distorted lines over the ground, and a large Palmetum, or collection of tall and graceful palms of various kinds, occupied several acres at one side of the garden; whilst a still larger portion of ground was being appropriated to a picturesque assemblage of certain closely allied families of plants, whose association promised to form a novel and attractive object of study to the botanist, painter, and landscape gardener."*

* *Himalayan Journals.*

In 1855 Dr. Falconer left the country on account of ill health, and was succeeded by Dr. Thomas Thomson, who held office till 1861. The next Superintendent was Dr. Thomas Anderson, whose untimely death in 1870 was caused by disease contracted during his efforts to introduce the quinine-yielding cinchonas into the Darjeeling Himālayas. For the two years subsequent to Dr. Anderson's departure from India, *i.e.*, from 1869 to 1871, Mr. C. B. Clarke, F.R.S., acted as Superintendent; and then Dr. (afterwards Sir George) King, K.C.I.E., F.R.S., was appointed, holding the office till 1898. His successors have been Lieutenant-Colonel D. Prain, I.M.S., the author of *Bengal Plants*, and Captain A. T. Gage, I.M.S.

From the first foundation of the garden it was understood that it was to be made a source of botanical information for the possessions of the East India Company, and at the same time a centre to which exotic plants of economic interest could be imported for experimental cultivation, and from which, in turn, they could be issued for distribution in the Company's possessions. It was also intended to assist in introducing indigenous Indian products to new markets. It was, in brief, intended that it should not only be a botanical, but also a horticultural and agricultural garden. At first, great hopes were entertained that the spices which rendered the trade of the Company with the Malaccas and other of the Malayan Islands so valuable, might be cultivated in Bengal. The earliest efforts of Colonel Kyd were therefore directed to the introduction of the pepper vines and of the trees which yield nutmegs, cloves and cinnamon. It was, however, soon proved that the climate of Northern India is quite unsuited to these equatorial species. The equatorial fruits, such as mangosteen, langsat, dukko and bread-fruit, were also tried with a similar result; and so were the temperate fruits of Europe. In fact, not the least of the benefits conferred on the country by the garden in its early days was the demonstration by practical experiment that certain natural products, many of them of a most desirable kind, cannot be grown in Bengal; much money and fruitless effort being thus saved to the country. The introduction of exotic timber trees also received attention, and the garden still contains a few of the teak and mahogany trees introduced in these early years.

The introduction of tea was one of the items put down in Colonel Kyd's original programme, and the garden bore a most important part in the final establishment of what has now become one of the most important industries in Northern India. "Among its greatest triumphs," wrote Sir Joseph Hooker, "may be considered the introduction of the tea-plant from China, a fact I allude to as many of my English readers may not be aware that the establishment of the tea-trade in the Himalaya and Assam is almost entirely the work of the Superintendents of the gardens of Calcutta and Saharunpore." Potato growing was also introduced through its agency, and the cultivation of the quinine-yielding cinchonas of the Andes was initiated and carried to a successful issue under the direction of its Superintendents. The garden authorities worked hand in hand with the Agri-Horticultural Society of India in the improvement of Indian cotton, and in the introduction both of that and of jute to the markets of Europe. By the introduction of some of the best kinds of sugarcane from the West Indies, and the dissemination of these to all parts of the country, a considerable improvement was effected both in the quality and quantity of the sugar crop of India. In this matter also the Agri-Horticultural Society worked in cordial co-operation with the garden authorities, for soon after the establishment of the Society, some land in the garden was made over to it rent-free, and on this land the Society conducted the greater part of its operations for forty years. In fact, it was not until 1872 that the Society's garden was transferred to its present site in Alipore.

It is unnecessary to discuss in detail the numerous experiments in the cultivation of economic plants which have been conducted in the garden since its beginning. A few of the products tried may simply be mentioned. Chief among these are flax, hemp, tobacco, henbane, vanilla, coffee (Arabian and Liberian), ipecacuanha, aloes, sarsaparilla, jalap, India-rubber, cardamoms, tapioca, and cocoa. As regards horticulture, it will suffice to say that a large proportion of the exotic plants now found in private gardens in India have been introduced through the agency of the garden, and that the improved methods of cultivation which now obtain were to a great extent initiated here. Within half a century after its foundation, the garden had attained a European reputation; and owing to the distribution of its Herbarium by Dr. Wallich among the museums of Europe it had, according to Sir Joseph Hooker, "contributed more useful and ornamental tropical plants to the public and private gardens of the world than any other establishment before or since. This is the most valuable contribution of the kind ever made to science, and it is a lasting memorial of the princely liberality of the enlightened men who ruled the counsels of India in those days." At the same time, however, the garden suffered, for the Herbarium was denuded of every specimen collected during the past 50 years, and it was not till the time of Sir George King that it was restored to a position commensurate with the importance of the garden.

In 1864 the garden was devastated by a cyclonic storm of extraordinary violence, which either uprooted or broke to pieces the majority of the trees in it, and, by blowing down all the plant-houses, hopelessly crushed their contents. The trees which escaped on that occasion were sadly reduced in number by a second cyclone which passed over the garden in 1867; and, at the present time almost the only trees dating from before 1867 are the great banyan and a smaller tree of the same sort, some *pīpals* and country almonds, about twenty mahogany trees, and some palms. Moreover, the destruction of all shade, which resulted from the removal of the trees, allowed the inveterate weed known popularly as *ulu* grass, and botanically as *Imperata cylindrica*, to take possession of the whole of the ground not occupied by roads or flower borders. Consequently, when Sir George King assumed charge in 1871, it was necessary to lay out the garden entirely anew. The liberality of the Bengal Government, under whose control it passed soon afterwards, and the tireless energy of Sir George King, combined with his genius for landscape gardening, in a few years completely altered the aspect of the place, increasing incalculably its value as a scientific centre and bestowing on it all the charms that as a pleasure ground it now possesses.

Botanically, the most important feature in the garden is its Herbarium, or collection of dried plants. As has already been explained, the species collected prior to Dr. Wallich's visit to England in 1828 were distributed by him to scientific institutions abroad. The commencement of the present collection dates, therefore, from his return to India in 1832. It consists of plants contributed by almost every worker at botany in India since that date and by a number of botanists in Europe. It is first and foremost an Indian Herbarium, but the plants of many other countries are represented. Constant communication and interchange of specimens have been kept up for the last 70 years with the great national collection at the Kew Garden in England; with other European botanic institutions, such as the Herbarium of the British Museum, of the Jardin des Plantes at Paris, and the Imperial Gardens at St. Petersburg and Berlin; and in the East with the Botanic Gardens at Buitenzorg in Java, at Peradeniya in Ceylon, and at Sāhāranpur.

The garden is walled in on three sides, and can be entered by three routes, the Howrah gate, the College gate, and the Water gate (on the river bank). It is intersected by a number of avenues named after distinguished botanists, or occasionally, after prominent trees, such as the banyan and palmyra. It has no wells, but gets an abundant supply of water from the river, and inside from 26 tanks. Among other noticeable objects are the grove of bamboos, the mahogany group, the great banyan, the Palmetum, the palm-house and the orchid-house. The finest bamboos, chiefly natives of Java, skirt the Collett avenue. The mahogany group near the middle of the Clarke avenue contains fine specimens 80 years old or more. The Palmetum devoted to the cultivation of palms contains some fine trees. In the palm-house, an octagonal structure with a central dome 50 feet high, are cultivated palms and other scandent plants that cannot be grown out of doors. The orchid-house in the centre, built on the model of native betel plantations, contains beautiful orchids, mostly natives of India, which flower chiefly during March and April. In the Herbarium, built in 1883, are arranged in scientific order a very complete collection of dried specimens of Indian plants, with a fair collection of those outside it.

The pride of the garden is the great banyan tree near its western limit. Its main trunk is 51 feet in girth at a height of 5½ feet from the ground, and it has no less than 562 aerial roots rooted in the soil. The circumference of its leafy head is 997 feet, and the diameter of the space covered by it at its longest is 287 feet and at its shortest 264 feet. It is not known exactly how old the tree is, but tradition says that it was in existence in 1782, when it was a small tree sprouting out from a date palm, under which a *fakīr* sat. Observations of the rate of growth of this tree and other trees taken since 1871 make it probable that it is even older; and this supposition is supported by the evidence of Lord Valentia, who visited Calcutta in 1803 and described it as "the finest object in the garden, a notable specimen of the *Ficus bengalensis*": in fact, he visited the garden chiefly to see it.

As regards the general appearance of the garden, the following description is quoted from Mr. Forrest's *Cities of India*:—"Trees of the rarest kinds, from Nepal and the Cape, Brazil and Penang, Java and Sumatra are gathered together in that spot. The mahogany towers there, and the Cuba palms form an avenue like the aisle of some lofty cathedral. Noble mango trees and tamarinds are dotted about the grassy lawns; and there are stately casuarinas, around whose stems are trained climbing plants. There are plantains of vast size and beauty from the Malay Archipelago, and giant creepers from South America. The crimson hibiscus and scarlet passion-flower dazzle the eye, and the odour of the champak and innumerable jessamines float upon the breeze. As Bishop Heber remarked, 'The Botanic Gardens would perfectly answer to Milton's idea of Paradise, if they were on a hill instead of a dead flat'."

Dumjor.—A village in the Howrah subdivision, situated about 9 miles by road and 10 miles by rail (Howrah-Amtā) from Howrah. It is an old place on the bank of the Saraswatī, being shown in Rennell's Atlas (Plate XIX). The village is the headquarters of an Union, and contains a police station, a post office and a District Board bungalow. It is a centre for the jute and rice trade of the neighbourhood, and exports a considerable quantity of milk to the towns.

The thāna of which it is the headquarters is densely populated, and contains several important villages. On the bank of the Saraswatī are Baluti and Jhāpardah with High English schools, and Mākardah at which a large *melā* is held on the fifth day of the *Holi* festival in March. West of the stream are Nārnā with a large *melā* held on the Charak Sankrānti day in April; Rājāpur (or Dakshinbār) on the drainage channel of the same name, with a railway station and a canal bungalow; and Begri with a large weekly *hāt*.

Fort Mornington Point.—A point in the extreme south of the district at the junction of the Rūpnārāyan with the Hooghly. On this point there formerly stood a fort, said to have been built by Lord Clive, which fell into the river owing to the erosion of the bank.

Ghusuri.—A quarter in the northern part of Howrah city and in the southern part of Bally, containing jute and cotton mills, jute presses, rope works and an old Buddhist temple described in the article on Bhot-bāgān. See also the articles on Howrah and Bally.

Howrah.—The headquarters of the district, situated on the right bank of the Hooghly opposite Calcutta in 22° 35′ north latitude and 88° 21′ east longitude. The municipality, as defined by a Government notification, dated 17th January 1884, covers an area of about 8½ square miles, and is nearly 7 miles long and 1½ to 2½ miles wide. In 1901 it had a population of 157,594, the largest in any town in the Province outside Calcutta, there being no less than 17,510 persons per square mile. In 1872 the population was returned at 84,069, and the increase is due chiefly to the immigration of labourers attracted by the numerous factories and other industrial concerns in Howrah, Calcutta and their neighbourhood. So great, indeed, has been the influx of immigrants, that it was ascertained in 1901 that no less than two-thirds of the inhabitants of Howrah were born outside the district. Further, the number of males has increased from 47,213 to 99,904, or by more than 100 per cent. since 1872, whereas the number of females increased from 36,856 to 57,690 or only by 56·5 per cent. Hindus predominate largely, numbering 116,002 or 73·6 per cent of the population, while Muhammadans account for 39,239 or 25 per cent., and Christians for 2,282 or 1·4 per cent.

The city lies in the revenue divisions (*parganas*) of Boro and Paikān. Boro appears in Todar Mal's rent-roll as Purah in *Sarkār* Sātgāon, with a revenue of 652,470 *dāms*, *i.e.*, at the rate of 40 *dāms* per rupee, Rs. 16,311-12.* Paikān, a name meaning "pertaining to military service" (from *pāik*, a soldier), cannot be traced in the rent-roll, but is mentioned in a list of villages prepared in 1714, which shows that it comprised land on both sides of the Hooghly.† In 1765, when the *Dīwāni* was granted to the British, Boro and Paikān formed part of the zamīndāri of Muhammad Amīnpur in *Chaklā* Hooghly, with revenues of Rs. 24,006 and Rs. 2,153 respectively.‡ Muhammad Amīnpur estate then belonged to two sons and two nephews of Rāmeswar, a Kāyasth by caste and the ancestor of the present Bānsberiā and Seorāphuli zamīndārs. At the Permanent Settlement Boro was assessed to a revenue of Rs. 82,414 and Paikān to Rs. 10,986. This large increase shows how valuable land had become in the first years of British rule, though the low assessment of 1765 may have been partly due, as Mr. Grant suspected, to the proprietors misrepresenting the rental of their estates.

The city is entirely of modern growth. It has been evolved from a congeries of villages accreting to the central village of Howrah; and traces of the original villages still survive in the different names of the quarters (*pārās*) into which the city is still divided, in spite of the western nomenclature of streets and lanes. For example, along the river bank there are the old *pārās* of Ghusuri, Sālkhiā, Howrah, Rāmkristapur, Sibpur, Shālimār and Bator; and further inland are Bāntrā, Khurut, Kāsundi, Sāntrāgāchhi, etc.

The earliest details of the town are found in an application made by the English in 1714 to the Emperor Farrukhsiyar for a grant of a number of villages near Calcutta. The list mentions (1) Salica (Sālkhiā), (2) Harrirah (Howrah), (3) Cassundeah

* *Ain-i-Akbarī*, Jarrett, II. 141; J. R. A. S., 1896., p 103.

† C. R. Wilson, *Early Annals of the English in Bengal*, Vol. II., pp. 172-4.

‡ Grant's View of the Revenues of Bengal, 1786, *Fifth Report of the Select Committee*, 1812, Madras Reprint, pp. 457-8.

(Kāsundi, west of Khurut), (4) Ramkrissnopoor (Ramkristapur), and (5) Batter (Bator), with an aggregate rental of Rs. 1,450. The desire to obtain land on the Howrah side of the Hooghly was natural enough, for apart from its close proximity to Calcutta, there were "docks made for repairing and fitting their ships' bottoms, and a pretty good garden belonging to the Armenians."* The concession was granted, but the English could not avail themselves of it owing to the refusal of the zamīndārs to sell their rights; and the lands continued under Mughal rule for nearly half a century more. In 1750, Howrah is said to have been "a line of mud banks reeking with malaria, corpses in all stages of decomposition floating up and down the stream by the dozen, jungle lining the shore, the abode of the snake and alligator."†

This is most probably the reason why this part of the river bank is shown as blank in Valentijn's map, and in the various old charts of the river Hooghly. In the Pilot Chart of Bowrey (1688) no villages are entered on this side of the Hooghly, but in that of 1703, jungles, indicated by ten trees, are shewn above Sumatra Point (the modern Shālimār Point) and next "Simple Tom's Tree" near the present Ghusuri. In 1767 we find a proposal put forward by the Civil Architect, Mr. Fortnum, to have a hospital established at Howrah. The proposal is referred to as follows in the Consultation of March 1767:—"The Buxey lays before the Board an extract of a letter which he has received from the Civil Architect pointing out two places on the opposite side of the river to build an Hospital upon—the one opposite Surman's Gardens, and the other opposite the Town—but recommending the former as the most eligible spot. Point Sumatra, opposite Surman's Gardens, is the most proper spot for an Hospital from its being a wholesome situation and contiguous to the River, by which the Sick may be easily transported to it and better supplied with necessarys." The Board accepted this recommendation and directed the Civil Architect to prepare a plan and estimate. Fortnum submitted a detailed plan for the erection of a hospital on Point Sumatra (the present Shālimār Point) with an estimate amounting to 5 lakhs, but reported —"Notwithstanding I attended the Sarcar sent down by the Fuzdar of Hughley and marked out the bounds of the spot (four months ago), nothing has been done towards clearing of the riotts' Hutts, on the contrary a number of others since that time

* Alexander Hamilton, *A New Account of the East Indies*, 1688 to 1723, Vol. II, p. 12.

† *Howrah, Past and Present*, pp. 18-19.

have been put up." Eventually, however, the scheme was abandoned, apparently because it was too ambitious and too expensive for the straitened resources of Bengal at that time.*

A few years later, Sālkhiā became a centre of trade, with docks and roperies, and in Rennell's Atlas, Plate VII (October 1779) and Plate XIX (August 1780), we find "Solkee" or "Solkey" printed in large letters and shown as a place from which several roads radiated, one starting north-west *viâ* Chanditalā to Burdwān, a second westwards *viâ* Mākardah to Adampur, and a third south to Thāna Muckwa and Sānkrāil. "Seebpur" and "Bathore" are also shown, but, curiously enough, not Howrah. "Howra ghaut" appears, however, in a map of Calcutta and its environs prepared from Upjohn's survey in 1792 and 1793, together with "Ramkissenpore's Gt.," "Sulkhia Ghat" and "Sulkia Point." This map also has the following entries. In Sālkhiā there are two lanes marked "Rope Walk"; in Howrah proper there are three entries, viz., "Burial Ground," "Orphans of Private Educated" (indicated by three towers), and to the south "Hospital." Inland, to the west of an unnamed road, which is evidently the modern Grand Trunk Road, there are "Mosulman's Burial Ground," and, a little south of it but on the east of the road, "Former Practising Ground of the Bengal Artillery," from which the modern name Chāndmāri is derived. This interesting map shows other roads and houses, but does not name them.

A proclamation dated 10th September 1794, evidently based on Upjohn's survey, laid down the boundaries of Calcutta Town.† According to it, the river Hooghly was included within the metropolis, its western boundary running from "Colonel Robertson's garden called Jackapoore, immediately opposite to the mouth of the brook called Chitpore Nulla or Baugbazar Nulla," and then along the low water-mark of the river up to "the south-east point of Major Kyd's garden" but "excluding the said garden and the village of Sheebpore," and also "the Ghauts of Ramkisnopore, Howrah and Sulkeah." As mentioned in a preceding article, Major Kyd was the founder of the Botanic Garden, and his private garden was contained in the grounds of Shālimār House, now occupied by a rope-work.

From other sources we learn that docks and roperies existed in Sālkhiā and Ghusuri, and there were two docks, one opposite

---

* Notes on the Origin of the Presidency General Hospital, Calcutta, *Indian Medical Gazette*, February 1903.

† *Calcutta Gazette, Selections*, Vol. II, pp. 130-2.

Fort William and the other a mile below it.* Distilleries were also started, one belonging to a Chinaman in "Sulky" being advertised for sale in the *Calcutta Gazette* in 1784;† while the present court houses are said to have been built in 1767 for a rum distillery. The Hooghly records also mention the existence of cotton screws at Sālkhiā. Gardens, belonging mostly to Armenians, had been laid out among the houses and fields, to which the residents of Calcutta came for a change; and, according to Walter Hamilton, there was an extensive teak plantation above the Botanic Garden. The Europeans lived chiefly along the river bank in Sālkhiā and Ghusuri, and later in Howrah and Rāmkristapur. The natives lived inland, round the present Khurut Road, which is still known as *Purāni Sahar*, *i.e.*, the old town, and in Sibpur including Bator. Howrah was at this time a dumping ground for the Brāhmanī bulls of Calcutta‡ which roamed about in such numbers as to become a nuisance, while the houses and gardens were infested by bands of monkeys.

Dacoities were common,§ the dacoits hiding themselves in the paddy fields and jungle, and committing depredations by night in armed bands. Their detection was rendered difficult by the league which is known to have existed between the dacoits and police officers; for the sessions records contain the names of many *chaukīdārs* among the convicted dacoits, while the district records show that several *dārogās* were degraded or dismissed on suspicion of complicity.

Among the earliest public institutions in Howrah were the Royal Military Orphanage, the cemetery attached to it, the Hospital to the south of the school, and the salt godowns. The school for soldiers' orphans was located in 1785 in a large house, known as "Levett's house and garden," which was built about 1767 and was originally a rum distillery. Mr. Levett had taken a lease of Howrah village, but found it so unprofitable, that in 1785 he begged the Board of Revenue to allow him to relinquish his title and to pay the rent in future to the zamīndār. His request was granted in August 1785.‖ In the meantime, his house, which had a compound extending over no less than 160 *bighās*, was sold to the Orphan Society for Rs. 65,000. The premises were occupied by the Orphanage till 1815, and were

* Walter Hamilton's *Description of Hindostan*, 1820, Vol I, p. 29.

† *Selections*, Vol. I, p. 45.

‡ *Selections*, Vol. IV, p. 401 (17th August 1815).

§ A very daring robbery in the village of Howrah was reported in the *Calcutta Gazette* under date July 28th, 1807. *Selections*, Vol. IV, pp. 198-9.

‖ *Bengal MS. Records*, Hunter, Vol. I, p. 122 (No. 1043).

subsequently divided into three portions, one being allotted to the Customs House Officers, a second to the Magistrate of the 24-Parganas to serve as a periodical court, and the third to the clergy of Bishop's College in consideration of the services they rendered by taking services in the Church. The Civil Court of Sālkhiā was transferred to the second portion, and later the Magistrate's Court, when a separate Magistrate was appointed in 1843. In 1851 the clergy of Bishop's College vacated their portion, and in 1859 the Customs Office was also removed. Since then the building has been in sole possession of the Criminal, Revenue and Sessions Courts. The ground-rent of the Court and the *maidān* is still paid to several co-sharing zamīndārs.

The cemetery occupied a part of the Orphan School compound on the north of these buildings. The oldest inscription in this cemetery is on the tomb of Mr. Henry Ackland, Secretary to the Orphan Society for eight years who died in 1791, and the next oldest is an epitaph to Mr. J. Wynne, who died in 1799. The hospital shewn in Upjohn's survey was removed in 1828 to a double-storeyed house at the Howrah Ghāt and remained there till 1852, when the site was acquired by the railway. The salt godowns at Howrah existed before 1801, when they were placed under the control of the Western Salt *Chaukī*, and were removed to Sālkhiā on the opening of the railway. Salt, it may be explained, was imported from Hijili, Orissa and Madras, stored here free of duty and then sold, so that the salt godowns were practically bonded ware-houses.

Among other early institutions may be mentioned Bishop's College and the churches. The foundation stone of the former was laid by the Bishop of Calcutta, Bishop Middleton, in December 1820, and it was opened in 1821. The first Church of England church was built, at the instance of the Principal of Bishop's College, by private subscriptions and a small Government grant, on five *bighās* of land separated from the Orphan School premises. It was finished in 1831 and consecrated under the name of St. Thomas' Church. The Roman Catholic Church in Cullen Place was built in 1832 by the Revd. Father Paul de Gradoli at a cost of Rs. 40,000 realized entirely by subscriptions, and was consecrated under the name of the "Church of Our Lady of Happy Voyage." The earliest church, however, was one built in 1821 by Mr. Statham, the first Baptist resident missionary; when the site was acquired by the railway, a new chapel was built, in 1865, at the junction of Dobson's Lane with King's Lane.

Howrah, which Bishop Heber described in 1823 as a place "chiefly inhabited by shipbuilders," and which in 1848 was referred to as "the Wapping of Calcutta inhabited chiefly by persons connected with the docks and shipping," began to expand rapidly in the middle of the 19th century. Not only did the docks increase in size and in number, but other large industrial concerns were started, such as engineering yards, sugar factories, flour mills, and, after the sixties of the 19th century, cotton mills, jute mills and jute presses. The selection (in 1850) by the East Indian Railway authorities of Howrah as the terminus of their line and the construction of the bridge over the Hooghly gave an immense impetus to its development, which in recent years has been further facilitated by the entry of the Bengal-Nāgpur Railway, by the opening of the two light railways, and by the starting of steamer services. The rapid growth of the town has necessitated considerable modifications in its administration. A separate Magistrate was appointed in 1843, who was vested with the powers of a Deputy Collector in 1860, and ultimately was assisted by a Joint-Magistrate, several Deputy Collectors and several Courts of Honorary Magistrates. The police force was reorganised in 1862, and placed under a District Superintendent in 1863. The jail, after various changes, has been made a third class district jail and located in a large building. The Civil Courts have been enlarged and placed in a separate building, where a Small Cause Court Judge also holds an occasional court. The town was constituted a municipality in 1862, and is now the largest outside Calcutta both in population and income.

The Zilā school was opened in 1845 for native boys, and the St. Thomas' School in 1864 for European boys. The Bishop's College was replaced in 1880 by the Engineering College, now the centre of high technical education in Bengal. The Howrah General Hospital was started in 1861, and is the largest hospital in Bengal outside Calcutta, with separate wards for Europeans, native males and native females. A veterinary hospital, named after its donor Kumār Rāmeswar Māliā, has also been established. Among other buildings may be mentioned the salt godowns at Sālkhiā, which contain enormous stocks of salt and are served by a siding of the East Indian Railway, and the Town Hall built by private subscriptions over the municipal buildings.

The city is roughly divisible into two parts, the river bank and the portion further inland, which are separated from each other by the Grand Trunk Road. The former contains the European residences, offices and other buildings of business firms, and the latter the native town. Howrah proper lies nearly midway;

and its centre, bounded by Grierson Road on the north, Telkalghāt Road on the south, the river on the east, and the Grand Trunk Road on the west, forms the focus of commercial life. Except for a small part to the south in the possession of John King and Co., the whole of its river frontage is occupied by the railway station and goods-sheds. Then comes the long overbridge ending in the Buckland Road, with the Magistrate's residence and the Civil Courts on the east, and various other public buildings on the west, viz., the post office, the municipal office, the old church and cemetery, the Criminal Courts, the police reserve lines, and the hospital. The rest of the land is kept open, except for the Railway Institute in the north-western corner and the new church, the Zilā school and the District Board office in a corner on the south. The portion left open may be regarded as the chief, if not the only, lung of the city, there being space for cricket, football hockey and lawn-tennis, and for the pitching of tents in the cold weather for circuses or other entertainments. This central section is surrounded by other large buildings, such as the staff residences of the Bengal-Nāgpur and East Indian Railways on the north; the distillery, St. Thomas' School and Howrah Club on the west; and Smith Stanistreet's branch office and the extensive shipbuilding yard of Messrs. Burn and Co., on the south.

From the Hooghly bridge northwards along the river front extend a series of docks with the salt godowns in the middle. Above them come other works, between the Grand Trunk Road and the river, viz., roperies, timber yards, engineering works and oil mills, ending at Ghusuri in cotton mills and jute presses. Behind the docks lie a large *dharmasālā* and the European quarters; and beyond them native houses with several overcrowded *bastis* like Tindelbāgān and Ghāsbāgān. At the extreme north end, houses begin to thin out, and fields with gardens appear. South of Burn and Co.'s yard, a considerable area has been reclaimed from the river by the Port Commissioners and is crowded with godowns for storing rice and molasses. To the west of the reclaimed *chars* are 46 *bighās* of land acquired by Government in 1907, on which have been located the new jail and the offices of the railway police, with the residences of the Civil Surgeon, the Superintendent of Government Railway Police, and a Deputy Magistrate. Beyond them lie a row of small sheds, in which is held the Tuesday *hāt* of Rāmkristapur, said to be the greatest mart for hand-loom cloths in Lower Bengal. Further south, are found various factories, such as flour mills, jute mills and presses, timber yards, etc., until Shālimār Point is reached with the Bengal-Nāgpur Railway goods yard and wagon ferry. On the river bend come other factories, roperies and paint works, ending in the large compound of the Engineering College at Sibpur.

The river and the Grand Trunk Road form the two main thoroughfares, the greatest congestion of traffic taking place on the Grierson Road leading to the Hooghly bridge. The river bank is similarly crowded with cargo boats, which load or unload an immense quantity of goods between Bāndā Ghāt at Sālkhiā and Sibpur Ghāt, and with small boats ferrying passengers to and from Calcutta or vessels in the river. The river frontage is lined with iron *ghāts*, long jetties and busy dock-yards, having a background of tall buildings and grimy chimneys. The Grand Trunk Road presents a similar busy scene with rows of small shops and several large markets, and carries a heavy traffic to and from the railways, the factories, the shops, and private houses.

On the west of the Grand Trunk Road live the majority of the native population. The land gradually slopes away from the river bank, the lowest level being reached near Shālimār. Ghusuri is 20 feet, while Sāntrāgāchhi and Shālimār are only 12 feet above mean sea-level. The natives consist of two classes, viz., resident Bengalis and immigrants, mostly mill-hands and railway employés. The immigrants generally live huddled together in dirty over-crowded and ill-ventilated *bastis*, the Muhammadans preferring the quarters north of Khurut Road. Among the resident population Kaibarttas predominate, but they are now retiring more and more to the outskirts. The higher castes live chiefly in Bāntrā, Khurut, Sibpur and Sāntrāgāchhi. Kāyasths and Rārhī Brāhmans are chiefly found in Sibpur, and Bārendra Brāhmans in Sāntrāgāchhi.

The outer fringe of the town is thinly peopled, being mostly occupied by low fields intermixed with gardens and villas. A good deal of the town drainage finds its outlet into these low lands; and when owing to heavy rain the swamp level rises, the drainage is checked and the roads flooded. In September 1900, the swamp level rose to 13 feet above mean tide level, and for days together water stood on most of the roads, causing considerable inconvenience and damage.

The derivation of the name Howrah is uncertain. According to one account, it is derived from the Bengali word *hābar*, meaning stumbling, with reference to the numerous ruts in the streets of Howrah city, which formerly caused the unwary pedestrian to stumble. This seems a far-fetched explanation. There is a word *hāor* used in Eastern Bengal for a marsh or a swampy depression filled with water in the rains, and this would *a priori* seem a plausible derivation; but the word does not appear to be known in Western Bengal.

Howrah Subdivision.—The headquarters subdivision, situated in the north-east of the district, between 22° 30′ and 22° 42′ N., and 88° 2′ and 88° 22′ E, with an area of 173 square miles. The subdivision is a low-lying tract with a slight and gradual fall of level from north to south-east. It contains two main portions—(1) the high riparian strips of land along the Hooghly, Saraswatī and Kānā Nadī, and (2) the extensive swamps separating them, which are now drained by the Howrah, Barajol and Rājāpur drainage channels. The land is generally fertile, yielding abundant crops of winter rice, jute, pulses, sugarcane, potatoes and betel-leaves. It contains four urban thānas, Howrah, Sibpur, Golābāri and Bally, three rural thānas, Dumjor, Liluāh and Jagatballabhpur, and three independent police outposts, Sāntrāgāchhi, Sankrāil and Pānchlā. The population increased from 297,064 in 1872 to 431,257 in 1901, when the subdivision contained two towns (Howrah and Bally) and 365 villages. The average density in the latter year was 2,493 per square mile, and was greatest in the tracts lying along the river banks, where it did not fall below 3,000 per square mile. These portions of the subdivision are, in fact, more like semi-urban than rural tracts.

Jagatballabhpur.—A village in the Howrah subdivision, situated on the left bank of the Kānā Nadī, 16 miles from Howrah. It contains a police station, a post office, a High school, and a small District Board bungalow. Among noticeable villages in the thāna, of which it is the headquarters, are Bargachhiā, a railway junction with a five-storeyed tower of brick, 165 feet high, clearly one of those erected nearly a century ago for long distance semaphore signalling; Adampur, with the remains of a fort, an old place shewn in Rennell's Atlas (Plate VII); Paintāl, one of the largest villages in the district; Bāliā, with an old temple liberally endowed by the Burdwān Rāj with some two thousand *bighās* of land, a place which probably gave its name to the *pargana*; and on the west bank of the Kānā Nadī, Nabasān, once well known for its fine cloth, and Māju, a railway station with a High school.

James and Mary Sands.—A dangerous shoal in the river Hooghly, situated in 22° 14′ N. and 88° 5′ E. between the confluence of the Dāmodar and Rūpnārāyan rivers. The origin of the shoal was apparently due to changes in the course of the two latter rivers. As explained in Chapter I, the main stream of the Dāmodar formerly flowed along what is now the Kānā Dāmodar (or, as Europeans called it, the Jan Perdo, 'a river for great ships') which had its outfall by the modern Sijberiā *Khāl* above Uluberiā. Gradually the main stream was diverted to the present channel, and thus brought close to the Rūpnārāyan, the distance between the two being reduced from 23 miles to 6½ miles. The Rūpnārāyan again had its south-western channel silted up, and discharged all its silt-laden water by the eastern mouth. The angles at which both river debouch into the Hooghly, are favourable to the deposit of silt, which the close proximity of the two mouths nearly doubled. The result was that extensive shoals were formed, and their mobility, with the strong eddies set up, tended to make navigation dangerous.

These shoals and eddies were noticed as far back as the latter half of the 17th century. In the diary of Streynsham Master, under date 8th and 10th September 1676, we find an entry:— "This evening with the tide of flood we got into that part of the river Ganges that come from Hugly. At the mouth of the said river there's 18 or 19 fathoms water without, but eight or nine within, but it shoals gradually shelvingwise, soe that oftentimes ships and vessels are turned or winded round by it for a good space of time, but seldom receive damage thereby (as afterwards I saw one further up the river soe winded), but wee coming neare upon a high water gott in without such winding, and they happen at the first of the flood and last of the ebb."* Thomas Bowrey also speaks of having been caught in September 1676 in an eddy off "the shoals of the river Tombolee (where the river is most crooked)," that being an old name for the Rūpnārāyan. He described his experience as follows:—"It happened at that time for the space of half an houre to be slack water, but then the fresh came down like a boare and hurried up away into a most impetuous eddy, when in a moment our ship turned round soe often and quick withall that not one of us cold stand to doe any thinge. One cable broke, and the other swum like to a piece of wood."† From the above description it is clear that shoals had been formed by the fourth quarter of the 17th century.

The shoals appear under the present name "James and Mary Sands" in the Pilot Chart of 1703. The name is evidently derived from that of a ship (called after James II and his queen Mary of Modena), which was lost here in September 1694. "The

---

* *Diary of William Hedges,* Yule, II, 23.

† *Countries round the Bay of Bengal,* Temple, pp. 173-74.

Royall James and Mary arrived in Ballasore Road from the west coast in August ... but coming up the river of Hughly on the 24th September, she fell on a sand on this side Tumbolee Point and was unfortunately lost, for she immediately oversett and broke her back, with the loss of four or five men's lives."*

The sands, which are three miles long and a third of a mile in width, occupy the centre of the river Hooghly, leaving channels on either side, known as the Eastern and Western Gut. Various schemes have been suggested for evading this dangerous shoal, and it has more than once been proposed to dig a short canal at the back of Hughly Point so as to avoid the sands, or to construct ship canals from the docks to Diamond Harbour or to Port Canning on the Mātlā river. The problem was examined in 1865 and again in 1895 by experts, who suggested the construction of walls to train the channel into the Western Gut, but this proposal was not adopted.

Liluāh.—A village in the Howrah subdivision, situated three miles from Howrah. It contains a police station, but is better known for the extensive carriage workshops and goods-yards of the East Indian Railway. Many garden houses have been built in the neighbourhood in recent years by Mārwāris and others; and a great part of the surrounding land, which was formerly covered with reeds and low jungle, has been brought under cultivation.

Mahiāri.—See Andul.

Mahishrekhā.—See Bāgnān.

Mandalghāt.—A village in the Uluberiā subdivision, situated on the left bank of the Rūpnārāyan opposite Tamluk. It must have been a more important place formerly, for it gave its name to the *pargana*, while the Dāmodar river was often called River Moundleghat, *e.g.*, in the Pilot Chart of 1703. Mandalghāt appears in the *Ain-i-Akbari* as a *mahāl* of *Sarkār* Mandāran with a revenue of 906,775 *dāms*, and is mentioned by Valentijn, who says:—"Calcutta, Mondelghat, and some other places below, supply most of the wax and hemp that we require"; The *pargana* is low-lying and was repeatedly flooded by the Dāmodar in the early British period, until protected by embankments. The village contains an independent police outpost.

Pānchlā.—A village in the extreme south of the Howrah subdivision, containing an independent police outpost. At

---

* Bengal Letter to Court, 14th December 1694, l. c., Yule, II, 183. Tumbolee Point is shown in the Pilot Chart 1703 at the present site of Fort Mornington Point.

Jujeswar, a large village in its jurisdiction, are found a few Tutiā Kaibarttas, who are still employed in silk cocoon rearing.

Sālkhiā.—Northern part of Howrah city, containing docks, Government salt godowns, salt crushing mills, jute presses and engineering and iron works. See also the article on Howrah.

Sānkrāil.—A large village in the Howrah subdivision, situated below the junction of the Saraswatī with the Hooghly, about seven miles by river from Howrah, and two miles from Andul station on the Bengal-Nāgpur Railway. From its position commanding the two rivers, it was formerly a place of some importance. It was mentioned by W. Schouten in 1664, by Charnock in his diary dated August 24th, 1690,* and by Sir John Goldsborough under the form "Sea Crowle" in 1693†; and it also appears in Rennell's Atlas (Plates VII and XIX). The only event, however, of historical interest attaching to it is that in 1715 the Portuguese seized a British vessel in the Sānkrāil Reach. It is inhabited by Muhammadans in considerable numbers, and contains an independent outpost. With Rājganj it is served by river steamers.

The following villages within the jurisdiction of the Sānkrāil outpost may be mentioned :—Andul already described; Rājganj, separated from it by the Saraswatī *Khāl*, which contains the National Jute Mill, and is a centre of the trade in *hilsā* fish; Mānikpur, where the Belvedere Jute Mill was opened in 1907, an old place shown on the Pilot Chart of 1703; and Sārangā, with brick-fields and a white-washed building dedicated to Pīr Sārang. This is also an old place, shewn in the Pilot Charts of 1688 (Bowrey) and of 1703 as "Serrango tree."

Sāntrāgāchhi.—A large village adjoining Howrah city on the west and partly included in the municipal area. According to tradition, the principal family of the village, the Chaudhris, settled there 200 years ago in the time of the Muhammadan rule, and being Bārendra Brāhmans, induced several other Bārendra families to take up their residence in the village. The village gives its name to the junction of the branches of the Bengal-Nāgpur Railway which run to Howrah and Shālimār, but is nearer to Rāmrājātalā station. At Rāmrājātalā, a quarter of Sāntrāgāchhi, a large *melā* is held in April and May and is attended by large numbers. It is called the *Bārwāri melā* because its cost is met by private subscriptions. The place is noted locally for its coconuts and yams (*ol*).

---

* *Early Annals*, Wilson, Volume I, page 124, note 1.

† *Diary of William Hedges*, Yule, II, page 91, note 3.

Shālimār.—A part of Howrah city lying along the Hooghly close to Sibpur. It contains rope-works and the goods-yards of the Bengal-Nāgpur Railway. A century ago it was a country retreat for European residents of Calcutta. Here Colonel Kyd, the founder of the Royal Botanic Garden, had a house and a garden, which, it is said, was intended to be a miniature of the Shālimār garden and pleasure ground laid out at Lahore in 1667 by Alī Mardān Khān, the celebrated engineer of Shāh Jahān. Colonel Kyd died here in 1793, and the house was occupied by Sir John Royds, a Judge of the High Court, till his death in 1817, and after him by James Sutherland, a nephew of Colebrooke. Shālimār Point was formerly known as Sumatra Point.

Sibpur.—The south-western suburb of Howrah city containing the Royal Botanic Garden described in a previous article and, north of it, the Civil Engineering College. The latter occupies the buildings and the site selected by Bishop Middleton, the first Bishop of Calcutta for Bishop's College. The site was then "a wilderness of high grass, creeping shrubs and stagnant pools," but was considered suitable on account of its distance from the distractions of Calcutta. The object of the College was to be "the education of Christian Youth in sacred knowledge, in sound learning, and in the principal languages used in this country, in habits of piety and devotion to their calling, that they may be qualified to teach among the heathen." In other words, it was to be a Missionary College for India.

The Governor-General, the Marquis of Hastings, presented 62 *bighās* of land on the east of the Botanic Garden, and liberal grants of money were given by the British and Foreign Bible Society and by the Church Missionary Society. The foundation stone was laid in 1820, and the college opened in 1824, the first Principal being Dr. William Hodge Mill. Subsequently, the grounds were extended further to the east by the free gift of a piece of ground on the banks of the Hooghly by Sir Charles Metcalfe; while in 1826 the Governor-General, Lord Amherst, at the special request of Bishop Heber, assigned a further space of 48 *bighās* on the bank of the Hooghly for the demesnes and out-offices of the college. Bishop Heber took particular interest in the college, which he wished to be not merely an ecclesiastical seminary, but a college from which "India would derive her parochial clergy, her professors of the liberal sciences, her philosophers, her well-educated merchants, gentry and statesmen." The college flourished for nearly half a century, but in 1872 there was 'only one tutor with about half a dozen students.'* In 1880 the land and buildings were acquired by Government and utilized for the Civil Engineering College.

The college occupies three sides of a quardrangle, the southern side being open and facing the river. It is of Gothic architecture, and with its turrets and smooth lawns is strikingly like an Oxford or Cambridge college. Its architect was William Jones, whose sympathy for Indians, and knowledge of their language and customs, earned for him the name of Guru Jones. He came out to India in 1800 and for 10 years worked as a mechanic. In 1810 he is described in the directory as a manufacturer, and next year as the proprietor of a canvas manufactory at Howrah. It was there that he first established himself to any advantage, and to his energy and example may be in a great measure attributed the prosperity of that city. When an expedition was about to be despatched in 1811 for the capture of Java, and its departure was impeded by the want of cartridge paper, Mr. Jones came to the assistance of Government. His mechanical skill enabled him to set up a little paper manufactory, from which he furnished all the paper that was requisite, closing his new works as soon as the object of the expedition was accomplished. Four or five years subsequently, Jones accidentally discovered the existence of coal in Burdwān, and with characteristic ardour determined to open mines. "It is chiefly in reference to our Indian coal, and in contemplating the vast benefit which Jones' labours have conferred on India, that his claim to the highest rank among her benefactors rests." His last public engagement was the building of Bishop's College, which he undertook in some measure from his desire to promote every object of public utility, but also because he aspired to the honour of erecting the first Gothic edifice in India. His active and useful life was brought to an abrupt close in the month of September 1821, in consequence of a fever contracted while superintending the building, which proved fatal in three days. "It will," wrote Bishop Middleton, "still be his monument."†

Considerable additions have been made to the college since its acquisition by Government in 1880. The most interesting building is the chapel begun by Jones, which contains memorial tablets erected to Bishops Middleton, Heber and Wilson, and to four *alumni* of the college who were killed during the Mutiny of 1857. One of these, named Cockey, was at the college in

* *Howrah, Past and Present.*

† J. C. Marshman, *Notes on the Right Bank of the Hooghly*, Calcutta Review, 1845.

1846 at the same time as another distinguished pupil, the Bengali poet, Michael Madhusudan Dutt.

The area of the college premises is 350 *bighās*, of which 219 *bighās* are high lands, 55 *bighās* are accreted lands, and 76 *bighās* consist of low swampy lands and tanks. Much of the area is very low-lying or consists of *jhils* and tanks. The locality is consequently unhealthy, and as it is unsuitable on other grounds for the work of the college, it has been decided to transfer the institution to Rānchī.

Singtī.—A village in the Uluberiā subdivision, situated on the bank of the Kānā Dāmodar in the extreme north-west of the district. It contains an independent police outpost, and is an old place shewn in Rennell's Atlas (Plate VII), as is also Sibpur, another large village on the same river. The outpost was transferred from the Khānakul thāna of Hooghly District to the Amtā thāna of Howrah in 1894.

Syāmpur.—A large village on the right bank of the Dāmodar, chiefly inhabited by Kaibarttas. It has a police station, a sub-registry office, a post office, a ferry, a charitable dispensary and a District Board bungalow. Within its jurisdiction lie Sasāti, with a High English school, a ferry and a Public Works Department bungalow on the Rūpnārāyan; Fort Mornington on the mouth of the Rūpnārāyan in the village of Makrapathar; and Pichhalda, two miles north north-west of Fort Mornington with a *hāt*. Sasāti is shewn in Rennell's Atlas (Plate VII), while Pichhalda is still older, being shewn in the oldest maps existing, viz., those of Gastaldi (1561), De Barros (1623) and Blaev (1650) In De Barros' *Da Asia*, printed in 1552, it is said—"Ganga discharges into the illustrious stream of the Ganges between the two places called Angeli and Picholda in about 22 degrees."* It is also mentioned in the biographies of Chaitanya as the place where he crossed the river; and from its position, just above the junction of the Rūpnārāyan and the Hooghly, it must have been an important village.

Tanna or Thāna Muckwa.—A village in the Sānkrāil outpost. It is an old place, frequently mentioned in European accounts of the seventeenth and eighteenth centuries. The earliest reference to the place appears to be contained in a letter from Hooghly dated 31st March 1674 stating that the sloop *Arrivall* had reached "Tannah."† The maps of the second half

---

* J. A. S. B., 1892, p. 112.

† *Factory Records*, l. c., Bowrey's *Countries Round the Bay of Bengal*, p. 208, note 4.

of the 17th century have entries of more than one Tanna. The map of Valentijn, based on materials obtained in 1660-65 A.D., shows Thanna and below it Kl. (*i.e.*, *kilā* or fort) Thanna; the Pilot Chart of Bowrey (1688) shows Great Tanna and below it Little Tanna; and the Pilot Chart of 1703 shows Great Tanna, below it Tanna Fort, and still lower down Little Tanna. The name Tanna is evidently a corruption of *thāna* or police station. The upper Tanna shewn near the bend of the river, on the site now occupied by the Civil Engineering College, Sibpur, was named Great Tanna, apparently to distinguish it from the Tanna lower down at the next bend of the river near Rajganj. A short distance below Great Tanna was the fort, the position of which is reasonably identified with the site of the house of the Superintendent of the Botanical Garden. Here the river is so much narrower, that a fort on this bank, with the help of another fort on the opposite side,* would easily command the waterway.

According to the diary of Sir Streynsham Master, dated 30th November 1676, an old mud walled fort was built at "Tannay" to prevent the incursions of pirates from Arakan, who ten or twelve years before had carried off people from the river-side villages, to sell them in the slave market at Pipli, "in consequence of which none durst live lower than this place." Master buried Mr. Callway at "Little Tanna" on 12th September 1676, because the boats could not go further up that day to "Tanna." Great Tanna is also mentioned twice in Hedges' diary, viz., on 23rd July 1682 and 31st December 1684. When war broke out between the English and Nawāb Shaistā Khān of Bengal, Job Charnock assaulted and took the fort at Tanna on 11th February 1687 and after demolishing it landed at Hijilī. Subsequently, when the war was suspended by a temporary peace, Charnock proceeded to Little Tanna on the way up to Chutanuti, and thence sent a despatch to the Governors on 10th September 1687. The war was not actually concluded till 1690, but even after that the Governor of Hooghly would not permit the English shipping to come above Tanna Fort for some time. However, on 24th August 1690, Charnock arrived at Chutanuti for the third and last time, and recorded that on his arrival the Governor of Tanna sent his servant to greet him.†

In 1696, when Subhā Singh and Rahim Khān rebelled, their forces besieged the Tanna fort, but were repulsed by its commandant, with the help of the vessel *Thomas* lent by the English

---

* *Hedges' Diary*, Yule, Vol. III, p. 215.

† *Hedges' Diary*, Yule, Vol. I, pp. 32, 174; Vol. II, pp. 62-65, 68, 233, 237, 283.

to serve as a guardship.* The fort is said to have been captured by the Marāthās in their early invasions in 1741-42, and is last heard of in the first war of Lord Clive with Sirāj-ud-daula. At that time the Tanna fort was of brick, while the fort opposite it (at Mātiāburuz) was of mud. On 1st January 1757, the seamen of the *Tyger* took possession of "Tannari Fort", which the Muhammadans had abandoned, and the boats of H. M. S. *Kent* took the fort on the opposite side. Forty cannon were found in the two forts, several being 14-pounders.† The English set fire to both the forts, but two years later (in 1759) Clive hearing of the approach of a Dutch force, strengthened the Tanna fort and Charnock's fort (the one opposite to it) and put them under the charge of Captain Knox. Since then all trace of the fortifications at Tanna is lost, Rennell's Atlas (Plates VII and XIX) showing only the village of Tanna or Tanna Muckwa on the spot now occupied by the Botanic Garden. The fort at one time gave its name to this part of the river, as may be gathered from a report of the 19th May 1704 that the English sloop *Cassimbuzzar* returned to Calcutta, "having sprung her mast at Tana reach, about 4 miles below the Factory".‡

Uluberiā.—The headquarters town of the subdivision of the same name, situated on the right bank of the Hooghly river, in 22° 28′ N. and 88° 7′ E. Population (1901) 5,395. It is 19 miles distant by river from Howrah and 20 miles by rail, and is accessible by boat, steamer and rail. One steamer service runs from Calcutta to Uluberiā, and another to Ghātāl *via* Uluberiā. The Orissa Trunk Road and the High Level Canal to Midnapore also start from this town, and there is a station on the Bengal-Nāgpur Railway at a short distance from it. The town, which is protected from the river by a high embankment, is rural in character and has no features of interest. Before the railway was extended to it, Uluberiā was a place of some importance, for pilgrims passed through it on their way to and from Jagannāth, and there was a large bazar to meet their wants. It still has a considerable trade in rice and fish, especially mango-fish and *hilsā*. In 1903 it was constituted a municipality; but in April 1907, the municipality was abolished as unsuitable to local conditions, and the place was made the head-quarters of an Union. It has the usual Subdivisional offices, Criminal and

* *Early Annals of the English in Bengal*, I, 124, note 1.

† Stewart's *History of Bengal*, 1847, p. 210. Captain Cope's *A New History of the East Indies*, (1758), Appendix VI, pp. 418, 420; Ives, p. 101, l. c. *Hedges' Diary*, Vol. III, p. 215.

‡ *Early Annals of the English in Bengal*, I., 251.

Civil Courts, Local Board offices, a sub-jail, a police station, a sub-registry office, a postal-telegraph office, a charitable dispensary, a High English school, and a Public Works Department Dāk bungalow. The name is probably derived from *ulu* (a kind of grass) and *bere* (fence), the *ulu* grass growing in abundance round the town. The derivation "Abode of Owls" given by Sir William Hunter is fantastic and improbable.

This little river-side town has an interesting history. It first came into prominence in consequence of Charnock's war with the Bengal Nawāb. The first campaign was concluded by an agreement between Charnock and the Nawāb's *Bakshi* Abdul Samad, by which the former handed over Hijilī and was permitted to proceed to Chutanati and to demand a new *farmān* with twelve conditions. Charnock accordingly proceeded on 17th June 1687 "with half the fleet to Ulleberrea and Little Tanna."* One of the twelve conditions was that the English should be allowed to establish themselves at Uluberiā, besides keeping their factory at Hooghly. This condition was granted by the Nawāb in a *parwānā* or order from Dacca dated 21st July 1687.† It was also tentatively approved by the Court of Directors, who on 27th August 1688, wrote:—"Your town of Ulabarreah, we understand, hath depth of water sufficient to make Docks and conveniences for the repairing of any of our biggest ships, and is a healthfull place, and therefore we have added a Paragraph to our letter to our Generall that, if he can obtain a Phirmaund from the Mogull for our holding that place fortifyed with the same immunities and priviledges we hold Fort St. George, we will be therewith content, without looking further, or being at any new charge in contending for any other fortifyed settlement in Bengall . . . We hope you may so manage that place or Town of Ullaberreah which you have articled for, that it may in time become a famous and well governed English Colony."‡

The truce, however, was a hollow one, and, as the war continued, the Bengal Council with all their shipping had ultimately to retire to Madras. In the meantime, Charnock and other members of the Council changed their minds, and in reply to the above letter of the Court wrote from Madras under the date 30th September 1689—"In our Generall Letter by the *Beaufort* and our diaries of that Yeare, wherein wee have layd downe Our reasons for the altering Our Opinion about Ullaberreah and pitching on Chuttanutte as the best and fittest up the River on the Maine, as We

* *Hedges' Diary*, II, 68.
† Ditto II, 71.
‡ Ditto II, 75.

have since experienced, and likewise been sattisfyed that Ulubarreeah was misrepresented to Us by those sent to survay it."* Uluberiā thus never became "a famous and well-governed English Colony." It continued, however, to be a place of some importance, for it is shewn in the Pilot Charts of 1688 and 1703 and in Rennell's Atlas (Plates VII and XIX).

Within the jurisdiction of the Uluberiā thāna there are several important villages, *e.g.*, Phuleswar with the New Ring Cotton Mills; Sijberiā at the mouth of the Rājāpur Drainage Channel with a canal bungalow; Garhbhabānīpur with a High English school; and Nunti with plantations of betel-leaf, well-known in Northern India for its fine flavour. All the early maps shew below the present Uluberiā a place named Pisacol, which may have given its name to *pargana* "Pechacolly"† on the other side of the river, one of the original 24 Parganas. There is no trace of this village in the maps published after the middle of the 17th century. The Pilot Charts of 1688 and 1703 show a village Rangamatte, a name which still survives in the Rāngāmete *Khal* opposite Māyāpur Magazine. Valentijn's map shows another village Basanderi, which is also mentioned by Alexander Hamilton :— "Basundri and Tresinddi ... are on that river, which produce the greatest quantities of the best Sugars in Bengal".‡ It probably gave the name to the large *pargana* of Bāliā Bassendhari, which formed a portion of the Burdwān zamīndāri, while a small part of it was included in Lord Clive's zamīndāri of the 24-Parganas.§

Uluberiā Subdivision.—A subdivision occupying the whole of south and the western half of the north of the district, between 22° 13′ and 22° 47′ N. latitude and 87° 51′ and 88° 12′ E. longitude, with an area of 337 square miles. The tract is generally low-lying with a gradual slope from the northwest, to the south-east. It is drained by the Dāmodar and its branch channels, and on the south-west by the Rūpnārāyan. The north-western part is exposed to inundation, the embankment on the right bank of the Dāmodar having been abandoned; but the rest of the subdivision is mostly protected by embankments. The subdivision is divided into four thānas, Uluberiā, Bāgnān, Amtā and Syāmpur, with three independent outposts, Bāuriā, Singtī and Mandalghāt. The population increased from 298,801 in

* *Hedges' Diary*, II, 86.

† Grant's View of the Revenues of Bengal, *The Fifth Report*, p. 491; *Statistical Account of the 24-Parganas*, Appendix, p. 384.

‡ *A New Account of the East Indies*, Vol. II, p. 6.

§ Grant, pp. 478, 491.

1872 to 419,257 in 1901, when it was contained in 1,086 village The north and north-west of Amtā suffer periodically from epidemics of malarial fever; and this thāna, on the whole, shews least progress. The predominating castes are Kaibarttas, Pods and Bāgdis; the higher castes being comparatively few in number. The subdivisional headquarters were for twenty years at Mahishrekhā, but were removed to Uluberiā in 1883. Khānākul thāna was then included in this subdivision, but was transferred to the Arāmbāgh (formerly Jahānābād) subdivision of the Hooghly district. The density of population in all the thānas is nearly the same, averaging 1,244 per square mile or less than half of that in the Howrah subdivision

INDEX.

A.

B.

D.

E.

F.

I.

J.

K.

L.

M.

N.

O.

P.

S.

B. S. Press—7-10-1909—3054J—536—R. G.